Philipp Assinge

C000001266

Education and Training Po

Studies on Education

Volume 6

LIT

Philipp Assinger

Education and Training Politics in Europe

A Historical Analysis with Special Emphasis on Adult and Continuing Education

LIT

Bibliographic information published by the Deutsche Nationalbibliothek
The Deutsche Nationalbibliothek lists this publication in the Deutsche
Nationalbibliografie; detailed bibliographic data are available in the Internet at
http://dnb.dnb.de.

ISBN 978-3-643-91170-4 (pb)
ISBN 978-3-643-96170-9 (PDF)

A catalogue record for this book is available from the British Library.

© LIT VERLAG GmbH & Co. KG Wien,
Zweigniederlassung Zürich 2020
Flössergasse 10
CH-8001 Zürich
Tel. +41 (0) 76-632 84 35
E-Mail: zuerich@lit-verlag.ch   http://www.lit-verlag.ch
Distribution:
In the UK: Global Book Marketing, e-mail: mo@centralbooks.com
In North America: Independent Publishers Group, e-mail: orders@ipgbook.com
In Germany: LIT Verlag Fresnostr. 2, D-48159 Münster
Tel. +49 (0) 2 51-620 32 22, Fax +49 (0) 2 51-922 60 99, e-mail: vertrieb@lit-verlag.de
e-books are available at www.litwebshop.de

Foreword

This publication is the revised version of my doctoral thesis handed in at the Faculty of Environmental and Regional Sciences and Education at the University of Graz, Austria. Rooted within the study of education and in particular the study of adult and continuing education, the research in this book examines education and training politics in Europe based on a transdisciplinary approach.

Due to its contribution to peace, democracy and economic prosperity in Europe, and its unmistakable presence in the everyday educational practice, the European Union presents itself as an alluring subject of research to students in the field of education and training. Many questions arise concerned with the political powers of the European Union and its contribution to the future of education and training in Europe.

The research in this book was born of the insight that it is necessary to recognize the history in order to understand the present. The purpose of this book is, therefore, to raise awareness for the historical dimension of education and training politics among scholars, students and professionals in all areas of education and training. It is hoped that this will encourage the readers to use the arguments made in this book as a springboard for their own work.

Philipp Assinger
Graz, November 2019

Inhaltsverzeichnis

List of abbreviations

ACE	Adult and Continuing Education
ALE	Adult Learning and Education
CoR	Committee of the Regions
EAC	European Atomic Energy Community
EC	European Communities
ECJ	European Court of Justice
ECSC	European Coal and Steel Community
EEC	European Economic Community
EESC	European Economic and Social Committee
ET	Education and Training
EU	European Union
IO	International Organization
LLL	Lifelong Learning
OLP	Ordinary Legislative Procedure
OMC	Open Method of Coordination
TEAC	Treaty establishing the European Atomic Energy Community
TECSC	Treaty establishing the European Coal and Steel Community
TEEC	Treaty establishing the European Economic Community
TEU	Treaty on European Union
TFEU	Treaty on the Functioning of the European Union
VET	Vocational Education and Training

1. Introduction

The *European Union* (EU) is a very influential political actor within the European *education and training* (ET) community.[1] Over the last three decades, the EU has driven forward many of the predominant academic and political discussions on ET and countless national ET initiatives. For instance, learner mobility, lifelong learning (LLL)[2] strategies, competences frameworks or workplace learning have been established topics at all levels of education politics, practice and research. Altogether, EU politics has contributed significantly to the formation of a European political framework and a common understanding concerning the social and economic function of ET.

The best-established governing instruments in the EU's political framework are financial schemes supporting mobility and employability of learners and workers. These financial schemes include for instance the *European Social Fund* (ESF) or the *ERASMUS+* program. Other governing instruments are non-binding legal acts like Decisions or Recommendations covering a broad variety of ET and ET related topics. More recent legal acts have established, for instance, the *European Qualifications Framework* (EQF), the *European Credit System for Vocational Education and Training* (ECVET) or the *Entrepreneurship competence framework* (EntreComp).

The functioning of ET politics at the European level has at all times depended on the member states' willingness to engage in political cooperation. Within the *European Communities* (EC) and the EU, however, this political cooperation was impeded by disagreement on how to govern matters of ET

---

[1] *Education and Training* (ET) is the term that the EU uses when it refers to the entire body of early childhood education, primary and secondary school, higher education, vocational education and training and adult learning. ET also refers to international cooperation and policy dialogue, innovation in education, multilingualism and education for migrants. The term ET integrates the broad areas of general education and vocational training. In this book, the term/abbreviation ET will be used when referring to the general discourse concerned with the body of topics related to the areas and issues mentioned above.

[2] *Lifelong learning* (LLL) is an abstract concept that was introduced in the late 1960s when it was called lifelong education (LLE). The EU has been using LLL since the early 1990s in a similar way as it has been using ET but with the focus on the individual rather than on ET areas, sectors and topics. This book refers to LLL only when concrete strategies for the promotion of LLL are examined.

up until the 1990s.[3] At the Lisbon European Council meeting in 2000, a solid agreement was eventually reached and the so-called *Open Method of Coordination* (OMC) was initiated to govern ET politics. This method has enabled the EU institutions to coordinate and monitor the performance of national ET policies on the basis of commonly agreed objectives, indicators, benchmarks and procedures since this point.

This framework, which has been very briefly outlined, has evolved over the course of seventy years. When the *Treaty establishing the European Coal and Steel Community* (TECSC) was signed in 1951, European politics had already shown rudimentary interest in ET. However, it took twenty years until the Member States actually committed themselves to establishing a very basic institutional framework for cooperative ET politics. At the 1969 summit in The Hague, the heads of state recognized the importance of ET and, in 1971, the first meeting of national education ministers took place. The same year, also the first working groups in the European Commission were established to prepare for the creation of an education directorate two years later.

Everything started to move in a new direction when the socio-economic and technological transformation strongly affected Europe in the late 1970s. A reorganization of the ET portfolio in the Commission of the EC took place at that time and the general mindset of Member States was in in the process of changing. Instead of opposing proposals, they slowly began to appreciate political cooperation. From this moment on, the status of ET within the context of European politics constantly improved throughout the whole of the 1980s.

The *Treaty on European Union* (TEU) signed in Maastricht in 1992, then, redefined the EU's governing capacities because it included previously non-existent legal provision for two overarching areas of general education and vocational training. Eight years later, the Lisbon strategy confirmed that ET had meanwhile become one of the EU's main concerns in relation to the future challenges of knowledge-based economies. Again in 2009, the signatories of the *Treaty on the Functioning of the European Union* (TFEU)

---

[3] The term *European Communities* (EC) was used from 1967 until 1992 to address the common structure of the European Coal and Steel Community (ECSC) established in 1951, the European Atomic Energy Community (EAC) and the European Economic Community (EEC) established in 1957. In 1992, the EC was integrated into the European Union (EU). This book uses the term/abbreviation EC when it examines the time before 1992 and the term/abbreviation EU when it examines the time since 1992.

reinforced their commitment to the treaty's preamble saying that they are "Determined to promote the development of the highest possible level of knowledge for their peoples through a wide access to education and through its continuous updating".[4] In the *Europe 2020 Strategy* launched in 2010, two out of the seven so-called flagship initiatives, promoting the three political priorities: smart growth, sustainable growth and inclusive growth, addressed the area of ET.

The study presented in this book recounts the historical advancement of *education and training* (ET) in the *European Communities* (EC) and the *European Union* (EU) from a marginal issue to a political priority. In so doing, the study looks particularly at the formation of policies and governance and at how *adult and continuing education* (ACE) have been addressed in the context of this historical advancement.[5]

The historical study is based on the view that current ET politics cannot be fully understood without reference to history because they have developed from and taken shape through the accretion of the governing capacities of the EU institutions. This refers to the quantitative increase and the qualitative improvement of the EU's capacities to exercise its powers in the field of ET.

It will be argued that despite the fact that ET policies have at all times responded to the demands of European labor markets or the progress in *Information and Communications Technology* (ICT) and therefore changed in accordance with these developments, the core topics are perennial topics, since they are firmly anchored in the principles of the European unification project. This is the case for learner and worker mobility, integration of workers into the labor market and mutual recognition of qualifications, all of which are related to the idea of free movement of goods, capital, services and people.

It will be argued, moreover, that the re-definition of the EU's formal governing capacity regarding ET in the *Treaty on European Union* (TEU) in 1992 formed the backdrop against which a soft type of governance has

---

[4] TFEU consolidated, Preamble.

[5] *Adult and continuing education* (ACE) refers to all learning, training and education of the adult population after the completion of an initial period of compulsory education. ACE can have a general and/or a vocational character and leads to the development of knowledge and skills, and to the formation of attitudes and competences. It can take place in the organized practice of ACE providers or in the workplace. ACE is therefore the most extensive part of ET. The term/abbreviation ACE will be used in this book when referring to the specific discourse concerned with the learning, training and education of the adult population.

slowly changed the roles and the tasks of the EU institutions with respect to ET. The supranational institution of the European Commission was struggling for long time and could not properly define its role, however the TEU marks a watershed while the Lisbon Council Meeting from 2000 represents a turning point with regard to governance. Notwithstanding the importance of these two events, there have been some significant occurrences, without which these events would not have been possible. This is why a special emphasis will be laid on occurrences such as the individuals who have promoted ET in the 1970s, the series of court cases before the *European Court of Justice* (ECJ) in the mid-1980s, and the *European Year of Lifelong Learning* (EYLL) in 1996.

The relevant academic literature and the documents of the EC give reason for the claim that ACE was a marginalized topic of ET up until the 1980s. This study will point out that the training and education of adults have been taken into consideration ever since the very beginning of the *European Coal and Steel Community* (ECSC). However, as will also be argued, it was only the rise of *lifelong learning* (LLL) in the mid-1990s that pushed ACE forward and led to specific policy action in this sub-area.

In order to put this study into context, it shall be stressed that the narrative presented is consistent with the relevant academic literature. Much has been said about the EU and its role in ET so that a valuable base exists on the topic. However, what distinguishes this study from that of other scholars is the combination of topics, especially the focus on ACE, and the fact that developments from the very beginning of the European unification project up until the present day will be covered. Altogether, thus, the innovative aspect of this book emerges from the arrangement of topics and the focus of the examination.

2. An outline of the academic discourse

The origins of the organized practice and the politics of *adult and continuing education* (ACE) go back to the time when nation states were formed. The well-known Florentine education scholar, Paolo Federighi, enumerates three original causes that promoted ACE in most European countries:[1] First, the industrial revolution and the demand by industries for educated and trained workers; second, the ambition of the working class to participate and emancipate within the context of industrialization; and third, the expectation from national elites that adult and continuing education contributes to nation building, national unification and the establishment of governing classes. Eventually, in each country, though, ACE has developed differently under the specific circumstances of national culture, national economy and national politics.

These specific circumstances have somewhat changed within the last four decades. Phenomena with a global scope, transcending national borders, have become as important for the development of ACE as the demands of the nation state. Such phenomena are demographic change, advanced ICT, global markets or international organizations such as the EU or the OECD. All of these phenomena have significantly encroached upon the organization of labor at the national level and, thus, upon the traditional condition under which ACE has developed. As a result of this, a tendency of convergence of the politics and the practice of ACE among European nation states can be observed.

In the relevant academic literature, both aspects are being addressed: the divergence and the convergence of the organized practice and the politics of ACE in Europe. The following is a précis of some arguments from the relevant academic literature concerning the field of ACE in Europe and the EU's ET policy and governance since 2000 as well as the history of ET in the *European Communities* (EC) and the *European Union* (EU). At the end, some research desiderata will be addressed in order to state the precise research questions of the historical study.

---

[1] Federighi 1999, p. 5.

2.1 Adult and continuing education in Europe

Ekkehard Nuissl, Susanne Lattke and Henning Pätzold emphasize that at the European level, ACE has neither a commonly shared history nor a homogeneous structure.[2] In spite of the fact that the origins of ACE are similar in most of the countries, – so continues the argument – a precise definition and description of the European landscape as it has historically evolved or as it exists today is not possible. These authors hold that even in the near future, it will not be possible to draw a coherent picture of ACE at the European level.

It is indeed the case that there are evident differences particularly with regard to political, theoretical and practical ideas concerning what ACE should achieve and with regard to the approaches for the organization of ACE.

Similar was the account given by Wilhelm Filla, Elke Gruber and Juri Jug in 2002 in the introduction to an editor's publication comprising of contributions on the history of ACE in Germany, Croatia, Slovenia, Poland, Czech Republic, Slovakia, Romania, Hungary and Austria.[3] Filla, Gruber and Jug emphasize that in these countries, ACE is extremely diverse. The institutions, the teaching methods, the overall objectives or the resources available to ACE providers were distinct and always related to a specific national context. Moreover, the three authors pointed out that the state of development of ACE as an academic discipline was also of importance for the development of the practice and the politics; however, they argued that also the academic approach to ACE varied significantly between the countries discussed in their publication.

Even though many more accounts maintain that the organized practice and the politics of ACE are always specific to a country, other research argues that an insidious convergence is happening concerning national policies and the organization of ACE, suggesting that ACE in the European nation states is becoming more similar. It is claimed that this insidious convergence has been the result of socio-cultural and economic globalization on the one the hand, and EU and OECD education policy and governance on the other hand.

Alexandra Ioannidou, a Greek expert on international ACE policy working for the *German Institute of Adult Education*, points out, that there is some evidence for convergence caused by international and European politics,

---

[2] Nuissl et al. 2010, pp. 16–17.
[3] Filla et al. 2002, p. 10.

however, it is not clearly discernible whether this convergence manifests at the level of structures, at the level of thematic discourse or at the level of single educational programs.[4] According to Ioannidou's research, if convergence from EU or OECD politics occurs, it is more likely that it finds expression in political discourse such as that concerning lifelong learning or concerning quality in education. While it is likely that political initiatives converge as the result of political rhetoric, convergence of structures or single educational programs are rather the consequences of the globalization of economies and markets, according to an argument put forward by another expert on international ACE policy, Marcella Milana, from Italy.[5]

In summary, it is perhaps most appropriate to say that common characteristics or shared patterns among national systems can be identified, but it is to be doubted that they suffice to describe ACE at the European level as a coherent field. In fact, what needs to be mentioned is that the configuration of the organized practice or the politics of ACE even within each nation state often shows such great diversity that it is, also for a confined area, hardly possible to provide a comprehensive description.

The Austrian professor of adult and continuing education, Elke Gruber claims that compared with other sectors of ET, like compulsory school, the dual-vocational system or higher education, ACE in Austria is the quantitatively largest and most differentiated of all sectors.[6] Creating a geographical map of ACE in several Austrian federal states, Gruber realized that it is hardly possible to count the number of organizations or even to classify them according to criteria such as legal personality, type of organization or courses they provide.

When talking about ACE, it must be kept in mind that particularly the organized practice is not strictly regulated by the state but tends to respond to the demands of the free market; and the market for ACE has been expanding in recent decades. Traditional adult education institutions and more vocationally oriented continuing education organizations are exposed to increasing competition with public educational institutions such as universities and private tertiary education organizations, as well as small and medium sized multi-purpose providers.

Kirsten Aust from the Technical University of Braunschweig and Bernhard Schmidt-Hertha, professor of education at the University of Tübingen,

---

[4] Ioannidou 2010.
[5] Milana 2012.
[6] Gruber and Lenz 2016, p. 47; Nuissl 2011.

advance that ACE is organized in the form of a quasi-market.[7] Aust and Schmidt-Hertha assert in a positive manner that it is arguably this quasi-market type of organization that guarantees the plurality of providers and of programs and, therefore, helps to improve the effectiveness and the relevance of the whole field since the quasi-market is forced to respond to learners' and stakeholder demands.

This précis of statements concerning ACE in Europe will be concluded by an account on political measures. To this end, extracts from the *UNESCO regional report on the state and development of adult education in Europe, North America and Israel* published in 2009 will be reproduced. For this report, 35 European countries (25 EU Member States) were analyzed. The author, Helen Keogh, a policy specialist from Ireland, identified three types of countries.

> At one end of the spectrum, a relatively small number of countries are adopting a systemic approach to ALE, formal and non-formal, whereby it is an integral autonomous sector within the overall education and training system, and is embedded in the wider social, economic, cultural and political domains. (…) At the other end of the spectrum are the countries where, for reasons of ideology, stage of development and/or resources, ALE provision is limited and, quite commonly, market-led. The legislative basis, policies, and financial support are disjointed, weak or absent; and structures are fragmented. (…) In between the two ends of the spectrum, ALE in the majority of countries in the region [UNESCO region: Europe, North America and Israel P.A] is located along the continuum of development on the key dimensions of policy, governance, legislation, financing, infrastructure, participation, provision, recognition of learning and quality assurance. In these countries, the broad politico-educational drive is towards the rationalisation of provision with a thrust towards increasing co-ordination, quantity and accountability.[8]

After all, in line with Helen Keogh, it must be remarked that by means of political initiatives and market forces the ACE in European countries is becoming more structured and equipped with more resources so that most likely the general quality of offers improves. Despite the still existing divergence, there are a number of indicators pointing toward progressively forward-moving convergence. This concerns primarily policies for the institutionalization of organizational structures, the introduction of laws and regulations or the promotion of professionalization and quality of ACE provision.

---

[7] Aust and Schmidt-Hertha 2012, p. 43.
[8] Keogh 2009, pp. 53–54.

2.2 European education and training politics

In the editorial of a 2014 publication entitled *Adult and lifelong education: the European Union, its member states and the world,* the editors John Holford, Marcella Milana and Vida Mohorčič Špolar contend that for "two decades, the European Union has been at the forefront of international policymaking on lifelong learning." During this period, "the EU has developed lifelong learning as an important policy tool", these authors argue.[9]

In its function as a policy tool, LLL had an effect far beyond the original scope of reforming ET by means of building bridges between compulsory schooling, VET, Higher Education and ACE. Lifelong learning has turned into an overarching principle of social and economic policy referring equally to employment, competitiveness, innovation, social cohesion or democracy building issues. Not so much the pedagogical implications of LLL but rather the transversal character it took on in the context of general EU politics and the subsequent translation into ET policies have significantly encroached upon the organization of national ET systems.

"It seems undisputed," asserts Alexandra Ioannidou, "that the primary driving forces behind current policy reforms in national education systems are external to the national systems themselves". Looking at the developments not from an EU but from a wider perspective of international ET politics, Ioannidou sees the driving forces in "global labor markets, modernization and transformation processes, regional integration processes – primarily within Europe – demographic trends and changing working patterns, [or] common societal problems".[10]

National governments, it seems appropriate to say, have apparently lost a good portion of their authority over national ET policy and governance. In recent years, the *Open Method of Coordination* (OMC), a governance instrument the European Commission uses to organize cooperation between actors at regional, national and supranational levels, has been subject to critical assessment in this regard.

While some authors argue that the OMC underpins a shift in policy power from national governments to supranational institutions like the European Commission, Martin Humburg, currently an economist at the education department of the European Investment Bank, stands against this. He contends, "the autonomy of the Commission and the ECJ within the OMC process is

---

[9] Holford et al. 2014, p. 267.
[10] Ioannidou 2014, p. 205.

too small to expand the Commission's competencies against the will of the Member States."[11]

It is self-evident today that national governments must consider global developments such as those listed by Ioannidou. However, the OMC adds one aspect as it confronts national authorities with the performance of other countries, thus, making them more inclined to rely on a comparison and on international standards. Taken together, these two aspects, the external influences from globalization and the comparison with the performance of other countries tend relax the political tensions between national and supranational authority over policy decisions and might altogether be another cause for the convergence of national policies.

Danny Wildemersch and Henning Salling Olesen, two prolific researchers of ET, expand the arguments summarized so far and indicate that when the nation state undergoes change, ET and ACE practice also changes. They contend "[t]oday the role of the nation state is changing in many ways, and it also affects the role assigned to education and learning arrangements." Wildermeersch and Salling Olesen observe "policies at the supranational level and market forces have had an increasing influence on the understanding of what adult education/lifelong learning is about."[12]

Returning to the EU, the records confirm that the EU has been promoting ET as a universal remedy to problems in the social sphere and a vehicle for success in the economic sphere of today's knowledge-based economies. In 2000, the *Conclusions of the Lisbon European Council* put forward that "Europe's education and training systems need to adapt both to the demands of the knowledge society and to the need for an improved level and quality of employment."[13]

Anja Jakobi, an international relations scholar, who conducted research on lifelong learning, points out that the rise of concepts such as knowledge-based economy and knowledge society in the late 1990s had two important longer-term consequences for ET.[14] First, the dynamics of an economy that is increasingly dependent on the knowledge of the labor force impinged on the demand patterns in labor markets, which consequently impinged the demand-supply patterns in ET. Second, the emergence of the notion of societies in which knowledge is the key to any kind of performance homogenized

---

[11] Humburg 2008, p. 24.
[12] Wildemeersch and Salling Olesen 2012, p. 97.
[13] European Council 3/23/2000, p. 7.
[14] Jakobi 2007, p. 47.

organizational patterns of societies resulting in the fact that countries started comparing their own performance with that of other countries. Both of the consequences argued by Jakobi, that of market supply and demand patterns and that of homogenization and comparison, have been considered in many EU policies and are recognized in the literature as important contextual factors for the economization of ET policy.

Scholars frequently criticize economization and the overall economic focus of the EU and its application on matters of ET. The Portuguese education experts, Licínio Lima from the University of Minho and Paula Guimarães from the University of Lisbon, forcefully argue that the EU has formed and promoted – what they call – a "human resource management rationale" underlying all education, learning and training policy. [15] Based on historical research, they contend that this "human resource management rationale" has driven out the social and emancipatory qualities of traditional ACE and early *lifelong education* policies.

Axel Bolder, Helmut Bremer and Rudolf Epping, proponents of a critical theory of education, are concerned with the relationship between public and private actors that the EU is promoting.[16] They assert that the governance arrangement the EU is bolstering up has contributed to shifting accountability for successful ACE provision from public actors to private actors and in the end even to the individual learner. It suddenly becomes the failure of the individual and not of the public or the community if education and training are not successful. One of the most respected adult education scholars, Peter Jarvis from Great Britain, goes even one step further and propounds that international ET politics only to respond to the needs of industrialists and the claims of powerful multinational corporations.[17]

Many more critical arguments concerning European ET politics exist. For instance, the French social scientists, Isabelle Bruno, Sophie Jacquot and Lou Mandin sustain that "[t]he main purpose [of the EU] is to create a Europeanization of problems, a comparison of situations in all the countries, allowing for the sharing of some common representations, opening the way to a common perception of problems".[18] According to Martin Lawn, externally caused convergence of policies as well as deliberate political attempts of standardization has led to the emergence of a European ET policy space. He

---

[15] Lima and Guimarães 2011.
[16] Bolder et al. 2017.
[17] Jarvis 2010, p. 23.
[18] Bruno et al. 2006, p. 533.

affirms that "[t]hrough the construction of European policy spaces, the European Union (EU) makes Europe governable."[19] A policy space – as Lawn conceives it – indicates a shift from subjective politics based on ideologies and convictions of politicians towards objective and evidence-based politics of standardization and comparison formed by experts, or the so-called *epistemic community*.

Ute Clement, a professor of vocational education and training, put forward the notion that political actors and the *epistemic communities* realized that in a field as complex as ET, traditional governance through legislation would no longer yield the desired outcomes.[20] They drew the conclusion, according to Clement, that governance approaches had to be adapted respectively. The construction of a political and practice environment based on management by objectives is now considered the most efficient and effective approach, maintains Clement. Underlying this approach is the assumption that development or reform can be facilitated when educational actors of all kinds are required to work towards the achievement of specific measurable goals while at the same time being free to choose the means to achieve these goals.

The literature consulted confirms once more that the EU is considered a powerful actor with regard to ET in Europe. Since the main interest of this study is on the history of ET in the EC and the EU, the next section summarizes scholarly accounts concerned with this history.

2.3 The history of education and training

While researching the literature on European ET politics, it was surprising to realize that there are rather few monographs examining the historical development of ET in the EC and the EU. One of the few monographs that recounts the history in a very detailed way was written by Luce Pépin, a longstanding official of the European Commission, and published by the Publications Office of the European Union.[21] Another monograph was written by Martin Lawn and Sotiria Grek, who were working at the University of Edinburgh in Scotland at that time. These authors provide a very valuable discussion in which they look at the transformation of governance and policies from

---

[19] Lawn 2011, p. 259.
[20] Clement 2015, p. 31.
[21] Pépin 2006.

a historical perspective and argue the creation of a European education policy space on the basis of experts and standards.[22]

Other monographs deal with the EU in the context of a much broader scope of research discussing also the work of other *International Governmental Organizations* (IGOs) such as the *Organization for Economic Cooperation and Development* (OECD), the *United Nations Education, Science and Cultural Organization* (UNESCO), the *Council of Europe* or the *World Bank* such as the highly recommendable 2007 publication by the German professor of adult education, Michael Schemmann.[23] Finally, there are some publications on historical aspects of lifelong learning,[24] mobility programs[25] or vocational training in the EU's predecessor, the *European Economic Community* (EEC).[26] The situation is, however, somewhat different with international journals or editor's publications. Here, plenty of work can be found.[27] Scholars seem to fundamentally agree on there are three key facts and three observations concerning the history of ET in the EU.

Three key facts

- The first key fact is that the *Treaty establishing the European Economic Community* (TEEC) from 1957 made provision for vocational training (Article 128) but neglected general education.
- The second key fact is that the *Treaty on European Union* (TEU) from 1992 introduced general education as an official policy field in addition to the existing, but amended, provision for vocational training.
- The third key fact is that the Lisbon European Council from 2000 made ET a political priority of the EU with regard to the objectives of economic prosperity and social cohesion.

Three observations

- First, the observation that the 1970s were an initial phase in which the core topics were formulated and the foundation of a governance arrangement was created;

---

[22] Lawn and Grek 2012.
[23] Knoll 1996; Schemmann 2007.
[24] Field 2006.
[25] Fritsch 1998.
[26] Fahle 1989.
[27] Brine 1995; Rasmussen 2014; Mohorčič Špolar and Holford 2014; Németh 2016; Volles 2016.

- second, the observation that the 1980s marked a rather sharp turn from an integrated approach towards diversification, vocationalism and labor market-oriented ET; and
- third, the observation that the rise of lifelong learning in the 1990s and early 2000s created expectations concerning the possibility of adding a more social side to the economic side of ET policies.

In a description of the genesis of EC and EU, the renowned expert, professor Joachim Knoll emphasizes that the *European Economic Community* (EEC) was founded with the purpose of achieving political integration by means of economic integration. The economy was, thus, the glue that held together the EEC in the early decades.[28] After the expansion of the economic focus, the importance of culture was recognized and so it was that also ET became of greater relevance. However, whenever ET was addressed in the 1960s, it was conceived as a part of either the employment or labor market restructuring policies and was not granted the status of its own policy field. This also had to do with the lack of competences in ET given that the Treaty provision for vocational training was rather insufficient and that the sovereignty of the national governments had to be respected.

With regard to the competences of the EC, Hubert Ertl, professor of vocational education and training research at the University of Paderborn, mentions that in the 1970s, ET actions "were undertaken by virtue of 'implicit competences'".[29] The legal basis for vocational training was ambiguous and non-existent for general education, but in applying instruments like the ESF or policies concerning mutual recognition of diplomas, at least some minor developments could be made on the basis of such "implicit competences". Again, Joachim Knoll reports that among those minor developments were documents dealing with guidelines for vocational training policy in the 1960s, directives on professional qualifications, the first regular meetings of education ministers as well as the integration of ET in the Directorate General for Research, Science and Education in the early 1970s.[30]

In 1976, the first action program was adopted and the *Education Committee* was established. Mark Bechtel, Susanne Lattke and Ekkehard Nuissl stress that this Education Committee was an important element in the development of ET politics.[31] Having comprised members of the Council of the

---

[28] Knoll 1996, pp. 192–193.
[29] Ertl 2006, pp. 6–7.
[30] Knoll 1996, pp. 206–207.
[31] Bechtel et al. 2005, p. 32.

European Community and of members of the European Commission, the Education Committee assured that political decisions respected the viewpoints of the Member States and of the Commission equally. On the one hand, the Member States benefited because no decision could be made without their consent. On the other hand, the Commission benefited because it could advance policy proposals and persuade Member States of the need to promote ET.

By the mid-1970s, the EC had a twofold ET portfolio consisting of the vocational and the general education track. As Luce Pépin reports, initiatives simultaneously developed in both tracks.[32] In the vocational track, there was, for instance, the foundation of the *European Centre for the Development of Vocational Training* (CEDEFOP) in 1975, and in the general education track there were the first joint study programs in higher education. A topic that concerned both tracks was that of mutual recognition of diplomas, which had been on the agenda from early on.

Bechtel, Lattke and Nuissl point also out that regarding vocational training policies in the second half of the 1970s and the first half of the 1980s, much was done to address specific target groups.[33] The Council adopted legal acts to support integration of handicapped people into the labor market, young people in transition from education to work, equal opportunity for women, people suffering from permanent unemployment, and lastly adaptation of workers to new technologies.

As time went by, the action programs (COMETT, ERASMUS, FORCE and later Socrates, Leonardo or Grundtvig) turned into the core activity of the EU and served as a stepping-stone for extending competences. Most of these programs concentrated on higher education and vocational training. Adult education had long been a sub-category and was eventually promoted in the mid-1990s with the Grundtvig action.[34]

According to Balázs Németh, the president of the *European University Continuing Education Network* (EUCEN), the original intention of the EC was to proceed on the basis of an integrated approach in which the policy focus in all areas of ET would be nearly the same.[35] He points out that the labor market crisis that hit Europe in the late 1970s and early 1980s forced the EC to abandon the integrated approach and instead address topics on an

---

[32] Pépin 2007, p. 123.
[33] Bechtel et al. 2005, pp. 33–34.
[34] Rasmussen 2014, p. 22.
[35] Németh 2016.

area-by-area approach. In this way it happened that in the areas of vocational training and adult education topics like career guidance and counseling, use of ICT or re-training and integration of unemployed were promoted while, for instance, in higher education, the concentration was on university-business cooperation or transnational cooperation between universities. In compulsory schooling, the main topics were languages and European identity. Németh, moreover, reports that in the early 1990s, issues of social cohesion became more important after a phase of strong vocational orientation and, consequently, ET policy became more balanced. The result of this balancing out of the two orientations was the concept of lifelong learning as it was proposed in the 2000 Memorandum on lifelong learning.

Regarding the history of lifelong learning, Vida Mohorčič Špolar and John Holford come to the conclusion that the EU and particularly "the Commission has appropriated – though it has also played a part in developing – a language related to adult learning which itself has a long history."[36] One has to know that when lifelong education, or *education permanente* as it was called in the beginning, was proposed by the Council of Europe in the mid-1960s, adult education was emphasized and considered vital for the future of societies.[37] In a similar way, Lee, Thayer and Madyun argue that the EU adopted ideas from the UNESCO, the Council of Europe and the OECD, and then formed its own version of lifelong learning with a much stronger instrumental function than the other concepts.[38]

The British expert in the sociology of education, Jacky Brine, examined the contribution of educational and vocational policy to the construction of the EU.[39] In her research, she identified two dynamics that have shaped both educational and vocational policies and the EU as a whole. These two dynamics are related to the tensions between the interests of supranational institutions of the EU and of the Member States and the tensions between an economic and a social policy orientation. Brine arrives at the conclusion that the variety of topics, ranging from ET for employability and competitiveness, to languages, to common cultural values or European citizenship, allow the EU to use ET to structure the relationship with the Member States and its citizens, to work on issues of social cohesion and exclusion and to strengthen the economic performance of the Union in the context of global competition.

---

[36] Mohorčič Špolar and Holford 2014, p. 35.
[37] Lengrand 1972.
[38] Lee et al. 2008.
[39] Brine 1995.

All of these issues have been among the major goals in the construction of the EEC and the EU and of European integration.

One of the perennial arguments in academic discourse of recent years is that regarding a policy space that enables the EU to govern European ET. The already mentioned Martin Lawn and Sotiria Grek noticed that from the late 1990s a policy space was slowly unfolding.[40] Palle Rasmussen, emeritus professor of education at Aalborg University, argues that there were attempts to create a sort of policy space even before the Lisbon European Council of 2000. These earlier attempts were not successful because the traditional governance approach based on legislative competences and subsidiarity did not allow for convergence of ET in the Member States. It was the Lisbon strategy and the OMC that made the emergence of policy spaces and the onset of convergence possible. Rasmussen states that "[t]his approach has allowed common policy objectives to be fixed and benchmarked and processes of policy learning to unfold 'beneath' the cumbersome negotiations between national governments."[41]

Ase Gornitzka seems to be of a similar opinion as Rasmussen. She posed the question: "Does this [the OMC] represent a fundamental change in how cooperation takes place within this policy area – is it a watershed in European education policy?"[42] In her research, Gornitzka arrives at the conclusion that the impact of the OMC must be assessed against the historical development of political cooperation in ET.[43] She holds that in the past political cooperation was based on the question: *should policies be coordinated among the Member States*? Since the OMC, the question seems to have changed. Now the issue is: *how can policies be coordinated among the Member States*? What the OMC achieves with its methodology is that it combines the quest for common objectives and integration with the freedom of Member States to choose the elements they consider adequate for their national contexts.

Scholars divide the history of ET in the EC and the EU into phases generally depending on the topics they focus on and the perspective they take. Anne Corbett, who conducted in-depth research on the history of higher education in Europe, divided it into six phases beginning with the origins of higher education politics (1955-1957) and ending with the implementation of the ERASMUS mobility scheme in 1987.[44] In between, she distinguishes

---

[40] Lawn and Grek 2012, pp. 83–84.
[41] Rasmussen 2014, p. 32.
[42] Gornitzka 2006a, p. 3.
[43] Gornitzka 2006a, pp. 48–50.
[44] Corbett 2005.

"conflicting visions on European higher education" (1958-61), "experiments with intergovernmental approaches" (1961-69), the creation (1970-72) and the stabilization of an own policy domain (1973-76). After this phase, she locates the first action programs (1976-84) and a phase dealing with the ERASMUS decision and implementation (1985-87) Her publication closes with an epilogue entitled "The Europe of Knowledge: A Renewed European Ambition".

Jacky Brine, who looks at the vocational and educational policy and their contribution to the construction of the EU, distinguishes three phases.[45] The criterion she uses is that of the labor market situation as the root cause for both vocational and educational policy. During the phase from 1950s to the late 1970s, the major concern was cyclical youth unemployment. For most parts of the 1980s, which forms the second phase, the major concern was structural unemployment and the third phase ranging from the late 1980s to the mid-1990s considered unemployment from the progress in ICT as the challenge and focused on the investment into and promotion of human resource development.

Martin Lawn and Sotiria Grek, who look at governance arrangements, also distinguish three phases, however they concentrate on the modes of political interaction and the actors involved in the governance of ET.[46] In the first phase, the authors argue that science and research on European education formed the basis of ET policy. Education and training policy "benefited from national research centres and researchers who had begun to work together (…) from their subjects of study, and their quantitative and qualitative research expertise; it used pre-existing institutions to work with and to model its own practices."[47] According to Lawn and Grek, the second phase from 1970 to 2000 was a phase of "chaotic uniformity" which resulted in the emergence of a European dimension in ET. "The key governing idea through this time is cooperation, initially taken as a weak response to national sensitivity and then growing into a distinctive governing approach in European education."[48] The third phase started in 2000 with the new governance idea of quantitative measuring. Key to understanding governance in this phase is to understand the power of data and comparison. Lawn and Grek assert, "[t]he flow of Europeanization is enhanced and shaped by the indicators and data

---

[45] Brine 1995, p. 149.
[46] Lawn and Grek 2012.
[47] Lawn and Grek 2012, p. 33.
[48] Lawn and Grek 2012, p. 35.

produced in the construction of Europe as a legible, governable, commensurate policy space."[49]

The last example of periodization comes from Luce Pépin, who wrote a very detailed report on the history of European cooperation in ET.[50] Given that the author was an official of the European Commission and the report a joint product of Commission staff, the periodization takes actual events as landmarks. The first phase actually started before the founding of the European Communities, namely with the founding of the Council of Europe in 1948 and ended in 1968. This phase is called "The Europe of education before European Community involvement". The 1969 Summit at The Hague initiated the second phase, which lasted until 1984. This phase, entitled "The early days of Community cooperation in the field of education", covers the first meeting of education ministers and the first joint study program. In 1985, the preparation for the adoption of the first action programs, COMETT and ERASMUS, began. At this point the third phase – "From the launching of the Community programs to the inclusion of education in the Treaty" – set in. The phase ended in 1992 with the Treaty on European Union and the introduction of Article 126 on general education. Phase number five, "Towards the knowledge society" started in 1993 and ended in 1999. The last phase in Pépin's report covers the years 2000 to 2005 where the Lisbon European Council initiated a new era of cooperation in ET and where the Lisbon strategy made ET a political priority. This phase is entitled: "Education and training are central to the Union's economic and social strategy for 2010".

2.4 Developing the research question

A corpus analysis in the EurLex data archive conducted by Michael Geiss, from the University of Zurich, has identified an incredible number of 294,059 individual documents released by the EC institutions in the period between 1968 and 2000. The analysis revealed that since 1972, more than 1000 and since 1985, more than 10,000 documents were released every year. Using the keyword search function for the keywords educat*, learn*, school* and training*, Geiss found that between 1974 and 1990, on average, seven percent of all Documents released by the EC referred to one or several of these keywords. Since 1990, the percentage has even doubled. Taking the

---

[49] Lawn and Grek 2012, p. 83.
[50] Pépin 2006.

whole period of analysis into account, the keyword "training*" is most often found in the corpus of the EurLex data archive.[51]

In conducting a bibliometric analysis, Bernd Käpplinger from the University of Giesen found that international ACE research during the last twenty-five years has made extensive use of policy documents.[52] References to national and international policy documents substantially increased in total, whereby EU documents attracted the most attention. Results show that the share of references to policy documents grew from 4.9 percent in 1995 to 5.8 percent in 2007. In 2010, a peak of 10 percent was reached. During that time the use of documents from the EU, OECD, and UNESCO doubled so that finally, in 2013, their share of citations superseded those of national policy documents. The EU has more than quadrupled its citation rate from 10 percent in 2007 to 42 percent in 2013 and has, therefore, become as relevant a source as any national government or agency.

According to Simona Sava, Ekkehard Nuissl and Anca Lustrea "[a]n important focus in the research is on governance and implementation of policy measures"[53] whereby most of this research is conducted in order to develop better means of managing policy implementation or evaluating policy outcomes. Such research has a rather strong tendency towards either justifying existing measures or furnishing evidence for the creation of new measures and can, therefore, go without proper reflection and critical assessment.

Although perhaps contrary to the passage above, Marcella Milana and John Holford claim that there has not been enough research on the EU's ACE policies. Neither ACE scholars, nor scholars from other disciplines have gone into detail on EU ACE policy. In particular, Milana and Holford hold that "[t]he complexity of policymaking as a co-production process remains largely unexplored."[54] They regret that serious policy research depends, for instance, on the access to data or to people. It is simply often not possible to receive secret documents or an interview from one of the important policymakers or from politicians. This restricts proper policy research, according to these authors. The former Austrian envoy to the ET 2020 adult education working group, Birgit Aschemann, also demands more research concerning the EU's ACE policies.[55] She indicates that despite the massive influence of

[51] Geiss 2017, pp. 216–220.
[52] Käpplinger 2015.
[53] Sava et al. 2016, p. 7.
[54] Holford and Milana 2014, p. 6.
[55] Aschemann 2015, p. 10.

the EU on national education practice, so far, research has not given enough consideration to the role of the EU within the formation of national policies.

Palle Rasmussen et al. outline an additional hindering aspect of policy in ACE when they say that policy agendas and the argumentation of policy-makers "[are] often conceptualised in too narrow and even ahistorical ways."[56] This appears to be an important point since it can be said that often-times too much attention is paid to short-term solutions without proper re-flection on evolutionary patterns, on what has already been completed unsat-isfactorily, or on what has already been completed successfully. From the viewpoint of research, Rasmussen et al. hold that "[i]n order to further un-derstand globalised and Europeanised education policy discourses and prac-tices it is important to study their historical origins and contemporary con-texts".[57]

The research of this study, thus, gains momentum with the notion that a lack of historical knowledge leads to a limited capacity for interpreting and critically reflecting upon transitory circumstances and contemporary issues. As concerns ET in the EU, this study will claim that the current politics are the result of the accretion of power innate in the evolutionary process, in the course of which the EU's specific policy focus and governance arrangements have taken shape. It is believed that an inquiry about the history of ET poli-tics by means of academic literature and official documents has the potential to provide knowledge useful for further empirical research as well as for pol-icy formation.

The following questions form the research interest: in what way have re-sults of certain events, of politicians' strategic behavior, of court decisions, or of conceptual shifts accumulated against the backdrop of the general evo-lution of the EU and the European unification project? How have these de-velopments incrementally piled up to become today's political objectives and the corresponding governance arrangements in education and training? What has been the role of adult and continuing education in this context?

In an attempt to identify historic patterns or find feasible explanations for the relations between past and present, four roughly defined phases will be examined between 1969, when the first idea for a center for the development of education was proposed at the summit in The Hague, and 2017, when the *New Skills Agenda* was launched. The four historical phases were derived partly from the relevant academic literature and partly from initial archival

---

[56] Rasmussen et al. 2015, p. 480.
[57] Rasmussen et al. 2015, p. 481.

research. The following are the research questions and the chapters of the historical study.

Research questions
- Which historical developments have shaped the current EU policy focus and the current EU governance in the field of education and training?
- In what way has the EC and the EU addressed adult and continuing education in the history of education and training?

Chapters of the historical study
- Primary law, vocational training and general education: ET related provision in the Treaties from the European Coal and Steel Community to the Lisbon Treaties.
- ET politics in the 1970s: The contextual development and organizational processes leading up to the adoption of the first Action Program in Education in 1976. (Focus 1969-1976)
- ET politics in the 1980s: The political events and judicial interventions that enabled the Commission to implement the first Action Programs in the late 1980s. (Focus 1981-1987)
- ET politics in the 1990s: The strategic work and learning of the Commission in the context of the 1990s policy work on lifelong learning and knowledge society. (Focus 1993-1997)
- ET politics after 2000: The Lisbon Agenda, the changing concepts of quality in adult and continuing education, the European Framework for Cooperation in Education and Training – ET 2020.

3. Methodology of the historical study

According to the internationally renowned expert in research methodology and evidence-based policy making Zina O'Leary, "[h]istorical analysis is a specific form of textual analysis"[1] that might include texts such as official data and records from various national or international organizations, as well as organizational documents and records such as websites, pamphlets, brochures or records from meetings. Keith Punch, a specialist of research methods in education confirms this, pointing out that "[d]ocuments, both historical and contemporary, are a rich source of data for education and social research."[2] The challenge in doing such historical analysis based on documents, though, is threefold: the research must ensure that what happened actually took place, it must inquire as to why things happened and it must give an account of the implications of the occurrences.

Types of sources used in the historical study

Historical sources are generally divided into primary sources and secondary sources. Primary sources are those sources that give testimony to an event or to the results of events. It is important to note that primary sources refer to records that were created in the past. Secondary sources, on the contrary, are sources, which give account of past events from a distant perspective. This means that secondary sources were written after the events had taken place. In this case, it also is important to note that secondary sources might already include interpretations. For the historical study in this book, extensive use of primary sources will be made, while secondary sources are used to support the argumentation and the narrative created from the examination of primary sources.

For the selection of primary resources, inspiration was taken from the review of relevant academic literature and from initial archival research. The identification and selection of primary sources was conducted in line with four predefined types of primary sources: primary sources of established significance, primary sources recounting events, primary sources indicating change concerning the policy focus or the governance arrangement and primary sources consolidating discourse.

---

[1] O'Leary 2010, p. 224.
[2] Punch 2009, p. 158.

Besides documents of established significance (e.g. the Treaty on European Union 1992, the White Paper on growth, competitiveness and employment 1993, the Lisbon Council Conclusions 2000 or the Memorandum on Lifelong Learning 2000), documents that indicate a change in the policy direction or the governance approach were considered most relevant (e.g. Conclusions of The Hague Summit of 1969, court of justice judgment in the Gravier case 1985, Rolling agenda decision 1999), followed by documents that consolidate existing discourses (e.g. Communication on education 1974, Action Plan on adult learning 2006, New Skills Agenda 2017), or simply recount events. The following is a list of primary sources used in the historical study.

- Primary law documents like the founding Treaties (TECSC, TEAC, TEEC, TEU, TEFEU), amended Treaties (Treaty of Amsterdam), and consolidated Treaties (TEU and TFEU consolidated 2016), and the Charter of Fundamental Rights of the EU
- Judgments of the European Court of Justice and Opinions of the Advocate General on the cases preparing judgments
- Binding secondary law acts like Directives and Regulations, Decisions
- Non-binding legal acts like Council Decisions, Council Resolutions, Recommendations, European Council Conclusions
- Official documents of non-binding soft law character produced by the EC/EU institutions like Communications, Memoranda, White Papers, or working programs
- Studies of political character written by academic scholars or politicians on behalf of EC/EU institutions like the Janne Report or the Adonnino Report
- Studies of research character written on behalf of EC/EU institutions by academic researchers or consultants
- Documents produced in the context of the OMC working groups like official working group mandates or final reports of peer learning activities
- Public speeches of politicians or high-ranking Commission officials

A few particularities must be taken into consideration when examining these primary sources. The documents are produced by different actors and serve different purposes. The original Treaties and amended Treaties are the result of political processes and must be signed by all Member States. Consolidated Treaties are documents put together by administrative staff integrating primary law documents like protocols, annexes or corrigenda into the existing Treaties. Treaties are the most formal type of documents.

Secondary law of binding character (Directives, Regulations and Decisions) is the result of formal legislative procedures like the former *Co-decision Method* or the current *Ordinary Legislative Procedure* (OLP), which are laid down in the Treaties. Non-binding legal acts of soft law character (Recommendations, Opinions, some Council Decisions, Resolutions and Communications) can be adopted after a formal procedure but can also be released by single institutions like the Council of Ministers, the Commission or the Parliament.

The Commission staff devises and releases documents like White Papers or Memoranda. These documents represent the views of the Commission and the Commission staff and not the views of the Member States and usually have a preparatory character. Having a preparatory character means that they contain proposals that might be based on research evidence or on consultation with stakeholders. When the Council and the Parliament agree on the Commission proposals in the formal legislative procedures, they might be translated into legal acts.

Legal acts, which are produced by the Council of Ministers or the European Council (Conclusions or Presidency Conclusions) represent the views of the Member States or at least the political views of the Member States' representatives in the Councils. As concerns the Council, it must be noted that in education and training, the composition of the Council has been unique since the Education Committee has included representatives of the Council and of the Commission.

Whenever it was possible during the research to identify an author, such is the case of some Commission staff documents, the name of this person will be mentioned because it helps to better understand the contents and arguments put forward in the document. Records such as public speeches are obviously the most transparent testimony of a personal viewpoint, while reports are supposed to be the result of methodologically correct research.

The origin and the purpose of a document also constitute its significance. Documents of the highest political significance are the Treaties and the Conclusions of the European Council because the European Council has the right to indicate political directions and priorities. Depending on whether a legal act is binding or non-binding, the significance can be substantial because the Member States must integrate the decisions into national law or must implement a new measure. Non-binding documents can unfold a soft law power and also lead to full compliance by the Member States. Commission staff documents can be of great significance because they initiate discourses or introduce concepts or terminology. Judgments of the European Court of

Justice can also be of great significance. Especially judgments of precedent character or those constituting case law have had a key function in the creation of the institutions and the deepening of European integration.

Against some initial worries, there were hardly any barriers to accessing primary sources. The EU itself has a very well-furnished databank (EurLex) in which legal acts, administrative acts or judgments dating back to 1952 are collected and provided for free access. Moreover, the online archives of the EU institutions and the online archives on European integration at the University of Pittsburgh, USA and the University of Luxembourg served the purpose of the study well. Below is a list of the places where primary sources were retrieved.

In addition to the rich corpus of primary sources, two types of secondary sources were used. The first type was that of academic research publications like monographs, editor's publications or articles in international journals written by academic scholars. The second type consisted of the same types of publications but written by officials of the European Commission or by politicians. For instance, the former French Minister of National Education Olivier Guichard laid down the ideas he put forward at the 1969 The Hague Summit in an article originally published in Le Monde in 1971. Also, the former Director for Education, Director General for Employment and Social Affairs and founder of the ERASMUS program, Hywel Ceri Jones, published several articles in international journals, in which he reported about the developments of ET policy. The same is the case of Alan Smith, Luce Pépin and Anders Hingel, all of which were previously high-ranking officials of the Commission.

Methodical procedure of the historical study

The methodical procedure that was applied in writing the historical study is based on the idea of a free document analysis. It comprised four steps: in the first step, text passages concerned with ET and/or ACE in the primary sources were identified and counterchecked with the research questions. In a second step, the selected text passages were examined according to three questions: (1) does the passage add further information to the narrative concerning the historical development? Does the passage address an event or statement that is not sufficiently covered in existing research? Does this passage indicate policy or governance change? Then, in a third step, extracts and commentaries were written and secondary sources were consulted to support the narrative unfolded from the primary sources.

The structure of each chapter of the historical study except for the first chapter is identical. In the beginning, an overview of contextual developments is provided. This overview covers developments in the general political environment, in the European Communities and the European Union,[3] and in the academic discourse concerning work, education and training. Then follows a description of the transition period, which refers to the years in between the core phases of the examination. The main part eventually contains the examination and discussion of the most important political documents. Lastly, a conclusion is constructed in which the most significant findings of the examination are derived and summarized.

Limitations of the methodological approach

The type of historical research conducted is based on the idea of free document analysis. Document analysis is widespread in policy and governance-oriented research in education, as well as in historical research, however this approach also comes with a few limitations. Since document analysis is used by many scholars, it might be argued that the method is not very innovative. Moreover, the depth of document analysis depends on the documents one can access and how close they come to the reality that is being recounted. It might happen, therefore, that such a methodical procedure may only produce superficial evidence. In fact, it can be acknowledged that more empirical research would also be needed in policy and governance research to get closer to the political reality.[4] Oral history could certainly be a possibility for an empirical approach to history that would give a voice to those who personally experienced the events.

What is innovative about this book, however, is not the method, but rather the focus on ACE as well as the selected events and documents and the way data was arranged. Fortunately, the archives on the European Communities and the European Union are accessible; this is why a rich corpus of documents was available.

Lastly, it must be mentioned that no specific theoretical lenses were applied in the analysis and interpretation of data. Since the history is so rich in events of great complexity intertwined with each other, looking at them with the necessarily limited terminological repertoire of a theory, would not have

---

[3] As far as the EC and EU are concerned in the description of contextual developments, the following was used European Union. The history of the European Union [website]

[4] Holford and Milana 2014, p. 6.

been appropriate. It is hoped that the relevant academic literature that was consulted could make up for this and moderate and support the argumentation to bring about a meaningful narrative.

4. The conceptual framework

The conceptual framework addresses terminology and concepts relevant to the historical study. At first, some remarks will be made concerning the three basic settings of international cooperation in relation to ET. Subsequently, the political system will be defined as a functional subsystem of society, which enters into a relationship with other functional subsystems through a cyclic process. Then, the three analytical dimensions of a politics – polity, politics and policy – will be outlined and lastly, the transdisciplinary concept of governance will be discussed.

4.1 International interaction and cooperation

Historically, the practice of education and training has always had a certain affinity towards cooperation at the international level. There is a long tradition of educators undertaking study travels to see how culture and teaching works in other countries and how education is organized elsewhere. Exchange, though, was not really institutionalized until after the First World War while the end of the Second World War gave new impetus for international cooperation. Since then, many international institutions arose in the area of *education and training* (ET) to frame exchange and cooperation.

The term *'international'* in this book shall denote that an organizational entity, a thematic subject, an interactive process or a discourse extends beyond national borders *or* has implications for developments by which several states, corporate actors or individuals are affected.[1] *Internationalization,* then, shall indicate the qualitative and quantitative intensification of interactions and relationships among nationally situated actors and/or national and supranational actors. This may materialize in a greater number of networks, cooperation, exchange of information and people, or the integration of new perspectives on education theory and practice. Analytically, three basic settings can be distinguished in which international interaction and cooperation occurs: the inter-governmental setting, the supranational setting and the transnational setting.[2]

Inter-governmental means that two or more governments, state-representing organizations or people officially cooperate with each other or enter into some kind of relationship or agreement. The modes of interaction can either

---

[1] Nuissl 2010, p. 162.
[2] Schmidt-Lauff and Egetenmeyer 2015, pp. 272–273.

be negotiations, bargaining or deliberation. Inter-governmental relations are mostly economically, politically or culturally motivated. In addition to bilateral or multilateral meetings, *International Governmental Organizations* (IGO) provide settings in which exchange takes place. Examples for such IGO settings are the European Council, the Council of the European Union, the meetings of the Committee of Permanent Representatives, the OECD Ministers' summits, the United Nations General Assembly or the Council of Europe Assembly.

Supranational refers to the fact of nation states conferring competences for political decisions and policy implementation upon an organizational structure that acts – according to its mandate – independently of the nation states but has the right to make binding proposals and legislation. Such supranational organizations can be political organizations (European Commission), economic organizations (World Trade Organization) or interest organizations (Greenpeace), or specific organizational units within IGO's like the Secretariat General or the Directorates of the OECD, the European Commission or the European Court of Justice.

Transnational settings are the least political of the three. Transnational interaction takes place when nationally based non-state actors or individuals, such as educational institutions, private businesses, teachers or researchers cooperate with each other. The ways of interaction such as at conferences, teaching or research mobility or online can be manifold. In many cases, transnational cooperation is facilitated by funding programs such as provided by the *European Social Fund* (ESF), or mobility programs like ERASMUS+.

International cooperation in all three settings is a reaction to the fact that actors have converging interests and share norms or values, which they try to pursue while interacting with one another. However, having a political goal, international cooperation can also be a situation in which actors have diverging standpoints on issues by which they are mutually affected. They try to argue against the standpoints of others on the appropriateness of their own standpoint in order to persuade the counterparts or to reach a compromise that suffices the demands at stake. Internationalization of politics, therefore, might lead to a stronger interdependence and an increased demand for justification of national action with regard to international developments, as well as to an incremental loss of national sovereignty.

4.2 The political subsystem

The approach taken in this book supports the notion that the political system is a functional subsystem of society.[3] A functional subsystem, such as the political system, the legal system, the health care system or the education system, contributes to society in accordance with the logic of its very own institutions, organizational structures, values and principles, processes and mechanisms. By character, a functional subsystem closes off externally from other subsystems and differs internally from further functional subunits. In the political system there are functional subunits like industrial politics, social politics, labor market politics or education politics. Societal subsystems and functional subunits, however, enter into a form of interdependent relationship with each other because they share concerns, their interests overlap or actors belong to several subsystems or subunits. One becomes aware of this interdependency when confronted with statements like: *the economic progress depends on the quality of education* or *the political culture in a country determines the organization of education.* Internal interdependency within a system is evident in statements like: *universities engage in continuing education and thereby compete with adult education organizations on the market* or *adult basic education has to make up for the failures of school education.*

The political system enters into a functional relationship with other societal subsystems through a cyclic process that consists of four elements: political input, political output, political outcome and political impact.[4] This cyclic process can be described as follows: first, a subsystem communicates a problem, a demand or forwards a request to the political system and therefore creates *political input.* Political input activates actors in the political system to invest institutional, constitutional, financial, and human resources in order to provide a solution to the problem, meet the demands or give an answer to the request, for instance, by means of formal decisions; this is termed *political output.* Political output, then, has to be implemented by the politico-administrative system in the form of policies in order to create a *political outcome*, which may finally have *political impact* in the subsystem, in which the problem was located or that forwarded the request.

---

[3] Holzer 2015, p. 55.
[4] Schneider and Janning 2006, p. 15.

4.3 Three analytical dimensions of politics

Political practice and scholarship distinguish three dimensions of politics: polity, politics and policy.[5] All three together constitute the context in which the governance of societal subsystems takes place.

The concept of *polity* refers to the institutional and constitutional dimension of politics that brings about the formal organizational structure in which political processes take place, and defines the formal principles and the informal cultural norms by which political processes are guided. The concept of polity, thus, refers to the institutions, the principles and the culture(s), on which the organization of a political system is based.

The characteristics of the institutions of a polity are stipulated in a constitution or constitutional treaty, which defines the various institutional structures and their relationships with each other, laying down the core principles and determining the rules and procedures of decision-making and the tasks of the institutions. As concerns the EU, the Treaties signed by all Member States are the constitution that defines the polity and regulates political interaction.

The most visible manifestation of a polity is the separation of powers into the legislative (parliament), executive (government and state bureaucracies) and judicial (courts) branches. In addition, the party system, public administration, interest groups or the social partners form parts of a polity.

The concept of *politics* contains all the complex processes of interaction by which political objectives, strategies or operational programs are initiated, negotiated, formed and communicated, and which lead to formal decisions and their implementation. In a democratic system, the actors of the polity, plus political stakeholders and the public interact with each other in different ways and engage in a debate over the means and ends of political action.

Politics refers to the interaction between actors like government, coalitions and opposition, negotiations and bargaining of political representatives with social partners, businesses and with other political or societal entities and the interaction of political actors with the public such as in the case of electoral campaigns. The interaction between all these actors can be regulated by means of formal arrangements (e.g. decision-making procedures, collective bargaining) or might be part of the legislative or executive tasks conferred upon the political actors or public authorities (e.g. policy implementation). It might also occur in rather informal settings (e.g. campaigning, public speeches).

---

[5] Blum and Schubert 2009, pp. 14–15; Knoepfel et al. 2011, pp. 45–48.

The concept of *policy* stands for the substantial and normative dimension, that is, political objectives, political content and the materialized results of political debate. Policy, thus, refers to the means and ends developed and formed in the course of political processes, adopted through formal decisions and usually implemented by public administration. The purpose of any policy is to have an effect on the subsystem it targets. Three types of policy can be distinguished: distributive, regulative, and redistributive policies.[6]

- *Distributive policy* is in most cases some form of financial support. It is attempted to make sure that public money is allocated evenly so that all potential beneficiaries can actually benefit from it. An example at the European level is the ERASMUS mobility program, which is open to all eligible candidates and gives financial support after a successful submission process.
- *Regulative policy* is the deliberate promotion of a topic through legislation or regulation leading to standardization or more rigid organization of measures concerning this topic. An example therefore is the EQF, which prescribes the introduction of complementary standardized frameworks at the national level.
- *Redistributive policy* is often policy that changes the allocation of capacities, tasks, rights or financial resources within the political organization. When – as will be argued later – the responsibility for education is transferred from one Directorate General to another Directorate General in the Commission, then the resources are redistributed so that it affects the politics of education in various respects.

What constitutes a policy or policies? The following explanation builds on the work of Knoepfel et al. Although, in accordance with these authors, only the term public policy is used, the term education policy shall be implicit. Knoepfel et al. list eight constitutive elements of public policies.[7]

1. *Solution to a public problem.*
   A public policy is an attempt to solve a problem that was acknowledged to be relevant in the political process. Political leaders and stakeholders, public administration and the public, agree on a problem, whereby the capacities for the decision, the implementation and management are conferred upon by public or semi-public actors.

---

[6] Schneider and Janning 2006, pp. 23–24.
[7] Knoepfel et al. 2011, pp. 48–52.

2. *The existence of an adequate target group.*
Public policy wants to change the behavior of actors and/or groups of actors. Among those are actors who are considered responsible for having contributed to the creation of the problem or those who are considered capable of contributing to its solution. Moreover, actors can be those who suffer from or are affected by the problem and consequently who will benefit from its abolishment.

3. *A certain degree of strategic coherence.*
Public policy should be based on a theoretical model for the explanation of causal relations. Such a model may be, for instance, the welfare state, functionalist theory or human capital theory. Operational action follows an attempt to achieve the policy goals by operationalization of the theoretical model and the consequent application of interventions created from it. When such operational action in various policy fields is consistent with the model, the policies are coherent.

4. *Numerous decisions and activities.*
Public policy consists in more than just one specific action like a written communication or regulation. This distinguishes public policy from a single policy measure such as a funding scheme. It is defined by its comprehensive character in regard to the problem. All measures together build a set of measures potentially more effective in solving the problem than single measures.

5. *Programs of intervention.*
Knoepfel et al. assert that a public policy without implemented measures can hardly be considered a policy. Concrete operational measures must be part of an overarching strategic plan and must be effectively implemented. A policy proposal, which does not result in a decision that leads to the implementation of a program will not have an impact and, thus, will not contribute to the solving of the problem.

6. *Public actors as key players.*
Actors who decide, implement and administrate have to be public actors, to which tasks and competences are formally delegated by public institutions. In the context of soft governance arrangements, however, private actors like educational institutions, private commercial enterprises or civil society organizations have steadily become more relevant in the formation of policies.

7. *The existence of formal decisions.*

The operation of public policies as well as the opposite – the absence of active measures – must follow formal procedures and formal decisions. Knoepfel et al. contend that the absence of measures is not equal to public policies, except a formal decision is made to abstain from any intervention.

8. *Binding character of decisions and actions.*
Public policy usually indicates an authoritative relation between the politico-administrative system and the public based upon legislative power. Given the diversity of interventions and actors and the diversity of instruments, however, non-binding elements of public policies have increased, so that arrangements of soft governance have become more relevant.

4.4 Old, direct and new, indirect governance

Governance is a transdisciplinary concept. It is being applied in law studies, political science, policy studies, public administration studies, sociology, economics, organizational theory, history or education. According to Julia von Blumenthal, a German professor of political science, governance is a hotly debated concept that lacks clarity and precision.[8] When a scientific concept is applied to a very broad range of issues and used by different disciplines, it encounters the danger of concept stretching and concept obfuscation. Claus Offe, another German professor of political sociology, advances the notion that governance might be an "empty signifier",[9] thus, a concept that could mean everything and nothing. Looking for definitions, it becomes evident that they generally refer to a broad continuum of arrangements by which the behavior of groups and individuals is guided or coordinated.

Oliver Williamson, a Nobel Prize winning organizational theorist contends "governance is the means by which to infuse order, thereby mitigate conflict, and realize mutual gains".[10] The legal scholars Victoria Nourse and Gregory Schaffer distinguish between an "old governance theory of law" and a "new governance theory of law". They argue that the „new governance theory of law focuses on efforts to move beyond a court-centric and rights-focused basis of law and toward new forms of problem solving involving institutional experimentation in a pragmatist sense."[11]

---

[8] Blumenthal 2014, p. 88.
[9] Offe 2008, p. 67.
[10] Williamson 2009, p. 456.
[11] Nourse and Schaffer 2009, p. 88.

The professor of law, Michael Waterstone provides an account that thoroughly captures what has been happening in the area of education in the last thirty years. He also refers to a new form of governance whose goal is „to get a broad range of stakeholders involved, including regulated entities, private interest groups, government enforcement agencies, and the class of people that the law is intended to benefit." He continues to suggest that "[i]deally, these various groups converge on a set of legal norms, and then utilize their collective energy in achieving effective and context-specific solutions."[12] The specialist for international education research, Marcello Parreira do Amaral emphasizes the abstract character of governance theory.[13] For him, governance as a theory is an attempt to assemble a conceptual framework to better describe and analyze how collective behavior is coordinated in the practice politics. According to Josef Schrader from the German Institute of Adult Education, the question that is of interest to scientific analysis with regard to education and training is: "who tries to purposefully influence and diminish the discrepancy between the given and the desired of what, how, and why[?]"[14]

In the case of education, it is most appropriate to understand governance in accordance with the last three references. This understanding has indeed diffused over the course of the last three decades and it has taken much impetus from global developments and from changes in public management.

The sheer number of actors with a stake in the formation of policies has increased in the last decades so that the diversity and heterogeneity of political actors has automatically grown. Private corporate and private civil society actors have obtained more power in the political sphere. Moreover, the accelerating speed of the globalization of economic activities and its repercussions in politics have made political actors aware that the traditional national modes of governing have to be complemented by international or supranational modes of governance. The British EU expert Ben Rosamund calls this "the emergence of private authority within the regional and global arenas" and "the advent of public authority above the nation-state."[15]

As a result of that growing complexity in the organization of political activities, public administration is being forced to adopt managerial techniques in order to maintain relevant, effective, efficient and transparent

---

[12] Waterstone 2007, p. 482.
[13] Parreira do Amaral 2017, p. 214.
[14] Schrader 2010, p. 44.
[15] Rosamund 2009, p. 92.

service amidst the changing societal, economic and political reality. Therefore, *New Public Management* (NPM) instruments are being applied to supplement traditional techniques and methods of governance and public administration.

The professors Guy Peters from the University of Pittsburgh and Jon Pierre from the University of Gothenburg argue that the growing powers of international markets and supranational organizations have diminished the capacity of national governments to autonomously steer economic and societal developments.[16] This argument implies a weakening of centralist political steering in favor of more decentralized participatory processes. Such a participatory process aims to coordinate social action rather than impose rules. Peters and Pierre list four constitutive elements, which indicate a shift from the "old" mode of direct, hierarchical governance to the "new" form of indirect, coordinated governance.[17]

1. Networks with homogeneous or heterogeneous actor constellations gain influence and bargaining power. It is not only that they can make their interests heard, they are also self-organized networks and may therefore reject governmental or centralized attempts to authoritative steering.
2. Central authorities have to shift the focus of action from control to influence. They are part of the networks, however direct control is replaced by the coordination of the networks and bargaining with network representatives. Central authorities try to influence networks through discourse, quasi-market instruments like benchmarking, incentive measures or facilitate action by means of financial support, rather than by imposing regulations or adopting legislation.
3. Public private partnerships and a blending of public and private resources structure a system of governance. In some cases, central authorities decide to create satellite agencies or to outsource tasks to network actors. In other cases, they prefer shared responsibility. This happens, for example, when projects are co-financed.
4. The use of multiple instruments helps to establish and maintain networks and to create and to sustain mutual benefit. Public policy is formed, for instance, by means of participatory research, funds are allocated through public tenders, or policy implementation is monitored through regular performance assessment.

---

[16] Peters and Pierre 1998, p. 223.
[17] Peters and Pierre 1998, pp. 225–227.

To summarize, it must be reiterated that the increasing shift in power from national to supranational, and from public to private leads to the opening of a continuum, in which various modes for coordinating an actor's behavior exist.

What – in this book – will be called direct or hierarchical governance refers to the 'old' modes of governance and carries the notion of *one* entity like government or central authority steering societal developments by exercising the rule of law, while the public or the stakeholders obey to these rules. In such a case, it is usually evident who governs and who is governed. As was indicated by Renate Mayntz, this implies a hierarchical relationship between the subject and the object of governance.[18]

On the other hand, what will be called indirect, or coordinated governance refers to 'new' modes of governance and indicates that action is cooperative and coordinated and aims at agreeing on mutually shared interests and adjusting societal processes to constantly changing situations. According to the German sociologist Thomas Brüsemeister, this form of governance is a deliberate attempt of a network to gain influence over policy developments.[19] Actors participating can be public (ministries, public administration, regional governments, social partners), private (business corporations, civil society organizations, education providers) or individuals (researchers, consultants, lobbyists). With this form of governance, it is not at all evident who is exerting influence on whom, since there is no real hierarchical order.

This means, in a nutshell, that hierarchical *direct governance* is formal and authorities can enforce compliance through the exercise of its formal competences and reach objectives by the application of democratically legitimate instruments. *Indirect governance* is rather informal and participating actors can attempt to convince or persuade others of the benefits of their ideas and apply instruments that facilitate discourse, interaction, cooperation or competition.

In the EU governance displays both forms: the direct and the indirect form of governance.[20] On the one hand, it refers to the formal procedures and mechanisms, which are in place to hierarchically govern a policy field by imposing rules and sanctioning non-compliance. These procedures are stipulated in the constitutional treaties and the mechanisms derive from the capacities of the institutions conferred upon them in the same treaties. This is

---

[18] Mayntz 2008, p. 43.
[19] Brüsemeister 2011, p. 13.
[20] Rosamund 2009.

equal to what will be called direct governance or hierarchical governance. On the other hand, governance in the EU refers to the non-formal or informal settings, in which institutional actors interact with external actors. Such governance abstains from imposing rules and from sanctions; rather it wants to coordinate action in a cooperative non-hierarchical manner. This is what will be called an indirect governance arrangement or non-hierarchical governance arrangement.

5. The system of the European Union

The EU holds a special position among international (governmental) organizations (IO/IGO). Concerning its constitutional and institutional character as well as concerning its political competences, it is distinct from other IOs/IGOs such as the *United Nations* (UN) and its satellite organizations like *United Nations Educational, Scientific and Cultural Organization* (UNESCO), or such as the *Organization for Economic Cooperation and Development* (OECD) and the *Council of Europe* (CoE). According to Werner Schroeder, professor of European Law at the University of Innsbruck in Austria, it is still disputed in academic literature whether the EU is more adequately described as a federal system with incrementally integrating federal states, or a supranational organization with a juridical status independent of the Member States.[1]

The institutional structure of the EU comprises seven official institutions and a number of additional organizational structures.[2] The following seven are the official institutions: the *European Commission* which forms the executive branch and which is a supranational type of structure, the *European Parliament* (supranational) and the *Council of the European Union* (intergovernmental) which form the legislative branch, and the *European Court of Justice* which forms the judiciary branch and which a supranational type of structure. The *European Council*, in which the heads of state convene, has a special status because it is neither involved in legislation nor in implementation of policies. In addition to the official institutions there are the ancillary institutions of the *European Central Bank* and the *Court of Auditors* and the advisory bodies of the *Economic and Social Committee* and the *Committee of the Regions*.

Other organizational structures relevant in relation to ET are European and national agencies. The two most important European agencies are the *Centre for the Development of Vocational Education and Training* (CEDEFOP) and the *European Training Foundation* (ETF). In the context of ET, national agencies coordinate and manage the implementation of funding programs, such as the *European Social Fund* (ESF) or the ERAMUS+ program at the national level.

---

[1] Schroeder 2015, pp. 26–27.
[2] TEU consolidated, Art. 13.

The competences and the tasks of the institutions, as well as legislative and decision-making procedures are stipulated in primary law, that is European Law. It is the law on which the EU is founded, thus, its constitution. It comprises of the official Treaties or the amended Treaties and the specific legal acts adding further provision to the Treaties, such as Annexes or Protocols. Since 2009, the *Treaty on the Functioning of the European Union* (TFEU) and the *Treaty on the European Union* (TEU) are the constitution of the European Union.[3] They were both signed in Lisbon in 2007 that is why they are also called the Lisbon Treaties, and came eventually into force on December 1st, 2009. In 2000, the *Charter of Fundamental Rights of the European Union* was presented.[4] It was integrated into EU primary law and went into force only together with the Lisbon Treaties in 2009.

Since EU primary law is public international law, it must be unanimously decided upon and signed by all Member States. Concerning the legal status, since the Lisbon Treaties, the EU has explicit legal personality and can therefore conclude agreements with states or other international organizations.[5] According to Klaus-Dieter Borchardt, a reader of law at the University of Würzburg, Germany, and Director of the Internal Energy Market in the Commission, five elements characterize the legal nature of the EU.[6]

- First, the institutional structure is to make sure that action reflects the overall interests of the EU in accordance with the objectives defined in the Treaty.
- Second, compared with other IGO's, greater powers are consigned upon the EU institutions, even in areas, which usually remain subject to the authority of national governments.
- Third, what distinguishes the EU from other IGO's categorically is that the EU established a legal order, which is independent of the legal systems in the Member States.
- Fourth, the law of the EU is directly applicable to all Member States. This means that all European citizens can invoke their rights in front of the ECJ and force the Member States to adapt legislation in accordance with EU law. At the same time, the direct applicability of EU law imposes obligations upon the citizens as well as on the Member States in the exercise of their rights.

---

[3] TEU consolidated, Art.1.
[4] EU Charter.
[5] TEU consolidated, Art. 1; 47.
[6] Borchardt 2010, p. 32.

- Lastly, EU law presides over national law in the sense that national law cannot amend or revoke the legal order of the EU in case the two should disagree.

5.1 The institutions of the European Union

Not all of the seven institutions have been equally involved in ET politics. For this reason, only those institutions will be presented, which have the formal competences to participate in the *Ordinary Legislative Procedure* (OLP), as far as ET is concerned, or that have historically had significant influence on ET politics. The institutions participating in the OLP are the European Commission, the European Council and the European Parliament. The European Court of Justice will also be presented because it has played an important role in the history of ET in the EC. Finally, a few words will be said about the *Committee of the Regions* (CoR) and the *Economic and Social Committee* (ESC), which are to be consulted in the legislative and policy processes.

European Commission

The European Commission is the executive organ of the EU. Performing its executive capacity, the Commission must act independently of national concerns or affiliation, shall actively promote the interests of the EU and work towards the accomplishment of the EU's main goals.[7] In terms of the overall outcome of EU politics, the interdependence of the Commission is expected to counterbalance the Council, which serves the interests of the national governments.

According to the TEU, the Commission has four competences.[8] Firstly, it has the so-called Right of Initiative. Legislative acts can only be adopted after a proposal by the Commission has been made. Proposals must contribute to the achievement of the Union's objectives. The Right of Initiative has established the Commission as the most forceful promoter of European integration. It further implies that the content of legislative acts and the content of policy is *de facto* almost exclusively developed by the Commission or in cooperation with other organizations acting under the auspices of the Commission. Since the Commission has the right to initiate legislation, it can

---

[7] TEU consolidated, Art. 17.
[8] TEU consolidated, Art. 17.

influence legislation to some extent even in the absence of formal legislative power.

Secondly, in line with the executive competences conferred upon it, the Commission is the only institution that has the capacity and legitimacy to implement, coordinate and administer policy and budgetary programs. Thirdly, the Commission has the competence to control the application of EU law within the Member States, which makes the Commission the so-called guardian of the Treaties. Finally, fourthly, the Commission officially represents the EU interests in external relations.

The political arm of the Commission is the *Commission College*, which comprises the Commissioners plus the Commission President. Members of the College, except for the President, are not elected, but appointed by the Member States' governments and accepted by the Parliament. Each commissioner is assigned a specific portfolio in which the responsibilities, tasks and the subordinate service institutions are defined. Subordinate to the commissioners are the Directorate Generals (DG). The DGs form the administrative arm of the Commission. Performing their tasks, the Commissioners and the Commission's civil servants are obliged to promote only the interests of the EU and must abstain from pursuing any national or partisan interests.

The Commission has a hierarchical structure. At the top is the Commissioner, who has a political function, followed by the Directorate Generals with civil service management functions. Each DG is divided into a certain number of directorates with coordinating directors. The DGs are again divided into a certain number of departments, with head of departments.[9] The DGs form what is often called "the EU" or "Brussels", i.e. they form the body of civil servants who are the motor of the Commission's work.

The DGs' civil servants are responsible for the preparation and evaluation of documents and policies and for the coordination of programs and political cooperation.[10] For instance, they prepare and write communications, or they draft proposals for legislative acts. Then, the DGs develop, implement and administrate action programs or financial programs, and evaluate the implementation, the compliance with, and the impact of policies and legislation at the national level.

---

[9] European Commission. The Commissioners [website]
[10] Kopp-Malek et al. 2009, pp. 49–52.

European Council and Council of the European Union

For people not familiar with the EU, the distinction between the *Council of the European Union* and the *European Council* creates confusion. While the *Council of the European Union* has been an official institution since the 1957 TEEC, the *European Council* had long been an informal meeting. Only in 1992 did the TEU officially establish the European Council. Since the 2009 ratification of the EU and the EC Treaties, both Councils are official institutions of the EU.

The *European Council* is the meeting in which the heads of state or heads of government, plus the President of the European Council, the President of the Commission and the High Representative for Foreign Affairs convene. The European Council has the role of the leading actor of the EU in the sense that it provides impetus and defines the political direction of the EU, the objectives and the areas of priority. The European Council, though, has no legislative capacity. Its decisions – if not provided otherwise – are made by consensus.[11]

The *Council of the European Union* (also known as the *Council* or the *Council of Ministers*) is the shorthand term to indicate the meetings where the Member States' ministers discuss their respective policy fields. There is, for instance, a Council of the ministers of finance, of social affairs, of home affairs, of foreign affairs, and of the ministers of education. Only the Council has legislative and budgetary functions, which are exhibited together with the Parliament in the *Ordinary Legislative Procedure*. If not provided otherwise, the Council acts by qualified majority.[12]

The Council is the most important among the EU institutions with respect to legislative aspects as well as with respect to political aspects. Both Councils should act on behalf of national interests, even though the Council of Ministers is to a larger extent accountable to its national constituency. According to Schroeder, this complicates the position of the Councils within the EU systems, since they are at the same time Union institutions.[13] Therefore, they take over a mediating function between supranational and national interests.

The *Council of the European Union* is supported by the *Comité des représentants permanents* (COREPER).[14] The COREPER consists of

---

[11] TEU consolidated, Art. 15.
[12] TEU consolidated, Art. 16.
[13] Schroeder 2015, p. 37.
[14] TEU consolidated, Art. 16.

Brussels-based national diplomats or civil servants representing their national governments and has an essential support function as it is responsible for preparing the work of the Council. Moreover, it is assigned tasks by the Council and can even make procedural decisions.[15] Organizationally, the COREPER is divided into two Committees, designated COREPER 1 and COREPER 2. In the COREPER 2, which is concerned with topics of political priority, the Permanent Representatives of the Member States convene. The COREPER 1 works on thematically more specific issues and assembles policy officers who are often envoys of a respective ministry or public authority.[16]

The COREPER has an important role since it can shape policies and decisions eventually taken by the Council. Johannes Pollack and Peter Slominsky point out that the permanent representatives give stability to the work of the Council because they have insightful knowledge on both the EU and national governments.[17] The COREPER facilitates smooth negotiations and decision-making, prepares dossiers and coordinates meetings.

European Parliament

For many decades the *European Parliament* did not have forceful competences to shape policies. In the 1950s, it was defined only as an assembly with consulting obligations, rather than a parliament of democratic character. It did not have legislative competences, could not exercise control over the executive branch, and did not have political instruments against the Council as national parliaments do.[18]

In 1979, universal suffrage was introduced and the first public elections of the Parliament took place; ever since then, its status has consistently improved. On an informal level, the work relations between the Parliament and the other institutions became better and the influence of the Parliament became slowly more discernible throughout the 1980s. On a formal constitutional level, in 1992, the Maastricht Treaty established the Co-decision Method, which assured the principle of parity in the legislative process. With the Lisbon Treaties in 2009, the Co-decision Method became the Ordinary Legislative Procedure. Since then, the Parliament has been an equal participant in deciding legislation.

---

[15] TFEU consolidated, Art. 240.
[16] Council of the European Union. Council preparatory bodies. [website]
[17] Pollak and Slominski 2006, p. 79.
[18] Maurer 2012, p. 78.

The main competences of the Parliament are the legislative and the budgetary functions it shares with the Council; the functions of democratic political control or supervision and consultation; and the election of the President of the Commission.[19] Through its legislative competences, the Parliament contributes to policies, however, always within the limits established by Treaty provision in respect to the different policy areas. Education and training, for instance, are subject to the principle of subsidiarity, restricting the EU competences to coordination and supplementation. These competences are exercised by the Commission. The Parliament is involved in ET when the legislative acts are decided and since this is only rarely the case, the Parliament has, thus, a rather marginal role in the field of ET.

However, using the so-called partial right to initiative, the Parliament can appeal to the Commission to become active on certain matters.[20] The Commission must follow up on that appeal; otherwise, it could be sued by the Parliament at the European Court of Justice.[21] In academic literature, the opinion is widespread that the Parliament has too little influence on the ET policymaking process. The fact, though, that the Parliament can force the Commission to become active after all, suggests that for the practice of policymaking it is very likely that the Parliament more often acts as the initiator of policy proposals than one might expect. Bechtel et al. point out that in the past, the Parliament has brought topics on the agenda by presenting initiative reports and that by this, the Parliament could influence policy decisions even though it has little formal leverage.[22]

Just as the Commission and the Council, the Parliament also has subordinate units occupied with preparation and coordination of policy work.[23] These subordinate units are Committees, in which the Members of the Parliament meet to discuss issues, develop joint positions and prepare their own proposals.[24] Parliamentary Committees often complement the Commission or DG portfolios, meaning that for almost every DG there is a respective Committee in the Parliament. Moreover, the committees are supported by service departments responsible for research and policy administration.

---

[19] TEU consolidated, Art. 14.
[20] TFEU consolidated, Art. 225.
[21] Maurer 2012, p. 111.
[22] Bechtel et al. 2005, p. 16.
[23] European Parliament. Committees. [website]
[24] Maurer 2012, p. 71.

European Court of Justice

The last of the institutions presented is the *European Court of Justice* (ECJ, sometimes called the *Court of Justice of the European Union*). Even though, the ECJ is not directly involved in policymaking, its contribution to the formation of ET politics has been of great importance. Throughout the 1980s, the major steps towards the implementation of action programs like COMETT or ERASMUS were enabled by ECJ interpretations and judgments.

The main task of the ECJ is to ensure correct interpretation and application of primary and secondary law by Member State courts. In this capacity, the ECJ is a supranational institution that exclusively promotes the interests of the EU and tries to reinforce political integration. According to Christian Ranacher and Fritz Staudigl, the juridical instruments and procedures are employed in a way that allows case interpretation as favorable as possible to the objectives of the Union.[25] Throughout the years, the ECJ has been innovative in promoting integration and further developing the competences of the institutions. Most of the characteristics of the institutions, as we see them today, have been shaped by the ECJ.

According to the Treaty, the ECJ rules when a Member State, an institution or an individual person invokes its rights; gives preliminary rulings in cases when Member State courts, or courts of final instance are in doubt about the correct interpretation of EU law; and it gives rulings in other cases that might come up in accordance with Treaty provision.[26] The preliminary ruling, also called preliminary reference procedure, is the ECJ's most significant contribution to integration. Preliminary ruling means that a national court communicates a request to the ECJ to take over a case in which it has doubts about correct interpretation. The consequent case interpretation and the judgment have binding character for the Member States.[27] By this preliminary ruling, the ECJ adds case law to primary and secondary law, and therefore proactively further unfolds the supranational polity. With regard to ET, this occurred several times during the 1970s and 1980s, most notably in the court cases Casagrande (1974), Forcheri (1983), and Gravier (1985).

---

[25] Ranacher and Staudigl 2010, p. 56.
[26] TEU consolidated, Art. 19.
[27] TFEU consolidated, Art. 267.

Advisory bodies

Important advisory bodies are the *Committee of the Regions* (CoR) and *the Social and Economic Committee* (ESC).[28] The CoR represents the interests of the European regions and local communities. Bringing their interests to the table, they form the counterpart to supranational and national interests represented by other institutions. Ranacher and Staudigl note that the heterogeneity of regional and local situations, or actors and interests complicate the work of the CoR and to some extent impede the formation of a uniform voice.[29] The ESC is comprised of representatives from various trades, business sectors or interest groups concerned with economic and social progress. In the policy process, especially prior to legislation, both committees must have the chance to express their views on the issues at stake and on the actions proposed by the Commission.

5.2 Governance in the European Union

Governance in the EU refers to the rules, procedures and practices used by the institutions in exercising their powers. In a reference from Ben Rosamund, it was indicated earlier that there are two forms of governance in the EU.[30] One is a formal form of governance usually represented by formal decision-making procedures and decision implementation practices, the other is a rather informal form of governance usually focusing on the coordination of action through discourse, statistics, comparison or performance monitoring. While the earlier formal governance involves a restricted group of legitimized actors, such as in the OLP, the softer variation of governance involves a network of variegated public and private actors, such as in the OMC.

In the following section, the OLP and secondary law will be presented as examples of the formal form of governance and the principle of subsidiarity, the soft-law effect and the OMC will be discussed as relevant in relation to the softer form of governance.

The OLP and secondary law

The OLP is a rather new legislative procedure. In the EEC, legislative acts were decided by the Council after a proposal from the Commission was

---

[28] TEU consolidated, Art. 13.
[29] Ranacher and Staudigl 2010, pp. 63–64.
[30] Rosamund 2009, pp. 91–92.

made. This was the case for all areas, which were regulated by the TEEC and, therefore, not for ET. With the constant improvement of the status of the Parliament, the legislative process was adapted to render the decision-making more democratic. The so-called *Co-decision Method* was then introduced by the TEU in 1992 and established the Parliament as the third party in the legislative process besides the Commission and the Council. The *Co-decision Method* was later reformed and became the *Ordinary Legislative Procedure* (OLP) in the TFEU in 2009. According to the TFEU, "[t]he ordinary legislative procedure shall consist in the joint adoption by the European Parliament and the Council of a regulation, directive or decision on a proposal from the Commission."[31]

As far as secondary law can be decided in ET, the OLP is to be applied to both areas of ET – general education and vocational training since the TFEU; however, the principle of subsidiarity does not allow the decision of binding secondary law, rather only non-binding legal acts. For this reason, the OLP is seldom used in the area of ET and, thus, not the most relevant governance arrangement.

The adoption and execution of secondary law is the prime governance instrument of the EU. While primary law is the law on which the EU is based, secondary law refers to those legal acts that – according to the principle of conferral[32] – can be created by the EU institutions themselves by means of the OLP. In the fields in which the EU has exclusive rights of shared competences,[33] it can use binding legal acts as the main governance instrument. If the institutions do not have the necessary formal competences, as is the case in the fields in which the EU can only support, supplement, or coordinate,[34] binding secondary law is not an option for governance. Besides ET, the fields in which the EU can only support, supplement, or coordinate are, for instance, protection of human health, culture, industry, or tourism. These fields are subjected to the principle of subsidiarity, as is also the topic of employment policy or social policy.[35]

Within the scope of secondary law, five different types of legal acts can be adopted: Regulations, Directives, Decisions, Recommendations and Opinions.[36] The difference between the five legal acts is that only

---

[31] TFEU consolidated, Art. 289.
[32] TEU consolidated, Art. 5.
[33] TFEU consolidated, Art. 3; 4.
[34] TFEU consolidated, Art. 6.
[35] TEU consolidated, Art. 5.
[36] TFEU consolidated, Art. 288.

Regulations and Directives have a binding character: Regulations are directly applicable to Member States and Directives have a prescriptive character, meaning they prescribe objectives and rules to be implemented by national law. Decisions, though, can have binding character, but only upon those addressed by the Decision. Recommendations and Opinions are not binding at all and are also not subject to any formal procedure; rather, the institutions can issue them in accordance with their internal procedures.

The principle of subsidiarity and soft law

The principle of subsidiarity is one of the main characteristics of EU education and training politics. It limits the competences of the EU and secures the authority of national governments. Kees Van Kersbergen and Bertjan Verbeek note, "subsidiarity appeared as the guiding principle to delineating the competences of Brussels versus administrative authorities, such as national states or regions."[37] Following the principle of subsidiarity, the Community must not intervene in affairs that could be dealt with sufficiently by any actor at a subordinate level. It is provided for in Article 5 of the TEU, which reads as follows:

> Under the principle of subsidiarity, in areas which do not fall within its exclusive competence, the Union shall act only if and in so far as the objectives of the proposed action cannot be sufficiently achieved by the Member States, either at central level or at regional and local level, but can rather, by reason of the scale or effects of the proposed action, be better achieved at Union level.[38]

According to Van Kersbergen and Verbeek, there are three possible interpretations of the principle of subsidiarity.[39] Firstly, it is possible to say it extends the EU's competences. If the increasing complexity of political, economic and social issues created a situation in which the regional and the national governments could no longer handle the tasks imposed on it sufficiently, the principle of subsidiarity would indeed allow the EU to become active without breaching the provision made in the Treaty. Secondly, it is possible to say it restricts the competences of the EU and protects Member States' interests. If the EU remains within the scope of competences conferred upon it in the Treaties, subordinate actors must be given the freedom to care for their own good as long as they are capable of doing so. Thirdly, it

---

[37] van Kersbergen and Verbeek 1994, p. 215.
[38] TEU consolidated, Art. 5.
[39] van Kersbergen and Verbeek 1994.

is possible to say that the principle of subsidiarity would even have implications for the relation between national and regional actors. Van Kersbergen and Verbeek contend that national governments would tend to be closer with the EU in securing its own competences against regional claims.

Soft law is a concept, which refers to the effect of governance and in particular to the effect of non-binding legal acts or policy documents. The proposals made in these documents cannot be enforced onto Member States. Linda Senden – a distinguished expert in soft-law research from the University of Utrecht – defines soft law as: "rules of conduct that are laid down in instruments which have not been attributed legally binding force as such, but nevertheless may have certain - indirect - legal effects, and that are aimed at and may produce practical effects."[40]

The Austrian political scientists, Johannes Pollak and Peter Slominski, point out that since the release of the *White Paper on European Governance* in 2001, the EU has demanded from its institutions the increased use of non-binding legal acts.[41] Since this time, the reliance on the soft-law effect has become more important in comparison to harder forms of governance.

It is often hypothesized by ET scholars that the soft law effect is used in order to bypass the principle of subsidiarity and by this increase the influence on national policies.[42] In formal terms, this is incorrect since non-binding legal acts can modify national law only when they are linked to binding Treaty law,[43] which, as mentioned above, cannot be adopted as far as ET is addressed in accordance with the TFEU. Only Decisions are to some extent an exception since they can be necessary in order to fulfill the tasks of coordination and support assigned to the Commission. This was the case of the ERASMUS+ scheme, which was established by Decisions following the OLP.

In terms of the actual effect, it is to some extent true that non-binding legal acts can have an impact on national legislation. A good example of this is the non-binding Recommendation by the Council and the Parliament calling upon the Member States to establish *National Qualification Frameworks* (NQF) in line with the European model.[44] For instance, in 2016, the Austrian Parliament adopted a national law on a NQF.[45] The soft-law effect occurred

---

[40] Senden 2005, p. 23.
[41] Pollak and Slominski 2006, p. 152.
[42] Milana 2014, pp. 73–79.
[43] Pollak and Slominski 2006, p. 158.
[44] European Parliament; Council of the European Union 5/6/2008.
[45] Nationalrat der Bundesrepublik Österreich 3/21/2016.

in this case because the proposal of a non-binding legal act was effectively turned into a national law.

In contrast to the potential of soft-law regarding the more open and less forced character, it must be noted that in terms of legitimacy, it raises some concerns. Especially the absence of the OLP in the formation of non-binding acts or policy documents, that means the absence of the Parliament, the only really democratically elected institution of the EU, is a negative aspect that is said to reduce the legitimacy of the whole EU soft governance.

The Open Method of Coordination

An *Open Method of Coordination* (OMC) is a governance arrangement, which is not exclusively used by the EU but that and can be implemented in various instances of international, national, regional or local policy for-mation, policy development and policy evaluation. The governance logic of an OMC is different from the logic of other governance arrangements, since it is a functional and flexible arrangement, which is not based on normative, predefined and rigidly framed procedures but rather on the willingness of participants to learn from other participants and from their own failures.

An OMC accommodates non-traditional and heterogeneous groups of participants and can include innovative instruments of control, coordination and evaluation. For the EU, this means that the OMC is not an intergovern-mental type of governance nor a supranational type of governance rather one that opens up for participants from all levels of the EU system and for meth-ods such as benchmarking or performance monitoring.

In the relevant academic literature, the EU type of OMC is classified in various ways. It is sometimes characterized as soft regulation or soft policy coordination[46] or is considered as new governance architecture or simply a third way of governance alongside intergovernmental modes and suprana-tional modes.[47] Moreover, the EU's OMC is classified as an experimentalist type of governance or as a direct deliberative polyarchy.[48] Adult education researchers like Nafsika Alexiadou usually consider the OCM to be a soft-law instrument.[49]

Variations of OMC's were applied in the EU as early as the 1990s, par-ticularly in the creation of the *European Monetary Union* (EMU) or the

---

[46] Jacobsson 2004.
[47] Radaelli 2003.
[48] Sabel and Zeitlin 2008.
[49] Alexiadou 2007.

European Employment Strategy (EES).[50] Looking beyond the EU, the OECD, for instance, has been operating a similar method of coordination in almost all of its policy fields ever since the 1960s. The OMC was officially introduced in the conclusions of the European Council Meeting in Lisbon 2000, where it was stated that the goal of the OMC is to help Member States develop their policies and with this achieve greater convergence towards the EU's objective. To this end, the OMC involves the following four methods.

fixing guidelines for the Union combined with specific timetables for achieving the goals which they set in the short, medium and long terms;

establishing, where appropriate, quantitative and qualitative indicators and benchmarks against the best in the world and tailored to the needs of different Member States and sectors as a means of comparing best practice;

translating these European guidelines into national and regional policies by setting specific targets and adopting measures, taking into account national and regional differences;

periodic monitoring, evaluation and peer review organised as mutual learning processes.[51]

In the 2001 Commission *White Paper on European Governance* it was submitted that the OMC be applied in policy areas, in which the principle of subsidiarity prevails. However, it should not be a replacement of the OLP but rather a complementary governance arrangement. In some areas "it sits alongside the program-based and legislative approach; in others, it adds value at a European level where there is little scope for legislative solutions."[52] Moreover, the coordinating role was assigned to the European Commission.

In fact, neither a single definition nor a single OMC exists. Erika Szyszczak, professor of law at the European Institute at the University of Sussex, identified four areas in which the OMC has been used:[53] (1) developed areas such as broad economic guidelines or the European Employment Strategy, (2) adjunct areas like modernization of social protection, social inclusion, pensions or health care, (3) nascent areas including innovation and research, education, information society, enterprise policy or immigration and (4) unacknowledged areas like tax. Still, there are some elements that all

---

[50] Hatzopoulos 2007, p. 311; La Porte 2011.
[51] European Council 3/23/2000, p. 10..
[52] Commission of the European Communities 7/25/2001, p. 22.
[53] Szyszczak 2006, p. 494.

of the OMCs have in common and which clearly distinguish the OMC from other EU governance approaches.

First, that which all types of OMC have in common is that the process does not directly result in acts of secondary law. In some areas, such as ET, it usually does not even result in policy documents, however it is possible that the materialized outcomes have an effect within the countries similar to the soft law effect. Of course, the outcomes of the OMC might be used to draft policy documents or even secondary law documents, but in order to turn them into binding legal acts, formal procedures such as the OLP must be applied.

Compared with soft law, the OMC furnishes a political environment in which mutual learning occurs through an exchange of practices, benchmarking, and peer learning or through compliance. This is supposed to facilitate cooperation, induce convergence and deepen integration. Complying with the principle of subsidiarity, the EU acknowledges and confirms state authority over national policy development nevertheless, at the same time, establishes "autonomous national decision-making arenas, coordinated by jointly produced best practice models."[54]

Second, in addition to the three major EU institutions (Council, Commission and Parliament), which form the triad of the Ordinary Legislative Procedure, the OMC involves – with varying intensity among the different areas – other EU agencies, a wide range of non-Community actors, such as European social partner organizations, national civil servants from various governmental departments, researchers, academic experts and consultants, private enterprises or civil society actors. This opening of the policy formation, implementation and evaluation process aims to ensure democratic participation, transparency, accountability and an evidence-based process. At the same time, involving the so-called epistemic community, the OMC attempts to avoid power politics and strategic behavior of politicians and tries to replace it with practical and theoretical expertise.[55]

Third, the performance and output orientation (e.g. benchmarks, best-practice examples, reporting mechanisms), which implies the possibility of rational evidence-based steering, qualifies the OMC as an arrangement in line with a *New Public Management* (NPM) philosophy. Such a philosophy suggests decentralizing, privatizing and individualizing actions and responsibility for the achievement of agreed objectives. According to Lange and

---

[54] Szyszczak 2006, p. 488.
[55] Preunkert 2009, p. 39.

Alexiadou, especially the education OMC is an "example of the managerialist approach of NPM for the delivery of public services."[56] The effect of this can be sensed in the methodology of the OMC. It can also be empirically observed at national level when Member States comply with agreed objectives and implement measures that meet the agreed-upon benchmarks.

Fourth, Nafsika Alexiadou argues that the OMC is a practice of reflection.[57] She refers to the fact that the OMC is subject to constant revision, which is a result of the processes themselves. In other words, whenever the Commission as coordinating actor and the participants gain additional knowledge about how to better promote formation or implementation of policies, the OMC arrangement can be adapted accordingly. This is what Peter May has captured in his famous article entitled *Policy Learning and Failure* with the terms instrumental policy learning, social policy learning and political learning.[58] Charles Sabel and Jonathan Zeitlin call this form of governance directly deliberative polyarchy by which they mean "(…) a machine for learning from diversity, thereby transforming an obstacle to closer integration into an asset for achieving it."[59]

[56] Lange and Alexiadou 2007, p. 326.
[57] Alexiadou 2007, p. 104.
[58] May 1992.
[59] Sabel and Zeitlin 2008, p. 276.

6. The historical study

The aim of the historical study is to raise understanding among the readership of the history of ET politics in the EC and the EU and the role of ACE in this context. It is hoped that other researchers, practitioners and policymakers will feel encouraged to utilize the argumentation presented to inform their own work. To this end, an overview of events, personalities and processes that have shaped European ET politics over the course of the last seven decades will be given. In accordance with the chapters presented in the methodological part of this book, the historical study is divided into five chapters.

The first chapter discusses how vocational training and general education were addressed by EC/EU primary law. Since primary law gives an account of how the Member States want the European institutions to act in relation to an area of common interest, it gives also an account of how the status of ET within the polity of the EC and the EU has evolved.

The second chapter covers the years from 1969 to 1976; a period in which the contribution of general education to the goals of the EC was acknowledged and fostered through the creation of institutional structures and the definition of topics of mutual concern. It will be argued that these years were shaped especially by individual actors and their political entrepreneurship.

The third chapter covers the years from 1981 to 1987. During these six years the political leadership of the EC started integrating general education and vocational training. The integration of the two areas was supported by external events such as labor market crises and by other EC institutions. The focus in the discussion is on the alignment of ET policy with the overarching objectives of the EC.

The fourth chapter covers the years from 1993 to 1997. The events of this rather short timespan indicate the final phase of the mainstreaming of ET within the EU's political framework. An analysis and discussion of the three most important policy documents and the role of the Commission will serve to argue that the governance of ET had changed significantly by the end of the 1990s.

The fifth chapter covers the years from 2000 until 2017. Given this long period of time, this chapter will focus on the discussion of three main topics: first, the new governance approaches of the Rolling Agenda and the OMC; second, the policies concerned with the quality in ACE; and third, the strategic framework for European cooperation in education and training ET 2020.

On the following pages, a timetable listing the most important events of the last seven decades.

6.1 Timetable of important dates

1951   The European Coal and Steel Community is founded in London

1957   The European Economic Community and the European Atomic Energy Community are founded in Rome

1963   The Council of the European Economic Community lays down principles for a common vocational training policy

1965   The three Communities are integrated to become the European Community

1969   The Hague Summit of Heads of State emphasizes the importance of culture and education in the unification process

1971   The first meeting of education ministers takes place

1973   The Directorate General for Research, Science and Education is established in the European Commission

1976   The Education Ministers within the Council of the European Community adopt the first Action Program in Education

1981   General Education and Vocational Training are merged within the Directorate General for Employment and Social Affairs

1986   The Council of the European Community adopts the program on cooperation between universities and enterprises regarding training in the field of technology – COMETT

1987   The Council of the European Community adopts the European Community Action Scheme for the Mobility of University Students – ERASMUS

1989   The Task Force on Human Resources is formed within the European Commission to work on the promotion of general education and vocational training

1992   The European Union is founded in Maastricht

1995   The Task Force on Human Resources becomes the Directorate General for Education and Training

1996   The European Year of Lifelong Learning takes place in all Member States

1999   The Council of the European Communities releases a Resolution concerning new working methods in Education and Training

2000   The European Council proposes the Lisbon Strategy at the Lisbon Council meeting

2009   The Council of the European Union releases the Conclusion on the Strategic Framework for European Cooperation in Education and Training – ET 2020

2010   The European Commission proposes the Europe 2020 Strategy

6.2 Primary law, education and training

The first chapter describes the evolution of ET within EC and EU primary law. It will be argued that primary law has played an important role in the background concerning the rise of ET from a marginal issue to a priority area of European politics. At the beginning, the *Treaty establishing the European Coal and Steel Community* from 1951 (TECSC) will be examined. At this point, ET was of little importance; nevertheless, it will be contended that it is possible to identify therein the roots of today's ET politics. Next is the *Treaty establishing the European Atomic Energy Community* from 1957 (TEAC). Scholarly accounts concerning the negotiations preceding this Treaty indicate how controversial European ET politics were and that there was a lack of commitment to supranational politics. Then, the discussion turns to the *Treaty establishing the European Economic Community* from 1957 (TEEC). The ambiguous Article 128 provided for vocational training, while general education was left out of the legal framework. Still, the TEEC is of great importance since it serves to show that European ET politics have effectively developed without addressing actual pedagogical issues.

The fourth document is the Treaty on European Union from 1992 (TEU). It is a landmark document in the history of ET in Europe because it officially made general education a policy field (Article 126) and consolidated the Union's competences in the field of vocational training (Article 127). Finally, reference will be made to the Treaty of Amsterdam and the Treaty on the functioning of the European Union (TFEU). These two documents have reinforced ET and they serve to indicate that ET has become a priority area in European politics. The summary at the end of the chapter points out some patterns along which ET politics have developed within primary law.

The TECSC and vocational training

In order to uncover the roots of EU politics, one must return to March 9th, 1950. On that day, the French Foreign Minister Robert Schuman presented a declaration in which he proposed his ideas of a united Europe. Still today, the following passage from the so-called *Schuman Declaration* is of great importance:

The contribution which an organised and living Europe can bring to civilisation is indispensable to the maintenance of peaceful relations (...) Europe will not be made all at once, or according to a single plan. It will be built through concrete achievements which first create a de facto solidarity.[1]

Schuman suggested that the reorganization of Europe after the war started with the reorganization of the coal and steel industries settled at the border region of Germany and France. He assumed that such reorganization would precipitate a spillover effect that would reach other European countries and help vitalize various industries so that the whole European economy would be stabilized and European states would integrate in a peaceful manner. One year after the Schuman Declaration, on April 18th, 1951, Germany, France, Italy, Belgium, the Netherlands and Luxembourg eventually founded the *European Coal and Steel Community* (ECSC).

The six Member States agreed that the mission of the ECSC should be "to contribute to economic expansion, the development of employment and the improvement of the standard of living".[2] In accordance with the Schuman plan, the ECSC institutional model was based on the idea that when the conditions for a common market of coal and steel are favorable, the production in this industry would almost automatically be distributed equally among the Member States. Of great importance, among other things, was the commitment of the Member States to pursue the maintenance of good working conditions and to protect employment, as these were considered important for economic prosperity and a good quality of life.

It must be stressed that the TECSC did refer to ET. Precisely, in Article 56 reference was made to technical re-training. Despite the fact that this issue has hardly ever been dealt with in education scholarship, it is worthwhile to mention this provision as it may help to hypothesize about how education, training and learning of adults was linked to European integration in the early 1950s.

Of course, compared to other topics and political areas, *technical re-training* was a side issue within the ECSC framework. Yet, the fact that it was considered an issue at all should not be underestimated. Article 56, TECSC stipulated that the ECSC would be entitled to take measures, if technological developments emerging from the Community's framework programs led to a significant decrease in employment in the coal and steel sector and, consequently, the situation required the development of new skill-sets in the labor

---

[1] Fondation Robert Schuman 2011.
[2] TECSC, Art. 2.

force in order to allow for the re-employment of laid off workers in other industrial sectors. The measures provided for were primarily of financial character. Financial assistance would be given in three instances:[3] (1) the creation and provision of re-employment programs, (2) technical re-training of those unemployed and forced to change their jobs and (3) to take over some of the costs that workers incurred during the transition period.

The history has shown that the connection between employment programs and re-training and the adaptation of workers to changing circumstances has been a recurring concern of ET politics. Article 56, TECSC arguably formed the basis on which the TEEC, in 1957, provided for the creation of the *European Social Fund* (ESF). As a matter of fact, as Josephine Shaw pointed out, most financial support for vocational education and training before the mid-1980s was provided by structural funds such as the ESF.[4]

The Treaties of Rome

European Integration politics were intensified when the *European Atomic Energy Community* (EAC) and the *European Economic Community* (EEC) were established by the Treaties of Rome, on March 23rd, 1957. The institutional model of the ECSC was further developed to meet the demands of the two new communities. The High Authority of the ECSC, which had supreme authority in organizing the common market, was replaced by the Commission, which in turn had to share authority with the Council. The Parliament, which was then still called the Assembly, had not yet acquired the status of a proper Parliament elected upon universal suffrage and had not yet been granted a participating role in the decision-making process.

The TEAC and higher education

The *Treaty establishing the European Atomic Energy Community* (TEAC) constitutes the basis for higher education politics. In particular, the TEAC laid grounds for the creation of the *European University Institute* and encouraged the Community to reconsider the role of general education in the European unification process. According to Anne Corbett, a British expert on higher education politics from the London School of Economics, the German government and its representative, Walter Hallstein, were keen on introducing a cultural dimension to the unification project and on founding a European university.

---

[3] TECSC, Art. 56.
[4] Shaw 1991, p. 3.

Among the negotiating partners, the proponents of economic integration were against the German proposal. Because of this, it was only by compromise that the part concerning a European university was inserted, however, not in the desired EEC Treaty but in the EAC Treaty.[5] There, it was stipulated that "[a]n institution of university status shall be established; the way in which it will function shall be determined by the Council, acting by a qualified majority on a proposal from the Commission."[6] In addition, the *training* of scientists was mentioned on various occasions linked with the establishment of a joint research center for the advancement of the nuclear energy sector. After a long period of difficult political negotiations, the *European University Institute* eventually started with the academic year 1976.

Discussions about general education lost impetus fairly soon after the enactment of the TEAC and the TEEC. Corbett mentions a meeting in 1961, where the EC leaders agreed "that decision-making on education was to pass from Community institutions to national governments cooperating on an intergovernmental basis — i.e. operating as sovereign States, rather than States bound by Community rules."[7] This agreement should have had long-term consequences, which are best described by Luce Pépin, a former official in the Commission. She reports, "the word 'education' remained 'taboo' for almost 20 years at Community level".[8] Even though education was not considered completely irrelevant to the purposes of the EC, Member States' governments were reluctant to acknowledge general education as an appropriate topic for cooperation within the economically calibrated EC framework.

The TEEC and vocational training

The *Treaty establishing the European Economic Community* (TEEC) projected a more comprehensive understanding of integration than the TECSC. The new objective was to bring economic policies of Member States into a converging state and to contribute to harmonious development and stability. The common market and particular the alignment of economic policies – this time targeting the whole economy and not just one industry – were considered the adequate means to generate prosperity and guarantee peace. There is no doubt that politicians were aware that ET would be important to achieve these goals, even if few concessions were made in respect to ET.

---

[5] Corbett 2003, p. 317.
[6] TEAC, Art. 9.
[7] Corbett 2003, p. 318.
[8] Pépin 2007, p. 122.

Article 3, TEEC, provided a list of eleven activities, which should help promote the goals of the EEC. Over the years, two of these eleven activities enforced ET policy in relation to the common market: firstly, the abolition of restrictions to the freedom of movement of persons, services, and capital, also termed the fundamental freedoms; and secondly, the installation of the ESF as an instrument of employment policy.

The four fundamental freedoms

Major elements of the projected common market were the so-called four freedoms: free movement of people, of services, of goods and of capital. The four freedoms have become fundamental pillars in European politics. In this context, the prohibition of discrimination of EC citizens, freedom of movement of persons, the right to establishment, and the right to receive services in other countries found application in order to enforce ET related policy. In application, all of these legal provisions could regulate the access to education rather than pedagogical aspects of education and training. This provision is altogether related to the objective that all community citizens should have the right to go to any place within Europe having the equal rights as the citizens of the host country.

In terms of integration, such an approach is subsumed under the term *negative integration*.[9] *Negative integration* means that potential barriers to integration are removed. On the contrary, *positive integration* means that integration is actively pursued with the help of policies. In order to raise understanding for evolutionary patterns in the relation between ET and European integration, a brief overview of this important legal provision will be given.

First is Article 7, TEEC on non-discrimination of EC citizens, which contained a fairly general statement prohibiting discrimination on grounds of nationality. It was used in the most important court case concerning ET by the plaintiff Gravier, a French national, who claimed equal access to ET in Belgium. The *Gravier Case* marked a milestone in the history of ET for many reasons. According to the legal scholar James Flynn,

> *Gravier's* significance is that, for the first time, the Court found a basis on which the would-be student could claim a self-sufficient right of access to education which was not dependent on his first demonstrating that he could derive other rights from the Treaty.[10]

---

[9] Shaw 1991, p. 2.
[10] Flynn 1988, p. 62.

Further information on the *Gravier* ruling and other ECJ judgments will be provided in a later chapter dealing with ET politics in the 1980s. For now, the next relevant provision is Article 48, TEEC, paragraphs 1 and 2 dealing with the freedom of movement of workers. It stated that workers should be able to go to another country and be treated equally to citizens of that country with regard to employment, remuneration and other conditions of work and employment. Education and training, being uncontested elements of work and employment, fell under the category "other conditions of work and employment".

This provision was implemented by the 1968 Council Regulation number 1612/68 on freedom of movement for workers.[11] Since a Regulation is binding secondary law, the provision therein was applied in some of the ET court cases. Article 7 of the Regulation from 1968 provided that vocational training and retraining must be considered in the pursuit of freedom of movement for workers. Every person should "by virtue of the same right and under the same conditions as national workers, have access to training in vocational schools and retraining centres"[12]

While the TEEC almost exclusively addressed vocational training, the only provision that bears relevance to non-vocational educational pathways can be found in Articles 52 and 57. They dealt with the mutual recognition of diplomas and qualifications and their relationship to freedom of establishment for those working in the professions and in entrepreneurial undertakings. In accordance with this provision, the Commission and the Council could develop and adopt Directives concerning the mutual recognition of diplomas, certificates and other evidence of formal qualifications.

With regard to these Directives, the British legal scholar Catherine Barnard points out that during the 1970s and early 1980s "the Council and the Commission proceeded on a 'profession by profession' sectoral approach".[13] From 1975 until 1985, seven Directives were adopted by the Council concerning mutual recognition of qualifications in medicine, nursing, dentistry, veterinary medicine, midwifery, architecture and pharmaceutical professions.[14] Only in 1988, did the Council set out to establish a general system for the recognition of higher education diplomas gained after having completed professional training of at least three years.[15] According to Barnard,

---

[11] Council of the European Communities 10/19/1968.
[12] Council of the European Communities 10/19/1968, Art. 7.
[13] Barnard 1992, p. 130.
[14] Barnard 1992, Appendix.
[15] Council of the European Communities 1/21/1989.

the Council and Commission based their later approach on the assumption "that a person who is fit to exercise a particular profession in one member state is fit to exercise it in the other eleven Member States, providing they have undergone a basic minimum of training."[16]

The next provision of relevance is that in Article 60, TEEC concerning the freedom to provide and receive services in the common market. In particular, it had to be applied to services of industrial or commercial character or to services of craftsmen or of the professions. In the court 1984 *Case Luisi and Carbone*, the Court ruled "the freedom to provide services includes the freedom, for the recipients of services, to go to another Member State in order to receive a service there". Furthermore, the ECJ stated, "tourists, persons receiving medical treatment and persons travelling for the purposes of education or business are to be regarded as recipients of services."[17] James Flynn critically assessed this ruling and emphasized that state-provided education would not fall under the provision of Article 60, since state-provided education programs are not primarily intended for profit but rather to implement national policies.[18]

In conclusion, in spite of the fact that all of the above-mentioned legal provisions are not directly associated with the organization of ET, the implications raise important and perennial questions such as: who should have access to ET and under what conditions? What kinds of diplomas and qualifications have to be recognized and on what criteria is the recognition based on? Are adult education and vocational training services part of the private sector or must public authorities financially support them in the implementation of public policies?

European Social Fund

In addition to the regulations concerning the four fundamental freedoms, the installation of the ESF would be of relevance to ET. The link to vocational training is obvious on a textual level since both the ESF provision in Articles 123 to 127 and that for vocational training in Article 128 can be found under the same heading, *Title II Social Policy, Chapter II European Social Fund*. The purpose of the ESF was "(...) to improve employment opportunities for workers in the common market and to contribute thereby to raising the standards of living (...)".[19]

---

[16] Barnard 1992, p. 132.
[17] European Court of Justice 1/31/1984, p. 403.
[18] Flynn 1988, p. 80.
[19] TEEC, Art. 123.

Since this point, the ESF has been administered by the Commission, while half of the costs incurred have been cared for by the EC and half of the costs by the Member States. In the first decades, financial support was made available to facilitate reemployment through vocational retraining and resettlement allowances. "The objective was to assist workers moving from one region to another in search of work and those needing to acquire new skills in sectors undergoing modernisation or conversion of production methods."[20]

In the first period after the installation of the ESF from 1960 to 1973, a number of 400 million ECU were provided for re-training of almost one million workers.[21] Until the first reform in the years 1977 and 1978, roughly ninety percent of the total financial support went into vocational training. The economic crisis at the end of the 1970s precipitated an increase in unemployment, especially among young people and in the southern and southeastern European regions. Consequently, the ESF funding scheme was adapted and from the early 1980s on focused more on the promotion of regional development and education-to-work transition.[22]

In the next two sections, Articles 118 and 128, which made provision for vocational training and the Council Decision on vocational training from 1963 will be presented.

Vocational training in the TEU
Article 118, TEEC, provided a list of policy fields in which close cooperation between the Commission and the Member States was desired. Basic and advanced vocational training was on the list together with other fields like employment, labor law and working conditions, social security or collective bargaining of social partners. The cooperating partners were to engage in "making studies, delivering opinions and arranging consultations both on problems arising at national level and on those of concern to international organisations."[23]

In the relevant academic literature, Article 118 is seldom dealt with in more than one line. It seems, however, as if it anticipated to some extent the *Treaty on the European Union* (TEU). The tasks and responsibilities defined in Articles 126 and 127, TEU, are in fact similar to the tasks assigned to the

---

[20] European Commission 1998, p. 14.
[21] ECU is the abbreviation for European Currency Unit, which was the specific reference currency or unit of account, the EEC and the EU used before the EURO was introduced in 1999.
[22] European Commission 1998, pp. 14–16.
[23] TEEC, Art. 118.

Commission in Article 118, TEEC. On the other hand, it is possible to imagine that in 1957, when the TEEC was signed, this form of cooperation in basic and advanced vocational training might only have had a declarative function.

As a matter of fact, Article 128 was the only provision that actually allowed the EC to act with regard to ET policy. Precisely, it asked the Council to lay down basic principles for a common vocational training policy. This provision is interesting in many respects. Catherine Barnard mentions, "as a legal basis for secondary legislation, [Art. 128] is unusual within the scheme of the Treaty of Rome (…)"[24] Below, the original passage is provided.

Article 128

> The Council shall, acting on a proposal from the Commission and after consulting the Economic and Social Committee, lay down general principles for implementing a common vocational training policy capable of contributing to the harmonious development both of the national economies and of the com-mon market.

For an analysis of this provision from the perspective of governance, two questions must be addressed. First, what did "laying down general principles for a common policy" mean? Second, what were the actual powers it conferred upon the actors?

To answer the first question, Article 128 will be compared with other Treaty provision. First, Article 128 did not comprise any policy content and did not define a target group or list any measures the institutions or the Member States had to take. However, it also did not lay down the general principles itself. What it did, was assign to the Council the task of laying down general principles. In fact, it took six years until the general principles were proposed in 1963.[25] In comparison, the ESF provision in Articles 123 to 127 was significantly less ambiguous since it clearly defined the content, the objectives, the target group and the measures. Only unmistakably defined tasks and responsibilities could have allowed the EC to actually form vocational training policy.

The rather ambiguous and cautious wording indicates that vocational training was a very sensitive topic. As James Flynn puts it, "[t]he Treaty draftsmen attached importance to vocational training but were unsure how

---

[24] Barnard 1992, p. 125.
[25] Council of the European Communities 4/20/1963.

common policy might be reached."[26] Even though vocational training was considered essential to Community goals, it was acknowledged that all kinds of ET depend on national idiosyncrasies and could not simply be made subject to supranational action.

To answer the second question, the decision-making procedure defined in Article 128 must be addressed. The EEC was a type of organization, which did not have sovereign law-making powers but was given powers only by the provisions made in the Treaties. For this reason, all of its legislative actions, enabling the implementation of policies, had to be based on the procedures defined in the Treaty. Provision defining legislative procedures had to include the following elements: who initiates action, i.e. who makes proposals; who legislates, i.e. who makes the decision; how will the decision be made, i.e. voting procedures; and who must be consulted, i.e. whose opinion must be heard prior to making the decision.[27]

Article 128 stipulated that the Council had to act after a proposal from the Commission would be made and after consulting the Economic and Social Committee. This was a rather insufficient provision as a further comparison indicates. The two articles that are of relevance in this respect are Articles 148 and 235, TEEC.

According to Article 148, TEEC, the Council had to act by majority voting in all instances for which no other procedure was defined. Majority voting meant that a simple majority of 51% of the votes would be sufficient to decide. Other possibilities for decision-making were qualified majority voting or unanimity vote. Since Article 128 did not provide otherwise, at least a simple majority voting had to be applied in all decisions on vocational training. The problem of such a voting procedure was that it was almost impossible for one country to veto a decision since it required more than half of the members to join the vetoing party. Whenever no precise legislative powers were defined in the TEEC, in order to promote the community goals, the Council had the option to apply Article 235 – the so-called "residual power article".[28] It read:

> If action by the Community should prove necessary to attain, in the course of the operation of the common market, one of the objectives of the Community and this Treaty has not provided the necessary powers, the Council shall,

---

[26] Flynn 1988, p. 60.
[27] Shaw 1991, p. 11.
[28] Shaw 1991, p. 3.

acting unanimously on a proposal from the Commission and after consulting the Assembly [European Parliament P.A], take the appropriate measures.[29]

This "residual power" was, in fact, used by the Council in many decisions. For instance, the Council Regulation establishing the *European Centre for the Development of Vocational Training* (CEDEFOP) was based only on Article 235.[30] The Council Decision adopting the student mobility scheme ERASMUS was based on Articles 235 and 128.[31] Applying Article 235, it was possible to bypass the limitations innate to the vocational training provision and to make proper binding decisions. In political debates, the Council's strategic move to apply Article 235 was perceived with mixed emotions. Especially the ECJ was not satisfied because it meant that only in very few cases, in which unanimity was reached, could ET policy be made. In conclusion, it is very likely that the insufficient provision of Article 128 was one among several reasons why vocational training developed so slowly and why general education lagged behind for many years.

A common vocational training policy

The Commission completed the task that it was given to lay down general principles for a common vocational training policy in a Council Decision from April 1963. This Council Decision is important due to setting some of the standards in the governance of education and training.

The Council and the Member States were required to "fulfil the obligation imposed on them by the Treaty". Concerning the economic sphere, it was stated that they "shall draw up programmes and shall ensure that these are put into effect in accordance with the general principles contained in this decision and with the resulting measures taken to apply them."[32] The Member States and the EC institutions were both given the responsibility to apply the principles. The Commission, though, was given particular competences as we see below in the summary of principles number four, five, and six.

"[The Commission] may propose to the Council or to the Member States (...) such appropriate measures as may appear to be necessary (...)". It may "carry out any studies and research (...) which will ensure attainment of a

---

[29] TEEC, Art. 235.
[30] Council of the European Communities 2/13/1975.
[31] Council of the European Communities 6/25/1987.
[32] Council of the European Communities 4/20/1963, p. 26.

common policy (...)".[33] Moreover, the Commission had the responsibility to collect, distribute and exchange "(...) any useful information, literature and teaching material (...)" as well as to encourage "(...) direct exchange of experience" for representatives of educational organizations and "(...) to acquaint themselves with and study the achievements and new developments in the other countries (...)".[34]

According to principle number two, a common policy should have the objective to establish conditions under which it would be possible for every person to receive education allowing for the full development of a person's capabilities. Vocational training and general education should be complementary in the sense that education should be envisaged to include the training of technical skills as well as civic education. By this it was expected that the needs of the economies and industries as well as the interests of the trainees could be adequately addressed.

In what follows now, the Treaty on the European Union (TEU) and the provision for general education (Art. 126) and vocational training (Art. 127) will be discussed.

The TEU and education and training

The *Treaty on the European Union* (TEU) signed in Maastricht in 1992 marked a milestone in the history of European integration and even more so in the history of ET. It completed a number of reform initiatives with the aim to give a more democratic face to the European unification project and, furthermore, it gave formal expression to the official recognition of general education as an indispensable matter of community concern. The education and legal scholar Philipp Eggers and the legal scholar Hans Hablitzel argued that it ended the role of general education as an *"ancilla oeconomiae"*[35], i.e. the servant of economic policy, and that it was the first step towards independent education and training politics. In Article 126, provision for general education was introduced in addition to the already existing, however, significantly altered provision on vocational training in Article 127.

After the 1987 *Single European Act* had already put forward reform plans and made suggestions on how to amend the existing Treaties, the TEU signed on February 7th, 1992 brought the proposals into reality. The main objective was to progress towards an even more integrated community in the economic

---

[33] Council of the European Communities 4/20/1963, pp. 26–27.
[34] Council of the European Communities 4/20/1963, p. 27.
[35] Eggers and Hablitzel 2002, p. 171.

sphere and this time, also, towards integration in the social, cultural and political sphere. It was clearly stated: "This Treaty marks a new stage in the process of creating an ever-closer union among the peoples of Europe, in which decisions are taken as closely as possible to the citizen."[36]

The tasks of the Community remained almost equal to the ones assigned by the TEEC; however, it seems that this time a more conscious approach to economic integration was taken. Central elements of this more conscious approach were the social dimension and the educational dimension, which have found acceptance as inevitable elements, without which the single market would not have been able to flourish.

The list of activities assigned to the EU comprised of 20 items. One of these referred directly to education policy. It was confirmed that in order to attain the objectives of the EU, "a contribution to education and training of quality and to the flowering of the cultures of the Member States"[37] should be made. Moreover, in Part III, entitled Policy of the Community, Title III was changed from Social Policy (TEEC) to Social Policy, Education, Vocational Training and Youth (TEU). Provision regulating the ESF remained almost the same, however, with a more pronounced emphasis on training and re-training.

Before Maastricht, Article 128, TEEC only regulated vocational training. Article 126 on general education, therefore, was a completely new provision and had no overlaps with the old article.

Article 126

1. The Community shall contribute to the development of quality education by encouraging cooperation between Member States and, if necessary, by supporting and supplementing their action, while fully respecting the responsibility of the Member States for the content of teaching and the organization of education systems and their cultural and linguistic diversity.

2. Community action shall be aimed at:

- developing the European dimension in education, particularly through the teaching and dissemination of the languages of the Member States;
- encouraging mobility of students and teachers, inter alia by encouraging the academic recognition of diplomas and periods of study;
- promoting cooperation between educational establishments;

---

[36] TEU, Art. A.
[37] TEU, Art. 3.

- developing exchanges of information and experience on issues common to the education systems of the Member States;
- encouraging the development of youth exchanges and of exchanges of socio-educational instructors;
- encouraging the development of distance education.

3. The Community and the Member States shall foster cooperation with third countries and the competent international organizations in the field of education, in particular the Council of Europe.

4. In order to contribute to the achievement of the objectives referred to in this Article, the Council:

- acting in accordance with the procedure referred to in Article 189b, after consulting the Economic and Social Committee and the Committee of the Regions, shall adopt incentive measures, excluding any harmonization of the laws and regulations of the Member States;
- acting by a qualified majority on a proposal from the Commission, shall adopt recommendations.

The professor of European law, Catherine Barnard, is of the opinion that the wording is "extremely cautious".[38] This style apparently helped to mitigate ambivalent feelings among national actors towards supranational intervention. The principle of subsidiarity and the prohibition of harmonization are other aspects that have strengthened the position of the Member States at least on paper. Philipp Eggers and Hans Hablitzel contend that even after Maastricht, the Member States further remained authoritative concerning education politics.[39]

The TEU introduced the principle of subsidiarity as a guiding principle of EU action.[40] Together with the principal of conferral and the principle of proportionality, it limits the powers of the EU institutions. The principle of subsidiarity must be applied in areas that do not fall under the exclusive competence of the EU. This means all of the measures that can be taken effectively at any level lower than the supranational level must be taken at that point and must not be made subject to EU intervention. Only if local, regional or national actors are incapable of acting is the EU allowed to intervene.

From the perspective of analysis, the line, which stated that the EU should "contribute to the development of quality education" must be addressed. There are many ways of interpreting quality in education; however, one can

---

[38] Barnard 1995, p. 17.
[39] Eggers and Hablitzel 2002, p. 176.
[40] TEU, Art. 5; TEU consolidated, Art. 5.

gain a clear impression of what the EU understood by "quality" from the *Commission Communication outlining guidelines for the period 1989-1992*,[41] and the *White Paper Growth, employment and competitiveness*.[42] Two ideas of quality can be extrapolated from these two documents: First, quality in education depends on the extent of cooperation and exchange; second, quality in education is important in pursuing strategies of competition. What is more, quality was integrated in the TEU as a topic that is not limited to a certain kind of education but is of equal relevance, for instance, in compulsory schooling and in adult and continuing education.

Going further, there is the definition of the formal decision-making procedure that needs to be addressed. First, reference was made to Article 189b, which defined the so-called "Co-decision Procedure". The "Co-decision Procedure" was introduced by the TEU and gave the Parliament the possibility to fully participate in the decision-making process. Article 189b provided that the Commission submit a proposal to the Parliament and the Council. The Council then acts by qualified majority after having received an opinion from the Parliament. The Parliament was given the right to be kept fully informed about the reasons, after which the decision would be made by the Council. Barnard holds that "[t]he Article 189b procedure incorporates a more extensive democratic element by gaining further institutional agreement on a proposed text."[43]

Applying the "Co-decision Procedure", the Council had the competence to adopt incentive measures, however, without harmonizing national legislation. For instance, upon qualified majority voting the Council could adopt Recommendations. According to Article 189, though, Recommendations have no binding force whatsoever. As Barnard points out, jurisdiction of the ECJ goes somewhat against this, as it rules, "that national courts must take recommendations into account".[44] This is the case, particularly when a Recommendation helps interpret national measures or functions as a supplement to a binding legal act. The best example for this is the already above-mentioned Recommendation on the establishment of a European qualifications framework for lifelong learning from 2008,[45] which, for instance, in Austria

---

[41] Commission of the European Communities 6/2/1989.
[42] Commission of the European Communities 12/5/1993.
[43] Barnard 1995, Endnote No. 51.
[44] Barnard 1995, p. 19.
[45] European Parliament; Council of the European Union 5/6/2008.

resulted in the adoption of the Federal Law on a nation qualifications framework in 2016.[46]

Comparing Article 126 on general education and Article 127 on vocational training, one gains some interesting insights with respect to the supposedly different handling of general education and vocational training.

Article 127

1. The Community shall implement a vocational training policy, which shall support and supplement the action of the Member States, while fully respecting the responsibility of the Member States for the content and organization of vocational training.

2. Community action shall aim to:

- facilitate adaptation to industrial changes, in particular through vocational training and retraining;
- improve initial and continuing vocational training in order to facilitate vocational integration and reintegration into the labour market;
- facilitate access to vocational training and encourage mobility of instructors and trainees and particularly young people;
- stimulate cooperation on training between educational or training establishments and firms;
- develop exchanges of information and experience on issues common to the training systems of the Member States.

3. The Community and the Member States shall foster cooperation with third countries and the competent international organizations in the sphere of vocational training.

4. The Council, acting in accordance with the procedure referred to in Article 189c and after consulting the Economic and Social Committee, shall adopt measures to contribute to the achievement of the objectives referred to in this Article, excluding any harmonization of the laws and regulations of the Member States.

Article 127 neither addresses quality of education nor encourages cooperation between Member States, as does Article 126. What is more, Article 127 mentions that the organization of vocational training must remain the responsibility of Member States, with the parts on cultural diversity being left out. Instead, the Community may immediately implement its own policy to support and supplement Member State action. It can be agreed with Jana

---

[46] Nationalrat der Bundesrepublik Österreich 3/21/2016.

Bektchieva when she states that in the area of vocational training, the EU was given the necessary competences to autonomously implement policy.[47]

Article 127 invests the Council also with the competence to adopt measures (see Article 126 "incentive measures") in accordance with Article 189c. The obligation to abstain from any form of harmonization of national legislation was still valid; however, the term "measures" implies a more targeted approach than the term "incentive measures". Barnard conjectured: "It is assumed that these 'measures' may include either legally-binding regulations, directives and decisions, or non-binding recommendations and opinions."[48] Article 189c did indeed provide for the adoption of all types of legal acts not limiting the legal character, as was the case with Article 126. On the other hand, this ambiguity has been relativized since Article 189c referred to the old cooperation procedure and not to the new co-decision procedure. This means that the simple majority voting procedure was exchanged for qualified majority voting. Qualified majority voting, in practice, makes it easier to veto decisions.

This examination has shown that on paper there is a fairly significant difference between the areas of general education and vocational training. Most evident are the differences with regard to cultural and linguistic diversity and to the types of measures that can be adopted. While the culture issue has always been key to general education politics, it has been less a matter of concern in vocational training. Concerning the types of measures, provision on both general education and vocational training is ambiguous, but that of vocational training did not clearly define whether only non-binding or also binding legal acts could be adopted.

Aftermath

The legal developments in relation to ET that took place since the Maastricht Treaty are summarized briefly in this shorter section. There was the *Treaty of Amsterdam* from 1997, amending the TEU, which mentioned the EU's commitment to ET in the Preamble. And then, there was also a slight change in the decision-making procedure that came with the Lisbon Treaties (TFEU) in 2009.

The Amsterdam Treaty in 1997 came as a reaction to the fact that Maastricht had made unsatisfactory and insufficient provision in some areas, especially since the pending eastern enlargement was bringing further

---

[47] Bektchieva 2004, p. 29.
[48] Barnard 1995, p. 20.

challenges. The Member States decided to provide for more efficiency and to further engage in the process of democratization. So it happened that the use of the Co-decision Procedure was extended. Moreover, in the preamble of the Treaty, the signatories confirmed that they are "[d]etermined to promote the development of the highest possible level of knowledge for their peoples through a wide access to education and through its continuous updating"[49] This phrase in the preamble is of relevance insofar as it marks the next step forward on the high-politics agenda and demonstrates an unmistakable sign of commitment.[50] In terms of the procedure, Amsterdam added one more aspect to Article 127 on vocational training. Since then, the Committee of the Regions must also be consulted in the policy formation process. This was something that had already previously existed in matters of general education.

The TFEU signed in Lisbon on the December 13th, 2007 replaced the Co-decision Procedure with the *Ordinary Legislative Procedure* (OLP), further extending the powers of the Parliament. As defined by Articles 289 and 294, TFEU, the OLP is based on what is called the principle of parity or joint adoption. None of the legislative actors – neither the Council nor the Parliament – could adopt decisions without full agreement from the other part. Since the Treaty of Lisbon, both areas (of general education and of vocational training) are subject to the OLP.

To avoid any confusion, it is important to point out that the numbering of the ET provision has changed twice since the TEU. With the Treaty of Amsterdam, the numbers changed from Article 126 and 127 to Articles 149 and 150. Finally, with the Lisbon Treaties the location changed again. Currently general education is regulated in Article 165 and vocational training in Article 166 of the Treaty on the functioning of the European Union.

Chapter summary

The development with regard to primary law started on the premise that the Member States agreed not to include general education but rather vocational training in the TECSC and TEEC. Until the TEU introduced general education and reformulated the provision for vocational training, this meant that the EC had some explicit powers to make policy with regard to the area of vocational training but only implicit powers to make policy with regard to general education. This, however, did not mean that nothing was done to

---

[49] Treaty of Amsterdam, Preamble.
[50] Bechtel et al. 2005, p. 38.

address issues equally related to both general education and vocational training.

By means of Treaty provision concerned particularly with the freedom of movement, some non-binding acts were adopted on the mutual recognition of diplomas but, most importantly, utilizing the direct applicability of EC law, the ECJ responded to the claims of citizens and, by this, issued binding case law that was of great relevance to the organization of ET in the Member States. The ECJ, so to speak, opened the backdoor and laid tracks so that the introduction of general education in the TEU was the logical consequence.

The TEU eventually defined the division of responsibilities between the EU institutions and the Member States on the basis of the principle of subsidiarity, which has since then been the key to understanding ET politics in the EU. The principle of subsidiarity is formally protecting the authority of the Member States with regard to the organization of ET against the increasing powers of the supranational institutions.

The developments, which will be recounted in the following four chapters, however, suggest the thesis that the TEU provision in Articles 126 and 127 encouraged the EU institutions to exploit their competences while still respecting the principle of subsidiarity. This could be achieved by introducing new and softer governance arrangements as those related to the Education Committee, the Ordinary Legislative Procedure or the financial support programs for mobility, cooperation and retraining of workers.

6.3 Education and training in the 1970s

Political discussions concerning ET were intensified at the end of the 1960s when the EC needed to balance its economic and political objectives to address new societal demands. In this context, particularly general education rose in importance together with the topic of culture because both were discussed in the larger context of a not only economy-oriented approach to European unification. Institutional structures dealing with general education were established in the early 1970s in order to work towards a common policy. With the action program on education in 1976 and the creation of the *Education Committee*, the first stage in the mainstreaming of general education was completed.

Outline of context developments

In the context of societal and cultural upturns taking place all over the western hemisphere during the 1960s, education entered the EC agenda as a means to many ends. The younger generation was raising claims and the existing institutions of society were being questioned. Many countries were confronted by the necessity to undertake a radical reform of their education systems. On one hand, they had to deal with new demands of economies and industries and, on the other hand, they had to deal with the increasing democratization of society. Moreover, technology and the mass media were about to turn the world up-side-down and demographic developments required an expansion of educational provision.

Looking into the academic literature, one finds many scholarly works discussing this new situation. In Germany, the pedagogue and theologian Georg Picht diagnosed the "catastrophe of education" (*„Bildungskatastrophe"*) and emphasized that a state of emergence concerning education means at the same time a state of emergence in the economy.[51] Ralf Dahrendorf, a German sociologist and politician, pronounced "education is a civil right" (*"Bildung ist Bürgerrecht"*). In his view, the right to education as a civil right automatically constitutes the need for an active public education policy.[52] Simultaneously, in the United States, Philip H. Coombs gave his point of view in the book *The World Educational Crisis*, in which he asserted "the crisis in the foreground is not simply a crisis of education, but one that embraces the whole of society and the economy."[53]

Concerning ACE, movements had emerged even earlier than this. Already in the late 1940s, the French adult education movement People and Culture (*'Peuple et Culture'*) started to work on the concept of *'éducation permanent'*. Led by organizations such as the Study and Research Group on Adult Education (*'Group d'Etudes et de Recherche pour l'Education des Adultes'*) or the National Institute for Adult Education (*'Institut National pour la Formation des Adultes'*) and driven by individuals like Paul Lengrand or Bertrand Schwartz, the idea of learning across the lifespan began to spread in the mid-1960s.[54] The Council of Europe and UNESCO picked up on these ideas and commissioned a number of academic studies among which the report *Learning to be* produced by a Committee chaired by the French minister of education, Edgar Faure, is the most well-known.[55] In 1973, also the OECD joined with its concept of *recurrent education*, while

---

[51] Picht 1964, p. 16.
[52] Dahrendorf 1965, p. 24.
[53] Coombs 1968, p. 8.
[54] Hausmann 1972, p. 18.
[55] Faure et al. 1972.

in the European Community discussions on permanent education took place at that time but only slowly gained momentum.

The late 1960s were characterized by cultural and generational clashes. In Europe, ongoing French military interventions in Southeast Asia upset the young and triggered serious riots in May 1968, turning Paris upside down. Around the same time, the Prague Spring gained strength but was eventually crushed by the Warsaw Pact Invasion a few months later. Internationally, the US won the space race and on July 21st, 1969 Neil Armstrong was the first human to land on the moon.

Very important for education were the events before the landing on the moon. In 1957, the USSSR successfully launched the first artificial satellite, the Sputnik 1. This event caused the so-called Sputnik Crisis or Sputnik Shock. Western countries, most of all the United States of America, realized the Soviet dominance in terms of technology. In reaction, various initiatives were launched, among which the so-called Space Race was the most well-know. More importantly, it was a major impulse for US and European governments to invest into education in the natural sciences and engineering to keep up with technological development in the Soviet Union. This was, among other reasons, a cause for the massive expansion of education during the 1960s.

The 1970s, then, were a decade of international turmoil, economically as well as politically. In 1971, cancelling the convertibility of the US-Dollar, the President of the United States, Richard Nixon, suspended the Bretton-Woods System and caused a currency crisis. The Arab-Israeli War from 1973 resulted in an OPEC oil embargo and triggered an international energy crisis with significant effect on the European economy. In Europe, important political changes occurred in 1974 and 1975, when the Greek Military Junta collapsed and the Portuguese Salazar Regime was turned over. After the death of General Franco in 1975, also Spain turned its back on the autocratic regime.

By the end of the 1960s, the EC had just overcome a troublesome period, which laid bare the weak spots of the framework for European integration. Throughout most of the decade, political tensions had become tangible regarding the question of how much supranational regulation was needed and how much sovereignty was supportable for achieving common goals. For instance, the extension of the majority vote procedure caused irritations since it was considered the prime instrument of supranational forces. In 1965, as France took over the Council Presidency, President Charles De Gaule strongly opposed the Commission's policy proposals and eventually recalled his Council representative. This move resulted in what is called the "empty chair crisis" leading to an effective deadlock in the Council.[56] The Luxembourg Compromise from 1966, subsequently, reestablished the balance by introducing the unanimity vote procedure.

The accession of the United Kingdom, the Republic of Ireland and Denmark in 1973 meant the first enlargement of the EC. Economically, however, the 1970s brought a "prevailing stagflation" meaning a "weak economic growth combined with high inflation and unemployment".[57] Following the 1972 Meeting in Paris, initiatives for environmental, social and regional policy were launched. The Davignon report on political cooperation allowed for soft forms of intergovernmental collaboration. The intergovernmental dimension was additionally strengthened in 1975 through the inauguration of the European Council, the meeting of the Heads of State, which soon turned into the primary agenda-setting body.[58]

Examination of historical developments

The first event that will be discussed is the summit of the heads of state that took place in The Hague in 1969 and the plan that the French minister for national education, Olivier Guichard, presented at the summit. Guichard wanted to establish a *European Center for the Development of Education*. Next, is the first meeting of the Council of Ministers from 1971, followed by a report on the first working groups set up under the Italian Commissioner Altiero Spinelli. It was Spinelli who asked Professor Henri Janne from Belgium to write a report on the possibilities of community policy in the field of education. Then, the program of the German Commissioner Ralf Dahrendorf is discussed and compared with Spinelli's plans. The last three sections deal with the 1974 Communication on education, the Education Committee and finally the Council Resolution adopting the first action program on education in 1976.

The Hague Summit and Olivier Guichard

A turning point in the history of European integration and of ET politics was the summit meeting of the heads of state that took place in The Hague, Netherlands, in December 1969. Statements from the final communiqué of the

---

[56] Dinan 2012, p. 34.
[57] Dinan 2012, p. 35.
[58] Dinan 2012, pp. 35–36.

summit are a testimony of the first major political commitment on general education at the European level.

For instance, the Member States' inherent transnational cultural bonds that unite the peoples of Europe were invoked. In addition to that, they emphasized preserving "an exceptional seat of development, of progress and culture"[59] in order to achieve the EC's objectives and contribute to a peaceful and balanced world order. Moreover, the role of the younger generation for the EC's growth ambitions was reinforced by governments and EC institutions. Even if education was not addressed explicitly, the statements were interpreted in favor of education and culture. They set into motion further action, eventually leading towards the introduction of education into the EC's policy portfolio.

At The Hague summit, Olivier Guichard initiated a discourse by which he wanted to encourage politicians to foster cooperation among the six Member States. In an article originally published in *Le Monde* two years after The Hague, in 1971, Guichard wrote about the observations that led him to become active and present his innovative ideas.[60]

Up until the end of the 1960s, the EC had neither paid much attention to general education nor to culture. Contrarily, other international governmental organizations (IGOs) like the UNESCO or the Council of Europe had already started to work on such issues and institutionalized an early outline of an international framework for cooperation in education. If there was cooperation between the EC and its Member States, it was on a bilateral basis and, hence, did not involve the EC institutions as the center of multilateral cooperation. It was without any problem, for example, for Germany and France to have an agreement on certain aspects of cooperation but it seemed impossible to have an agreement involving all Member States and multiple aspects.

Guichard expressed his discontent towards the non-existent multilateral supranational cooperation. He was neither satisfied with the work of the IGOs, which he thought had produced too few concrete actions, nor was he satisfied with the bilateral approaches preferred by the EC Members, which he considered insufficient. For him, the EC was the adequate forum and capable of combining the supranational with the bilateral dimension. He stressed his viewpoint saying that Europe (meaning the EC) had to be more

---

[59] Commission of the European Communities 01.1970, p. 12.
[60] A version of this article was accessed that was published in the Italian *Rivista di Studi Politici Internazionali* in 1972.

than a large administration taking care of the present state of things, rather it needed to invest in a common future including education and training, especially for those who would be leading the continent in the future.[61] It was with this that he demanded a stronger commitment and effort on the part of the EC.

The first idea he forwarded was to organize a meeting of the six Member States' education ministers during the period of the French Council Presidency in the first half of 1971. An ad hoc committee consisting of high-ranking member state officials was soon established and began to work. Guichard's intention was to place the education ministers at the helm of any further action and in charge of all issues related to cooperation. Even though possible dates for the meeting in May 1971 were suggested, his initiative failed and the meeting did not take place because the ministers could not agree on an appropriate date. At the time Giuchard was writing the article (July 1971), he didn't know that later on in the same year, in November, the first meeting of education ministers would actually take place. However, more important was his second idea. He proposed to establish stable administrative structures in order to facilitate a better coordination and promotion of education issues at the community level. He conceived it as a *European Centre for the Development of Education*. Guichard wanted the center not only to be an administrative and coordinating structure but a place where education was promoted pro-actively. Among the tasks that were to be assigned to the Centre were, most prominently, the improvement of research methods and the production of education statistics, provision of services for teacher and researcher mobility, coordination of mutual recognition of diplomas and development of a system of equivalents, work on modern teaching techniques – for instance the use of audio visual media – and pedagogical research on continuing education.

Most of Guichard's ideas, particularly the *European Centre for the Development of Education*, remained firmly within the framework provided by the constitutional Treaty. The mobility of teachers, i.e. education work force and the recognition of diplomas were implicit within the provision for freedom of establishment, and the general improvement of statistics was also an objective defined in the Treaties. The problems arising from his proposition, however, reflect some of the long-term issues in ET. Precisely, he wanted a permanent organizational structure, equipped with the necessary means to

---

[61] Guichard 1972, p. 123.

establish contracts, which would work on the basis of education ministers' decisions.[62]

Establishing contracts was a sensitive topic because the TEC (Art. 128 on vocational training) conferred no legislative competences upon the Community. The idea with the leading role of the education ministers, on the other hand, caused irritations with other EC institutions, particularly the more powerful Council and the Commission. This was most likely the reason why the *European Centre for Development of Education* was never implemented even though it had been discussed up until 1976.[63] In spite of the various obstacles Guichard's ideas faced, the following years proved that he was one of the individuals who laid tracks for future activities in the field of ET.

The first meeting of education ministers

The first official meeting of the education ministers took place on November 16th, 1971. The topic of the meeting was cooperation in the field of education. Pépin mentions that, since it was an event outside the Treaty framework, the meeting was not fully acknowledged within the Council of the EC. The result of this meeting was entitled "Resolution of the ministers for education within the Council".[64] This meant that it was a purely intergovernmental agreement among the Member States' representatives with no binding effect and only very little political leverage.

In the just mentioned Resolution, the education ministers stressed that already existing measures in the field of vocational training must be supplemented by a closer cooperation in matters of general education.[65] They decided to set up a working party for education and teaching, associated with the Commission and reporting to the education ministers. The working party took over conceptual work for the establishment of Guichard's *European Centre for the Development of Education*. The agreed upon conceptual tasks included the planning of legal requirements and organizational structures and the financing of the center, as well as its relationship with other community structures and nation states.

Four months before the meeting of the education ministers in July 1971, the Council adopted general guidelines for a community program on vocational training pursuant to Article 128, TEEC.[66] Dissatisfied with the general

---

[62] Guichard 1972, p. 123.
[63] Pépin 2006, p. 64.
[64] Pépin 2006, p. 63.
[65] Ministers for Education 1987.
[66] Council of the European Communities 8/12/1971.

principles laid down by the Council in 1963, a new attempt was made to link (particularly adult) vocational training more tightly with social policy and active employment policy. The Commission was aware of its lack of abilities to operationalize and implement the 1963 principles, as well as insufficient resources to actually convert those principles into effective measures. Congruent with Guichard's proposal, the Council Conclusions on adult vocational training issued in November 1970 demanded concrete work at the community level to coordinate research, collect and exchange data and information and elaborate ways for dealing with the issue of mutual recognition of diplomas.

Even if there hardly existed a formal basis for policy-making, neither stipulated within the Treaties, nor structurally within in the EC institutions, the statements made in The Hague were somewhat revolutionary since they sparked discussions and initiated action. Brad Blitz, professor of international politics and education policy, who looked into the events in detail, highlights this when he says that "[a]fter the Hague summit a de facto educational policy evolved from a series of non-binding resolutions in which the Council of Ministers for Education first identified the goal of defining a European model of culture that correlated with European integration."[67]

It did not take long for the Commission to take up the various impulses and start investing in administrative structures. The following six years from 1970 to 1976 saw immense progress, primarily attributed to the merit of a small number of key figures: Altiero Spinelli, Henri Janne, Ralf Dahrendorf and Hywel Ceri Jones. These personalities had similar plans for policy topics but different visions of and approaches to the *finalité politique* of EC action in the field of education.

Rudimentary structures and Altiero Spinelli

From 1970 until 1973, the Italian Altiero Spinelli was the Commissioner first for Industrial Affairs and Trade, and then for Industrial Affairs and Research. In this capacity, he was in charge of the Directorate General in which the first rudimentary structures for ET were established. Because of his more than 40 years of commitment to and involvement in various European institutions, Spinelli is considered one of the most influential figures in the history of European integration. Together with Ernesto Rossi, he co-wrote the Ventotene Manifesto. Soon after its publication in 1941, the Manifesto became one of the most influential ideological documents of the post-World

---

[67] Blitz 2003, p. 200.

War II period and the founding document of the movement of European federalists. Being a federalist, Spinelli had argued consistently throughout his entire political career in favor of a supranational solution to European unification as opposed to the continuation of nation state sovereignty. His approach to education was also centered on the idea of pooling competences within Community structures (Commission and Parliament). Moreover, his ideas turned away from the focus on vocational training and placed more importance on culture and higher education.

According to the research of Anne Corbett, Spinelli was the first member of the Commission to show real interest in matters of general education. [68] She reports that Spinelli won a bid against other competitors over the allocation of the education portfolio and could therefore, in 1971, arrange to establish two working groups on education under his direct responsibility. The first of the two working groups had the task of conducting studies and working on proposals for potential action with regard to education and teaching. The second, an interdepartmental working group, had the task of dealing with cooperation and coordinating the exchange of information across several DGs who had a stake in ET.

Information concerning Spinellis' intentions comes also from the research on cultural policy by Ana Gaio, who reports that Spinelli considered education pivotal in both areas of EC interests: the economic and the social. [69] He was particularly interested in the equal recognition of educational and cultural products and services on the market and argued that it was possible to apply Treaty provision in that respect. By this, according to Gaio's argument, Spinelli created a link between future policies in the educational and cultural domain and the already existing common market project. The intention was to utilize education as a sort of spillover creator into the area of culture and, by doing this, contribute to the achievement of overall Community objectives.

A document discovered in the Archive of European Integration at the University of Pittsburgh adds to the impression of Spinelli's understanding of education as given by Gaio. In the magazine 'European Community' from March 1972, Spinelli speaks about ideas on education, and education as a basis of European unity. Below, are two sections reproduced from the article.

Education should enable man to develop his personal, intellectual, and professional abilities. It should also enhance his capacity to live creatively in a

[68] Corbett 2003, p. 320.
[69] Gaio 2015, pp. 187–188.

world where traditional ideas of society, knowledge, and work are changing swiftly and radically. (...) Constantly refining and improving education, especially adult education, could help to mold a new civilization.[70]

Why should the Community need a common education policy of its own, when international organizations such as the United Nations, the Organization for Economic Cooperation and Development (OECD), and the Council of Europe have for years been going over similar ground? The answer is that the Community, although no better qualified than any other organization to come up with the right solutions, faces a greater need for such a policy. The logic of economic union demands it, and, in the longer term, it must be one of the factors in turning the concept of separate European identity into something more than a nebulous dream.[71]

In December 1972, Spinelli released a Communication in which the first results produced by the two working groups were presented to the Commission. In addition to a first outline for a long-term action plan, an institutional framework was put forward. According to Luce Pépin, with this framework, the Commission reacted to Guichard's proposition of the *European Centre for Development of Education* and demanded on its own part the lead in educational cooperation, arguing that it would be much better equipped to accelerate processes than any intergovernmental meeting of the education ministers.[72]

After Spinelli had managed to establish the two working groups and clarify his intentions, he sought some current policy measures that would have had the potential to break from the intergovernmental procedures. In July 1972, he commissioned Henri Janne, professor of sociology and former Belgian minister of education, to conduct a study and provide a report for a common European education policy. This report will be examined in the next section.

The Janne Report and its findings
Commissioner Altiero Spinelli asked Henry Janne to write a report identifying the best possible education policies at community level. [73] For this purpose, Janne set out to conduct an inquiry among 30 experts from the wider international and European education and scientific community. The sample of experts was drawn up in agreement with the head of the Working Group

---

[70] European Community Information Service 1972, p. 18.
[71] European Community Information Service 1972, p. 19.
[72] Pépin 2006, p. 65.
[73] Janne 1973.

on Teaching and Education – who, in turn, was the chief assistant to Spinelli. Composing the sample, it had to be assured that the opinions expressed by the experts neither represented the Commission's position nor the view of any Member State but gave account of and reflected the whole spectrum of concerns attached to EC policy. The final sample consisted of experts who either had a high reputation in the field of education or had long-term experience in other scientific fields. By nationality, they were citizens of the nine Member States or of the Nordic Countries Sweden and Norway, plus one American.

The report started with a list of developments that had taken place in the preceding years. On one hand it was acknowledged that "at the level of principles, a great step forward" had already been made. On the other hand, the intergovernmental nature of EC education politics was made responsible for "developments" that "are very limited in importance, [and] extremely slow". The report went on to state that the present situation constituted "the irreversible recognition of an educational dimension of Europe and the irreversible initial movement towards an education policy at European Community level (...)".[74]

The experts asserted that the Treaty provision was fully adequate and sufficient to make education politics. They pointed out that a common policy on education must consider the regulations on free movement of people and freedom of establishment of workers as well as the mutual recognition of qualifications. Moreover, they wished to see measures concerning the coherence of national and international policies as well as the coherence of education and other policy fields such as education and culture, or education and science. In the original words: "It can be seen that it is a whole Education-Culture-Science sector which must tomorrow be covered by a Community policy rendered indispensable by the requirements and consequences of the development of economic policy (with its social aspects)."[75]

The consultation produced findings in various categories. A first category concerned the extent of EC power. Here, the experts agreed that the existing Treaty provision was fully adequate and suggested not demanding further provision only to force a community policy into being. Altogether, the experts raised concerns as to whether a community intervention would harm recently established education systems or the autonomy of educational organizations.

---

[74] Janne 1973, p. 10.
[75] Janne 1973, p. 13.

A second category of findings referred to the EC institutions. It was widely agreed that some structure in charge of policy preparation, consultation, planning and implementation must exist in every EC institution (Commission, Parliament, Council). Staff and resources should be allocated to these structures in accordance with the size of the activities and the tasks conferred upon them. One expert wished to see an Educational and Cultural Committee equal to the Economic and Social Committee.

A third category of findings referred to the types of powers. While there was broad agreement on the previous two categories, the experts' views diverged on the types of powers. Some preferred a global policy that would encompass all levels of education from primary school to adult education, while others thought it was better to focus on specific areas, particularly those, which could not effectively be handled by any lower national or regional level of administration. One thing that the majority agreed upon was the need to have a program for teacher and student mobility.

From today's perspective, it is noteworthy that the general policy topics that emerged from Janne's consultation have been conspicuously consistent over the years. They provided the direction, which European education policies have followed ever since. In the report's conclusion, for instance, there are issues such as strengthening the European dimension in terms of social cohesion, knowledge of languages and the use of mass media and new technology. Moreover, the report emphasized the relevance of learner and teacher exchanges and equivalences of diplomas to guarantee freedom of movement and permanent education.

Altogether, four aspects stand out within the report. Firstly, a transversal understanding of education was favored since issues are inseparably linked with other policy areas like economic, scientific and cultural policy. Secondly, national idiosyncrasies had to be respected but an incremental harmonization was advisable in order to successfully apply the global approach to education policy. Thirdly, the role of EC policy should be complementary and compensatory in relation to national policies and should offer a link between economic and social policy. Fourthly, promoting Member States' involvement with other international organizations, however, without duplicating efforts was regarded as a desirable objective.

The directorate general and Ralf Dahrendorf
In 1973, the first enlargement of the Community was completed when the United Kingdom, the Republic of Ireland and Denmark joined the six founding members. As a result of this enlargement, a restructuring of the

Commission had to be conducted, which, as it turned out, proved beneficial for the growing aspirations in the field of education. The number of Directorate Generals (DGs) was increased from eight to thirteen, the importance of education was confirmed and firm organizational structures were established. Ralf Dahrendorf took over as Commissioner for the new Directorate General Research, Science and Education (DG XII). Prior to his political career in the European Community, Dahrendorf – a sociologist and university professor by profession – had served as Secretary of State and Foreign Affairs in the German government and was a leading figure in the field of social sciences. In this capacity, he wrote the book *Bildung ist Bürgerrecht* ('Education is a civil right' 1965), in which he expressed his view on how politics should deal with education in the context of a modern society.

Within the motive for establishing the new Directorate General, Dahrendorf was clear: "[T]here was political purpose in this decision".[76] Indeed, all three fields, namely research, science and education, were scattered all over the wide range of other policy areas even though they were obviously closely related to each other. Merging the three fields in one Commissioner's portfolio made it possible to deal with the issues independently, however, as part of a coherent Community policy.

There seems to be some disagreement on Dahrendorf's role. According to the German professor Joachim Knoll, it was Dahrendorf's vigorous efforts that led to the official introduction of education into the Commission portfolio.[77] The accuracy of this statement, however, cannot be proven. On the contrary, in an interview from February 2017, Hywel Ceri Jones, who was at that time the head of the Education Division, gave the credits to Altiero Spinelli for having initiated the education endeavor.[78]

Within the DG, four Directorates were formed, whereby one was dedicated to education: the directorate for training, education and external relations in the field of research, science and education replaced the two existing Working Groups on education. This directorate's agenda was divided into four thematic sectors:[79] (1) Education, training and youth policy, dealing with policy and mobility programs, (2) mutual recognition of diplomas in charge of professional and adult training, and freedom of establishment, (3)

---

[76] Commission of the European Communities 5/23/1973, p. 1.
[77] Knoll 1996, p. 206.
[78] ERASMUS+ UK 2017.
[79] Commission of the European Communities 1973, p. 47.

problems of the cultural sector focusing on the promotion of a common culture and (4) bilateral and multilateral external relations.

Luce Pépin reports that this Directorate had a staff of 20 officials, among which Hywel Ceri Jones was the most important figure. As head of the Education Division, Jones – a former University administration officer at the University of Sussex in Great Britain – would be the architect of education policy at the community level for the next twenty years, obtaining all posts from Director of Education, founder of Erasmus to Director General for Employment, Social Policy and Industrial Relations in the period from 1993-1998.[80]

In May 1973, the first working program was presented. It was a personal statement by Commissioner Dahrendorf, who expressed his views on the challenges education was facing, his political stance, and his plans for future activities.[81] It is difficult to estimate whether or not the document drew from the Report Henri Janne had submitted in February just three months earlier. What is certain, though, is that the two perspectives were not consistent. It would be valid to argue that Dahrendorf's document very much reflected his own political and educational views. On the political side, he took on a position that can be classified as in favor of strong intergovernmental cooperation and critical about supranational intervention. On the educational side, especially with regard to the objectives, he strongly advocated broader access to education.

The program stressed three things. Firstly, action in education must have a medium- and long-term perspective. Secondly, action need not necessarily be taken at the European level. Thirdly, action must be in accordance with Treaty provision, should respond to demands from other policy areas, and should concentrate on cooperation without bypassing the EC competences. The following quotation from the program reproduces the list of issues to which the program intended to give an answer.

> [G]iving effect to the civil right to education and the equality of opportunity for all;
>
> coping with the problems of a new order of magnitude ('mass problems') in secondary and tertiary education;
>
> the relationship between education and job (subject matters of education, demand patterns, career prospects, etc.);

---

[80] Pépin 2006, p. 92; ERASMUS+ UK 2017.
[81] Commission of the European Communities 5/23/1973.

exploration of new technical and organizational methods to open the road to 'permanent education';

changes in the quality of the subject matters of education and in the organisation of the educational system to take account of the demand for more democracy and the tendency towards a critical view of economy and society.[82]

From this list, the medium-term measures were defined. Overall, these measures were built around core issues contained in the Treaty on the one hand, and the demands from the changing social environment on the other hand. The first measure was to build up an information system within the Member States' education systems, to encourage permanent education, inquire the use of new technologies, and to promote open universities. The second measure was to create a European dimension of culture furthering integration. In this context, vocational training was intimately linked with the freedom of establishment, mutual recognition of qualifications and diplomas and exchange programs for students and teachers. All issues were closely related to the overall goals of the EC. A last measure concerned cooperation with third countries, referring to countries that were not Members of the EC. On governance, Dahrendorf was very clear, as can be gathered from the following two statements:

The mere mention of these problems is enough to show that at the moment the European Community can make only very limited contribution to their solution.[83]

Many of the projects in the field of educational and cultural policy, especially those which are connected with reforms and can only be put into effect in the medium-term, exceed the capabilities of the Directorate General for Research, Science and Education responsible for day-to-day routine work.[84]

The DG's capacity was limited, but Dahrendorf made two suggestions to overcome these limitations. First, in order to support the work of the Commission he suggested installing an advisory committee of experts working on Janne's proposal of the European Educational and Cultural Committee. Second, concerning the Council of Ministers, he encouraged meetings on a regular basis. Here, reference was apparently made to Guichard's idea for a European Centre for Educational Development.

---

[82] Commission of the European Communities 5/23/1973, p. 4.

[83] Commission of the European Communities 5/23/1973, p. 5.

[84] Commission of the European Communities 5/23/1973, p. 9.

In summary, the aspirations of the new Commissioner were in some respects contrary to what his predecessor had aimed at. To be more precise, it was Spinelli's drive for harmonization (supported by Janne's report) that left Dahrendorf with ambivalent feelings. According to Anne Corbett, Dahrendorf and the head of the education division, Hywel Ceri Jones, were "horrified by the mention of harmonization."[85] When, in 1974, the *Communication Education in the European Community*, containing the proposal for a working program, was forwarded to the Council, the future direction had already been decided.

The Commission Communication

The second document that emanated from the work of 1973 was the Commission Communication presented to the Council on the topic of education in the European Community.[86] The Communication made clear that harmonization of both the structure and the content of Member States' education systems was no option. What was required was "a common commitment to the development of a strategy of educational cooperation supported by a more systematic interchange of information and experience."[87] Consequently, the proposed program focused on three broad areas: first, mobility and recognition issues; second, as a new topic, education of children of migrant workers especially in foreign languages; and third, the fostering of European topics as part of school curricula and the cooperation among higher education institutions. Systematic interchange of information was additionally envisaged to link the three areas. This time, the governance dimension was extended to the wider education community. Consultation and cooperation was to include teachers, administrators, researchers and, likewise, officials. Moreover, working groups and institutionalized contacts with the Council of Europe, Unesco and OECD were also suggested.

It seems as if Hywell Ceri Jones' experience as a university administrator had been very influential because cooperation among universities and mobility of students, researchers, teachers and administrative staff was strongly emphasized. Anne Corbett found in her analysis of the Communication that defining the EC's role as a complementary role to national action, and the use of facilities from other policy areas created new opportunities for action.[88] For instance, the use of the ESF to set up joint study programs and

---

[85] Corbett 2003, p. 322.
[86] Commission of the European Communities 3/17/1974.
[87] Commission of the European Communities 3/17/1974, p. 6.
[88] Corbett 2003, p. 323.

short study visits based on bilateral contracts was innovative in many respects. It was a way to make the best out of the Commission's available resources and competences, while simultaneously serving as a strategy to align objectives. For universities, it was an equally attractive possibility to have a stronger international dimension.

The Education Committee

Jones also elaborated on the idea of the European Committee for Educational Cooperation, as was suggested in the working program. A draft decision was then adopted in the resolution of the education ministers on June 6th, 1974.[89] They agreed on a committee composed of three representatives from each Member State plus three alternates. Interestingly, the Communication wanted a Commission official to chair the Committee; in the Resolution it had previously been agreed upon that the chair should come from the office of the Council President. The tasks were to discuss pending questions and advise the Commission on further programmatic action. Moreover, they were given the power to initiate discourses and to entrust other actors and experts with the delivery of studies.

The Education Committee had a unique structure since it was the only committee in which Commission officials worked together with Member States' governmental representatives and their permanent representatives in the Council. According to Pépin, this was possible because the Member States had shown willingness to enter into a formal cooperation on the basis of a non-binding decision.[90] That the field of education was not categorized under the Treaty framework might have been an additional reason that facilitated the cooperation. In practice, work was advanced on the interplay between the Commission and the permanent representatives, as emphasized by Pépin. While the former provided input and pushed its agenda, the latter accommodated political tensions and tried to establish consensus among the parties.

The first action program in education

On February 9th, the final step towards the first EC action program was taken. The Council, together with the education ministers, adopted the resolution on the program that had been suggested two years earlier.[91] By this, they

---

[89] Ministers for Education 8/20/1974.
[90] Pépin 2006, pp. 88–89.
[91] Council of the European Communities 2/19/1976.

completed the framework for policy action and the basis of a governance arrangement.

Concerning policy, a rather global approach was attempted. The six pillars were: (1) education of migrants and their children, (2) closer relations between education systems, (3) closer cooperation in the field of higher education, (4) compilation of statistics and documentation, (5) teaching of foreign languages and (6) equal access to all forms of education.

To support the implementation of the measures within the six pillars, the Commission was given the responsibility to coordinate mobility schemes (short study visits, joint study programs), or to support research projects providing information about the national situation. Furthermore, they had to promote cooperation, encourage a European dimension in education and organize consultations. To establish a proper governance arrangement, the Education Committee was assigned the task of overseeing the implementation of measures.

Chapter summary

The examination of the 1970s produced some noteworthy findings. In the first place, it could be shown that the establishment of education in terms of institutional structures and policy topics was very much the result of the commitment of individual politicians or public servants. Since Member States communicated only little interest in engaging in European cooperation in general education, the initiatives of these few individuals were crucial for the formation of a basic framework and the advocacy of general education. Moreover, the *Education Committee* was a viable governance arrangement and made it possible to build a stable form of cooperation. An actual legal basis for decision-making, though, had not yet been provided for. The decisions made in the Council of ministers were arguably of little importance in the short- and medium-term but, very likely, of great significance in a long-term perspective. Notwithstanding its marginal role in the first years, the blueprint of topics created by the first action program on education in 1976 is, to certain extents, still demonstrated today. The topics it comprised were closely related to general EC interests since access to education and recognition of qualifications or foreign languages were to a great extent prerequisite for the achievement of other EC integration goals outside the narrow field of education and training, such as the free movement of workers.

6.4 Education and training in the 1980s

During the 1980s, the most significant stage in the mainstreaming of ET took place. Economies around the world were suffering from recession and rising unemployment rates. A closer liaison between employment, vocational training and general education turned out to perhaps be the key to raising ET to one of the highly valued political topics of the decade. The *European Court of Justice* (ECJ), whose judgments helped the Commission to implement cooperation and mobility programs and arguably laid grounds for the introduction of general education in the 1992 Treaty on European Union, played a crucial role in this advancement.

Outline of context developments

The 1980s saw the final stage of the Cold War and the disintegration of the Eastern Bloc. Prospective planning for integrating the Eastern European nations into the EC began. After the accession of Greece in 1981, Portugal and Spain in 1986 and the abatement of the previous period of recession, Europe was facing competition on the global markets because of the US and Japanese economic upturn and increasing potential for innovation. The European leaders wanted to boost the economic performance of the member states. Reinforcing policy areas, like research and technology, was considered an adequate response in regard to the innovation issue. The completion of the Single Market was considered an appropriate answer to the issue of competitiveness.

A very important year was 1985, when Jacques Delors was elected President of the European Commission. Upon starting his new position, he declared that in order to move forward, the European single market was inevitable; however, it demanded the removal of national borders. In June 1985, at the Intergovernmental Conference in Milan, the new Commission President presented a White Paper on the completion of the internal market. At this Conference, broad commitment among participants was reached in order to put an end to the long-lasting gridlock that had impeded earlier attempts of market liberalization. Proposing mechanisms for the removal of physical, technical and fiscal barriers laid track for the full implementation of the four fundamental freedoms.[92]

---

[92] Dinan 2012, p. 36.

Also in 1985, Germany, France and the Benelux countries signed the Schengen-Agreement to allow free movement of people between these five countries.

The Single European Act (SEA) from 1987, marked the first reform of the TEEC. Most importantly, it set the anticipated deadline for the completion of the single market for December 31st, 1992. In addition to that, the SEA introduced environmental policy, research and technology and foreign policy cooperation to the EC agenda. At the institutional level, the new 'cooperation procedure' "(...) was intended to improve democratic accountability at a time when the EC's remit and visibility were about to increase dramatically."[93]

Transformation of work and society were characteristic of the social science and adult education discourse of the late 1970s and early 1980s. In his famous work on the post-industrial society, Daniel Bell predicted a sustainable change in the structure of societies emanating from changes in the organization of work.[94] He had observed that theoretical knowledge and service tasks were slowly replacing labor and production, which had been the most important factors of the economy, and that these were slowly spilling over into society where they caused changes in the social structure. This observation led Bell to pronounce a shift in the organization of societies from an industrial logic based on work to a post-industrial logic based on knowledge.

Ralf Dahrendorf asked the question: „What will the working society do when it runs out of work?"[95] He did not suggest the end of work or that we actually would run out of work. What he suggested was that, in the future, there would be fewer occupations and fewer jobs while the population would still continue to grow. Some occupations would disappear while new ones would emerge. In general, the function of work in individual life and society would change, including: (1) the reduction of hard work to a necessary minimum, (2) the expansion of education without adapting it to the new demands of working life, (3) the balancing-out of work and leisure time and (4) the prolongation of the retirement period as a result of longer life expectancy and a shorter working life.

Peter Faulstich, a German education scholar, argued that production and work were becoming independent of the things produced or the actual work

---

[93] Dinan 2012, p. 37.
[94] Bell 1979.
[95] Dahrendorf 1978.

and, thus, some sort of self-referential activity. Consequently, ET provision could no longer be derived from and targeted at simply qualifying people for job positions. It was no longer useful to conceive of curricula as the simple translation of job profiles into educational concepts.[96] Education and learning for work were to be seen in a much broader sense.

By the end of the 1970s, awareness for global problems was rising. The Club of Rome argued the necessity to rethink human action in the context of overpopulation, environmental pollution, exploitation of natural resources and nuclear armament. In the 1979 book *No limits to learning*, the authors from the Club of Rome, James Botkin, Mahdi Elmandjar and Mircea Malitza proposed a new concept of learning.[97] They had no doubts that the 1980s were going to be the decade of learning, however, they thought that the major question was not whether learning will become more important but rather what kind of learning will become important. According to the authors, innovative learning was needed. Such innovative learning comprised of anticipatory and participatory learning, facilitating the achievement of two important goals: that of autonomy and that of integration.

The Austrian adult education scholar Werner Lenz argued that adult education as a profession was trying to find a new way to see itself.[98] In 1978, at a time when learning and education of adults was being instrumentalized as a means for dealing with economic problems, Lenz appealed to the adult education community that a definition of its role in society had to be found. Regarding its position within economic, social and education politics, adult and continuing education needed to recognize itself as political education, according to his argument.

Examination of historical developments

First in this analysis is a presentation of the most important events that occurred in the transition period from 1977 to 1983. During this period, among others, a crisis occurred in the Council of Education Ministers and the Directorate for Education was transferred from the DG Science, Research and Education to the DG Employment and Social Affairs. This strategic move was very beneficial for ET. After the transition period, the general political framework of the 1980s will be outlined. Some of the major political actions like the Genscher-Colombo Plan or the strategy of a People's Europe helped

---

[96] Faulstich 1985, p. 17.
[97] Botkin et al. 1979.
[98] Lenz 1989b.

to further promote ET within the EC framework. Subsequently, secondary law will be examined to extrapolate important policy proposals of the 1980s. The last section of this chapter is dedicated to the *European Court of Justice* (ECJ) and the cases that helped to define the competences of the Commission and to launch the first mobility programs.

Transition period from 1977 to 1983

The period in between the adoption of the first action program in 1976 and the rulings in the Forcheri law case in 1983 was a formative period. Despite some difficulties, overall a number of positive developments in regard to ET took place: Most notably, the implementation of Joint Study Programs in higher education, the re-organization of the educational departments within the Commission and the growing support by the European Parliament. Hereafter, the course of events during this period is summarized by reference to academic literature.

A pragmatic approach

In an article from 1980 with the meaningful title *"From 'Europhoria' to Pragmatism: Towards a New Start for Higher Education Co-operation in Europe?"*, Alan Smith, the operations manager of the Joint Studies Scheme in the Commission's education division, described some of the early developments in respect to cooperation in higher education. He put them into context with some of the prevailing tensions between national and supranational actors. Smith's estimation of the developments swung between disillusion and hope. What he had observed was a shift from an initial élan, tangible after having launched cooperation in the mid-1970s, towards a certain kind of pessimism as far as multilateral cooperation in education was concerned, after the crisis years at the end of the 1970s. This observation led Smith to argue that pessimism had always been intrinsic to the field of education particularly "in the interplay between exalted European idealism and concomitant despondency".[99]

Despite the fact that ET – particularly vocational training – had been on the Community's agenda ever since the early 1960s and even though the response from the political leadership in the 1970s had been relatively constructive, Smith stated that "the practical results remained stubbornly conspicuous by their absence".[100] However, what gave reason for optimism was that against the lack of material resources for implementing any policy at the

---

[99] Smith 1980, p. 77.
[100] Smith 1980, p. 77.

community level, there was an intensification of efforts at the national and the European level, but most of all at the level of universities.

In the end, however, Smith remained optimistic for the future since he sensed the onset of a more pragmatic approach to cooperation, instead of the rather idealistic one that had dominated the preceding decade. The pragmatic approach included the insight that efficient use must be made of the available resources and that the emerging movements from within the higher education community must become a valuable factor in promoting education at Community level.

Generally, Smith identified four main trends in respect to the development of higher education policies, which he reiterated in a 1985 article. [101] The first trend was that inter-institutional arrangements of cooperation were of greater applicability than agreements of national governments. A second trend was that, in respect to unstable economic circumstances, awareness had grown regarding the relationship between higher education and the labor market. Thirdly, within the field of higher education, the diversity of types of educational offers had increased and, consequently, bottom-up initiatives had emerged from within the higher education community. Lastly, a general observation was that regional trans-border cooperation and bilateral agreements had become greater in quantity in almost every policy area.

Joint study programs for short period mobility
By 1980, joint study programs and a short study visits scheme had been established. Both measures were part of the strategy to promote arrangements for short period student and teacher exchange on the basis of bilateral agreements between higher education institutions. For the year 1984, the joint study program was allocated a budget of roughly two million ECU. In spite of a relatively modest budget for the period from 1976/1977 until 1984/1985, a number of 413 joint programs were activated. The Commission officials Karen Fogg and Hywel Ceri Jones emphasized the "cumulative effect of these activities" that brought about a "change in attitudes" towards cooperation at all levels.[102] The pilot projects had attracted not only the interest of academics, but were also gaining more and more popularity among politicians.[103] As Alan Smith suggested, arrangements of short period mobility were considered "especially well-suited to solving problems concerning

---

[101] Smith 1985, p. 267.
[102] Fogg and Jones 1985, p. 295.
[103] Corbett 2003, p. 324.

tuition fee differentials, the award of appropriate recognition and credit and accommodation shortage for students."[104]

A crisis in the Council

Given the agreement articulated in the Resolution from 1976, one might expect that cooperation would have developed positively but it was not long until the flaws of the political framework became evident. Education was not accounted for in the TEEC, therefore, it was formally not an area MS desired to be a subject of integration. For that reason, the 1970s ended with a crisis that paralyzed the Council of Education ministers for nearly three years.

It all started in November 1978, when the Danish and the French governments forwarded a request that the next meeting of education ministers be cancelled. The Danish government was vehemently opposed to proposals for which financial implications were to be expected on the categorical argument that no decision should be made without having a TEEC basis. Pépin reports that "[t]he criticism was not, moreover, limited to education, but extended to all fields situated in the 'grey zone', starting with health, for which Denmark considered that the proposals made by the Commission overstepped the limits fixed by the treaty."[105] The Danish government was not entirely against cooperation, but it was afraid of any kind of harmonization of broader social policy, which they expected to be the result of a common policy. According to Pépin, "[t]his was no minor deadlock, and there was a real risk of seeing the nascent cooperation and all the efforts to set up the first action programme reduced to nothing."[106]

Education ministers finally resumed meeting in June 1980. Denmark agreed to participate only under the condition that no further decision with budgetary consequences be made. Paradoxically, the crisis could be resolved as it was agreed to turn away from traditional issues of education, which were considered too sensitive for a common policy, towards labor market issues, which were affecting all MS on equal terms as globalization was taking up speed. An agreement could be found on topics such as transition from education to work, career guidance, the impact of demographic change and technology on education or mutual recognition of diplomas, which were linking education and the world of work and thus could be promoted more easily by reference to the TEEC.

---

[104] Smith 1985, p. 274.
[105] Pépin 2006, p. 90.
[106] Pépin 2006, p. 90.

The strategic merger of education and training

In the late 1970s, negotiations started with the aim to merge education, training and employment affairs and to transfer education matters, particularly the education division, from DG XII Science, Research and Education to DG V Social Affairs and Employment. The intention was to create stronger bonds between education and vocational training and to overcome their separation so that it would be possible to further advance education policies on the back of employment policies. On one hand, linking education more closely with vocational training corresponded well with overarching socio-economic and political trends; on the other hand, it could help to overcome intergovernmental sentiments in the Council of Education ministers because it put plans for education into a different context. In early 1981, when the new Commission was appointed, the move was completed and welcomed with open arms. As Karen Fogg and Hywel Ceri Jones – who was the chief negotiator – comment:

> These decisions heralded the beginning of a new period during which the Commission has taken every opportunity to stress the interrelationships between education, training and employment and to place strong emphasis on the need for a new partnership and sharing of responsibilities for training policy, its planning and implementation.[107]

Jacky Brine argues that the reorganization of the Commission was beneficial in the political, an administrative, and an educational sphere.[108] *Politically*, the result was that the interrelation between education-training-employment against the background of social policy became tangible to the respective national ministries of employment, education *and* social affairs. In the sphere of *administration,* the re-organization was felt at all levels – supranational, national and regional. A new set-up emerged and facilitated the allocation and administration of financial resources and funding programs. Finally, in the sphere of *educational practice*, the effect was that the combination of education, training and employment linked compulsory schooling with the world of work and, thus, to vocational, adult and continuing education. According to Brine, this was a first move towards lifelong learning in the EEC.

---

[107] Fogg and Jones 1985, p. 297.
[108] Brine 1995, p. 149.

The mixed formula and the Parliament

With the adoption of the 1976 action program, also the *Education Committee* was introduced and served as the institutional policy making forum. Consisting of representatives of the Commission and the Council it represented an acceptable compromise to the interests of the EC and the Member States. However, the Education Committee had initially not provided for the contribution of the Parliament. Due to this, it was unsure whether enough financial resources could be allocated, since the Parliament had the right to co-decide on these resources. Moreover, on the side of the Commission, worries existed as to the extent to which the Council would dominate the Education Committee. By the early 1980s, the so-called mixed formula had proven an adequate instrument. Fogg and Jones remark:

> As regards the Community budget, for instance, in so far as any real growth in the allocation of financial resources for education could be expected, the European Parliament retained its vital influence over budget negotiations and the Commission remained autonomous in its use of any resources allocated.[109]

This situation made it possible for the Commission and the Parliament to set up a productive dialogue. Indeed, the parliamentary committee concerned with education and culture showed great interest in promoting education policy and intervened in the budgetary discussion in the interest of the Commission. The support provided by the Parliament turned out to be crucial since "neither the Commission nor the Education Ministers would alone have had the political influence required to build up the education budget from virtually nothing in 1976 to over 12 million ECU's in 1985."[110]

This summary of the period from 1976 to 1983 points out that ET was developing positively and the situation was in favor of a greater extension of Community action. However, what was still missing was a legal basis on which a respective extension in the policy as well as in the governance dimension could be made. Moreover, as will be shown in the next section, strategies in high-level politics of the Council were rendering the circumstances even more favorable.

The general political framework

A 1970 report on foreign policy – the Davignon Report, named after the Chair of the reporting commission, the Belgian Etienne Davignon – wanted

---

[109] Fogg and Jones 1985, p. 294.
[110] Fogg and Jones 1985, p. 294.

to revive plans for a political union. However, plans in the direction of a political union ossified quickly since the political climate was not yet favorable enough for any integration, other than economic. Facing new political challenges in foreign policy and security, closer cooperation became again a debated issue by the end of the 1970s. Moreover, with the first Parliamentary elections in 1979, a process of further democratization was initiated. In 1981, then, the *German-Italian Proposals*, also known as the *Genscher-Colombo Plan*, reactivated discussions about a political union. The intention was to have closer cooperation on political issues, an institutional reform making work more efficient, a community more approachable for European citizens and the eventual completion of the internal market.

Against the backdrop of these developments, ET became more important, primarily in relation to labor market problems and the plan for a so-called *People's Europe*. First, promotion of ET was considered part of a cultural policy, but later it became its own strategic policy field. In what follows now, it will be reconstructed how ET was integrated into the general political framework. To this end, documents produced at high-level meetings in the early 1980s will be consulted: the German-Italian Proposals, the Solemn Declaration, the Fontainbleau Conclusions, and the Report Adonnino on a People's Europe.

The German-Italian Proposals
In January 1981, the German Foreign Minister Hans-Dietrich Genscher delivered a speech, in which he appealed for the strengthening of political cooperation.[111] He proposed that political cooperation must go beyond the scope of existing political areas. An adequate response to the challenges Europe was facing must overcome the limited scope of action, which had been focused on agriculture or the internal market, and must seriously integrate culture policy to *forma proper* 'European Union' – according to the argument put forward by Genscher.

Shortly after Genscher's words, the Italian Foreign Minister Emilio Colombo delivered another appealing speech. For Colombo, the best strategy to handle the challenges was to find joint solutions, thereby extending cooperation in many policy areas. "Building a European awareness means making sure that the integration process makes its way in to [sic] all sectors of human activity," he stated. "The plans we have made for Europe could not be brought to fruition unless there was a real political will to make them a

---

[111] Freie Demokratische Korrespondenz 1981.

success and a joint effort to strive for common goals and solutions to our political, economic, social and cultural problems."[112] Genscher was more concerned with common foreign and security policies; Colombo, on the contrary, stressed the need for technological innovation, research, industries and global competition.

Solemn Declaration on European Union

In response to Genscher's and Colombo's speeches, the German and the Italian governments provided a joint document for discussion at the European Council in late 1981 – the *German-Italian Proposal*. After some deliberations, the proposal led to the *Solemn Declaration of the Heads of State* issued at the Stuttgart European Council in June 1983. The Solemn Declaration was an expression of a common will rather than an actual policy or strategic plan. Nevertheless, the contents are significant, since they provided for intensified cooperation in ET.

The Solemn Declaration was the document that set the pace and formulated early goals for a closer political Union. In the Preamble, the heads of state declared that the creation of a united Europe "(...) is more than ever necessary in order to meet the dangers of the world situation", and that "(...) in order to resolve the serious economic problems (...) the Community must strengthen its cohesion, regain its dynamism and intensify its action in areas hitherto insufficiently explored." They, therefore, declared themselves "resolved to accord a high priority to the Community's social progress and in particular to the problem of employment by the development of a European social policy (...)"[113] Policy fields such as culture, education, youth, research or technology had existed before but only within the context of a closer political union; the EC expressed the intention to fully integrate these topics into the political framework.

As the two quotations below indicate, among the four policy foci defined by the Solemn Declaration, two related to ET. These were general community policies with a focus on reducing unemployment and increasing competitiveness and particularly cultural cooperation, learner mobility, languages and cultural awareness – as the quotation below indicates.

> *Cultural cooperation*: "closer cooperation between establishments of higher education, including exchanges of teacher and students; (...) intensified exchanges of experience, particularly among young people, and development

---

[112] Europe Documents 1981, p. 2.
[113] European Council 6/19/1983, p. 2.

of teaching of the languages; (...) improving the level of knowledge about other Member States (...) and of information on Europe's history and culture so as to promote a European awareness.[114]

The Fontainebleau Council meeting

1984/85 placed another topic of ET on the political agenda. The recognition of diplomas and qualifications became an issue, not only in education ministers' meetings, but also in the meetings of the heads of state. Among education ministries, and even more so within the Commission, mutual recognition of diplomas and qualifications had been discussed for more than a decade. High-level politics, however, had disregarded this topic. At the Council meeting in Fontainebleau in 1984, an ad hoc committee under the chairmanship of the Italian lawyer and member of the European Parliament, Pietro Adonnino was commissioned to write a report on the idea of a "People's Europe". Among the issues to be worked on by the Committee was "a general system for ensuring the equivalence of university diplomas, in order to bring about the effective freedom of establishment within the Community."[115] The resulting two Adonnino Reports were presented at the Council Meetings in March (Brussels) and June 1985 (Milan).

The first of the two reports dealt with mutual recognition of diplomas and professional qualifications in the section on community citizens' rights. This section comprised of four topics: (1) freedom of movement in working life, (2) the right of establishment, (3) professional qualifications and (4) the right of residence. The qualification issues were joined with the freedom of movement because it would have been a matter of great difficulty for those moving across borders to find a job or to establish their own business in a host country without having recognized their completed education.

Contrary to the expected importance given to university degrees, the first Adonnino report only mentioned professional qualifications. It demanded an intensification of "efforts towards greater transparency of evidence of professional qualifications, (...)" and "to consider the introduction of a European vocational training pass for craftsmen and workers with special qualifications."[116] With regard to the liberal professions, such as doctors or architects, some progress had already been made.

The second report also made proposals in the area of education, youth, exchanges, culture, communication and European identity. Intending to form

---

[114] European Council 6/19/1983, p. 8.
[115] European Council 6/25/1984, p. 3.
[116] Adonnino 1985, pp. 13–14.

the views of the younger generations, the section on youth, education, exchanges and sport emphasized the importance of involving young people in Europe. Proposals were made on six topics: language teaching, exchanges between schools, voluntary work camps for young people, the European image in education, university cooperation, vocational training and exchanges of young people and professional exchange.

The report suggested the EC promote cooperation of higher education institutions, such as inter-university schemes, rather than cooperation concerning higher education between national governments. The reason for this can be found in the following statement: "Higher-education establishments and universities enjoy a high degree of autonomy. It is therefore necessary to take as a starting point the fact that a decisive role in the matter must be left to the establishments concerned."[117] In addition to such inter-university schemes, the Committee requested authorities to consider a system for the transfer of academic credits. Again, the credit system should be based on bilateral agreements between higher education establishments rather than agreements between member states.

Regarding vocational training, the primary concern was the labor market situation of those young people in transition from the compulsory school system into the labor market. "The encouragement of suitable vocational training should make it possible to assist with the transition to working life and hence contribute to a reduction of unemployment."[118] Through measures such as periods of practical training complementing compulsory schooling, it was expected to facilitate the transition from education to work and to combat youth unemployment. Addressing the political actors in the Member States, the proposal was made "to ensure that all young people wishing to do so receive one year's [sic], or if possible two years' [sic], vocational training in addition to their compulsory education."[119]

Education and training policy
The first action program in education was adopted in 1976 and defined the priority areas for Member State and EC for the preceding decade. In the 1980s, measures at the community level targeting these priority areas were further developed and eventually integrated into the first specific policy programs like COMETT (university industry cooperation), ERASMUS (higher education student and teacher mobility) or PETRA (education, vocational

---

[117] Adonnino 1985, p. 24.
[118] Adonnino 1985, p. 25.
[119] Adonnino 1985, p. 25.

training and work transition), all of which were implemented in the second half of the 1980s.

The priority areas reinforced in the 1980s were primarily university cooperation, teaching of foreign languages, education and technology and equal opportunities to access all forms of education. The last area also included issues regarding the transition of young people from education to work, which represented the link between education, training and employment. Other key areas such as documentation, data collection and statistics, closer relations of educational systems or offers for migrants' children were largely integrated as transversal issues in all of the priority areas. The transversal character of these topics is evident, especially for the migration issue, in connection with questions concerning prohibition of discrimination, freedom of movement, and freedom of establishment.

A further topic that rose to significance during the 1980s was the topic of technological change and questions on how ET could best support the adaption of workers to new demands at the workplace. This topic was of greater relevance in the area of continuing training than, for instance, the measures promoting a European dimension, which in turn were essential in relation to compulsory school policies.

At their meeting in June 1981, the Council and the education ministers expressed their commitment to strengthen ET. [120] The education ministers discussed how national ET systems should respond to the transformation of work and the effects this had on labor markets. In addition to this, demographic change, caused by steadily sinking birth rates, was defined as a further challenge for ET systems. From the meetings' summary, moreover, one learns about the education minister's reaction to the merger of ET and employment in DG Employment and Social Affairs.

The summary serves to indicate prevailing standpoints. Particular emphasis was placed on the contribution of ET to economic growth and social development, whereby both aspects were held as equally important. Education and training were attributed with the potential to moderate the consequences emerging from structural unemployment. Moreover, an "urgent need" was identified "to remove internal rigidities in the education system". This passage referred to the division between general and vocational types of education. It was suggested "to pursue an integrated approach to education, training and employment policies". Such an integrated approach included opening up education systems to potential partners for cooperation or

---

[120] Council of the European Communities 1987, p. 75.

consultation like "manpower authorities (…) parents, the social partners, and agencies at local level." Another element of this integrated approach was to take account of the value of ET "in stimulating innovation and creativity in social and economic life, whilst not neglecting their fundamental contribution to personal development, cultural values and democratic stability." It was therefore determined that policies should avoid a rigid separation and instead promote "the broadest possible education", namely one that integrated elements of general education and of vocational training.[121]

Moreover, one reads that the ministers of education appreciated the greater attention and opportunities given to general education, particularly as the social and employment department was better equipped with resources, thus, making it easier to pursue an integrated strategy. Ministers welcomed the already existing pilot projects implemented to facilitate the transition of young people from education to work. They also appreciated the proposals made by the Commission to promote continuing education as an essential part within the guidelines for vocational training policy. In addition to that, they expressed their contempt with being more closely associated with the European Social Fund and appealed to the Community to take up joint discussion with the ministers of employment and social affairs.

Eventually, it was agreed to intensify the comparison of national policies, and the Commission and the Education Committee were given the task of strengthening the exchange of experience among educational actors. Moreover, they were asked to put forward recommendations dealing among others with

> ways of extending education and training opportunities for adults by exploiting the potential of the new information technology and by extending access to paid educational leave or other methods of enabling adults to acquire new skills.[122]

For the meeting of the Council with the ministers of education in July 1982, youth unemployment and measures for disadvantaged groups of young people were the topics of highest priority.[123] The period for pilot projects, which ran from 1976 until 1981, was extended and it was agreed to implement further projects with the aim to assist national policies in combating youth unemployment. Six target areas for the new program were defined:

---

[121] All parts in Council of the European Communities 1987, p. 75.
[122] Council of the European Communities 1987, pp. 75–76.
[123] Council of the European Communities 7/28/1982.

the use of the out-of-school environment as a learning resource enabling both young people and teachers to gain experience of the world of work

the involvement of adults, including parents, employers and trade unionists, in activities taking place within the school in order to increase understanding about the role of education institutions

the coordinated provision of information and guidance about post-school opportunities for young people, and the development of systematic guidance

the development of practical cooperation between education authorities and employment and social agencies and with other bodies active in this field in order to provide direct work experience

the development of systems of certification or credit units flexible enough to make possible the assessment of the variety of learning experience

the development of continuous in-service training and personnel policies designed to enable teaching staff to adjust, individually and collectively, to the new demands made of them.[124]

At the first joint session of the ministers for labor and social affairs with the ministers of education in June 1983, the Education Committee and the Commission provided reports on the first phase of pilot projects concerning the education-work transition. After discussing the results from the reports, it was agreed "on the fact that unemployment can only be combated by means of a comprehensive strategy covering economic, financial and employment policies."[125] In such a comprehensive strategy, general education and vocational training policies were attributed two functions:

equipping all young people, in school as well as in supplementary out-of-school measures, with the knowledge, abilities and skills which are a prerequisite for successful access to further vocational training and entry into working life, also helping them to develop the personal and social attributes needed to face with self-confidence and initiative the increasing difficulties of transition and to find their place as young adults;

providing to all young school-leavers either the opportunity to obtain a supplementary vocational qualification or systematic work experience.[126]

The conclusion from the joint session stressed the need to install arrangements of cooperation between national, regional and local authorities, as well

---

[124] Council of the European Communities 7/28/1982, p. 1.
[125] Council of the European Communities 1987, p. 95.
[126] Council of the European Communities 1987, p. 95.

as between educational institutions and establishments of industry and communities. Moreover, guidance, inclusion of disadvantaged and under-achieving youth and in-service teacher training should be accounted for in ET policies. Only one month later, in July 1983, the Council of the European Communities set three general objectives for vocational training policies in the 1980s. Thereafter, vocational training was:

> an instrument of an active employment policy designed to promote economic and social development and adjustment to the new structures of the labour market;

> a means of ensuring that young people are properly prepared for working life and their responsibilities as adults;

> an instrument for promoting equal opportunities for all workers as regards access to the labour market and engaging in various occupations.[127]

In this document, member state representatives found a common ground to define their responsibilities. They agreed on measures to extend the scope of vocational training for workers of all ages, to give equal attention to training and re-training of workers who already had a job but may be in danger of becoming unemployed. Moreover, they also agreed to support measures helping workers to adapt to technological change as well as measures to support people becoming self-employed or establishing their own small and medium-sized businesses. Last but not least, there were measures on the training of instructors, of guidance personnel and of so-called development agents who should take care of activities at the local level.

The responsibilities assigned to the EC covered a broad range of actions. The Commission was encouraged to contribute "to greater consistency between, on the one hand, vocational training policies at national and Community level and, on the other, activities in receipt of assistance from the European Social Fund."[128] Altogether, the Commission was provided with the opportunity to further promote already initiated activities, particularly those with the objective to improve the exchange of information.

To point out how adult and continuing education was acknowledged, statements made in the *Council Resolution of June 3rd, 1983 concerning vocational training measures and new information technologies* and the *Conclusion of the Council and the Ministers of Education meeting within the Council of June 4th, 1984* will be recounted. The Council Resolution stated:

---

[127] Council of the European Communities 7/20/1983, p. 3.
[128] Council of the European Communities 7/20/1983, p. 4.

new technologies have an impact on employment and there is a need in this connection to ensure that systems of education and vocational training, both initial and continuing, take into account the potential of new technologies in such a way as to supply the labour market with the necessary skilled manpower for the future[129]

General guidelines referred to three issues: equipping workers with a broad set of skills potentially facilitating the adaption and accomplishment of work tasks in the context of new technologies, their re-employment in the case of losing employment and the need to understand the implications of new technologies in the social sphere. Member States were requested to support companies, particularly small and medium-sized enterprises, or young people entering work and skilled workers in need of continuing training.

In the Conclusion of June 1984, the Ministers wished "to emphasize the importance of continuing training given the advance of technological change and the need to define new relationships between general education and technical and vocational education and training."[130] Overall it can be said that adult, and even more so, continuing education and continuing training have found entrance to Community policy through measures concerned with the adaption of workers to technological change in the workplace. This was confirmed by a Michael Geiss in an article from 2017.[131]

The same Conclusion prepared grounds for the implementation of the COMETT program two years later. Prior to the meeting, the Commission had submitted a communication to the members in which it proposed that the Community and the member states should implement measures to strengthen the cooperation between universities and industry. It was considered "that this cooperation should lead to better adaption of education and vocational training to the changing needs of industry, particularly in favour of small and medium enterprises."[132]

The role of the European Court of Justice

The next section deals with some of the important judgments from the European Court of Justice (ECJ) in relation to ET. They had a significant effect on policy since the implementation of programs like COMETT or ERASMUS would not have been possible, if the ECJ had not intervened in favor of the Commission and thereby extended their competences. The Court

---

[129] Council of the European Communities 6/25/1983, p. 1.
[130] Council of the European Communities 1987, p. 115.
[131] Geiss 2017.
[132] Council of the European Communities 1987, p. 116.

cases *Casagrande, Forcheri* or *Gravier* will be presented to exemplify the role of the ECJ. As it was discussed earlier, the TEAC provided for higher education policy, however, only with respect to a European University. Eventually, the reference to vocational training, but most importantly, reference to legislation concerned with the four fundamental freedoms made it possible that higher education was emphasized and that the ERASMUS student mobility program could finally be implemented.

The Casagrande case

The first judicial precedent was the 1974 case of *Casagrande v. City of Munich*.[133] The case dealt with questions about the equal treatment of children of EC migrants with regard to the access to compulsory school. In short, the son of the plaintiff Casagrande – an Italian by nationality, but living in Germany since his birth – was refused a so-called inductional grant giving financial support to pupils for attending a comprehensive school. According to Bavarian Federal Law, children of German citizenship were eligible to receive this grant as were also specially defined other groups of children; however, children of EC migrants were not eligible to receive the grant. The case eventually came before the ECJ with the following facts and questions. According to Article 12 of Regulation 1612/68 on free movement of workers, children of migrant workers were to be given access to education under the same conditions as children of regular residents of the country.[134] Did this Article 12 contain a prohibition on discrimination and should this prohibition concerning access to education be interpreted strictly or broadly? After having decided that the prohibition on non-discrimination existed and was of significance, the ECJ came to the following groundbreaking conclusion that James Flynn termed the *Casagrande Formula*.[135]

> Although educational and training policy is not as such included in the spheres which the Treaty has entrusted to the Community institutions, it does not follow that the exercise of powers transferred to the Community is in some way limited if it is of such a nature as to affect the measures taken in the execution of a policy such as that of education and training.[136]

> Further, since Regulations, under Article 189 of the Treaty, have general application and are binding in their entirety and directly applicable in all

---

[133] European Court of Justice 7/3/1974.
[134] Council of the European Communities 10/19/1968, Art. 12.
[135] Flynn 1988, p. 64.
[136] European Court of Justice 7/3/1974, p. 779.

Member States, it is irrelevant that the conditions in question are laid down by rules issued by the central power, by the authorities of a country forming part of a Federal State or of other territorial entities, or even by authorities which the national law equates with them.[137]

The *Casagrande* judgment was groundbreaking for a number of reasons. According to Article 189, TEC, if there is binding Community legislation in place, such as that of Regulation 1612/68, it has to be implemented and executed at the national level first, no matter if it contradicts any existing national or federal legislation, and second, in a way that allows individuals to invoke their rights on the basis of this Community legislation. This is called the direct effect of EU law. Whenever the execution of any national policy was affected by binding Community legislation, however, the latter had to be recognized and considered in the implementation of the former.

The *Casagrande* case was the first extension of the EC governance power because national legislation had to recognize the judgment and national policies had to take it into consideration that EC principles such as the fundamental freedoms have implications for national ET systems. Referring to Article 12 of the Regulation 1612/68, James Flynn asserted in his analysis that "the Court appeared to treat Article 12 as only one of a number of Community rules potentially affecting Member States' freedom to formulate and execute 'educational and training policy.'"[138]

The Forcheri case

The *Forcheri* law case of July 1983 dealt with the issues of non-discrimination of EC citizens with respect to student fees.[139] It sparked discussions on whether general education and vocational training could both be dealt with under Article 128, TEEC. Forcheri, an Italian by nationality and wife of a Commission official, was required to pay fees at a Belgian higher education institute. She then invoked Articles 7 (discrimination on nationality) and 48, TEEC (freedom of movement) and Article 12 of the Council Regulation No. 1612/68 (freedom of movement of workers). The ECJ derived the judgment that in addition to vocational training, also education might be regulated on the basis of the Treaty.

> It follows that although it is true that educational and vocational training policy is not as such part of the areas which the Treaty has allotted to the

---

[137] European Court of Justice 7/3/1974, p. 780.
[138] Flynn 1988, p. 63.
[139] European Court of Justice 3/15/1984.

competence of the Community institutions, the opportunity for such kinds of instruction falls within the scope of the Treaty.[140]

This fairly broad interpretation gave a new twist to the Casagrande Formula so it would support the Commission's standpoint. In the following section, some developments that additionally pushed the Commission's efforts to launch action programs will be reported.

Interlude

At its meeting of March 13th, 1984, the European Parliament passed a 34 points strong resolution concerning cooperation between higher education establishments, in which it confirmed its support for all Commission action necessary for the creation of joint study programs.[141] The Parliament further endorsed Commission action in its Resolution of May 20th, 1985, in which it encouraged the European-wide recognition of school and university diplomas and professional qualifications as a means to guarantee freedom of movement within the Community.[142]

As mentioned in the preceding section, already in 1984, at the Fontainebleau meeting of the European Council, the strategy a People's Europe had been launched. An ad hoc committee was installed and given the task of conducting a study on a general system ensuring the recognition of university diplomas and enabling freedom of establishment within the Community.[143] The findings of the ad hoc committee encouraged the Council to invite the Commission to progress its activities and Member States' universities to follow up on their part by recognizing certificates from foreign students.

Moreover, Andre Kirchberger – a former Commission official in the division for vocational training – informs that an inter-institutional agreement was issued in early 1985, which obliged the Commission to base all forthcoming proposals on one of the stronger Treaty instruments, such as Decisions.[144] Around the same time, it became obvious that the budget, usually allocated annually, would not satisfy the needs of a bigger action program. It was necessary to receive funding that could cover a whole program period of three to four years. When the ECJ intervened in favor of the Commission, the legal situation changed and Article 128 was declared an appropriate basis

---

[140] European Court of Justice 3/15/1984, p. 2336.
[141] European Parliament 4/16/1984, p. 55.
[142] European Parliament 5/20/1985, pp. 121–122.
[143] European Council 6/25/1984.
[144] Statement by Andre Kirchberger in: Pépin 2006, pp. 114–115.

for decision-making. Consequently, it was possible to receive the financial support vital for the implementation of programs. The following section looks in more detail at the most important law case *Gravier vs. City of Liege*.

The Gravier case

The following were the circumstances in the *Gravier* court case. The facts are presented in accordance with the Judgment of the ECJ of February 13th, 1985.[145] Starting with the academic year 1982/83, Francoise Gravier, a French resident and national, registered for a four-year study program on the art of cartoon strips at the Académie Royal des Beaux Arts in Liège (Belgium) – a non-university higher education institution. Upon registration, she was asked to pay a so called '*minerval*' – an enrolment fee that would have had enabled her to take up the study program. Following a circular by the Belgian Minister of Education, this fee was only demanded from non-Belgian nationals. Gravier's request for being granted an exemption from paying the minerval was rejected. Gravier did not pay the fee and was not accepted for the following academic year. Moreover, as a result of this, her Belgian residence permit was not extended.

On the grounds of these circumstances, Gravier appealed to the Court of First Instance in Liège and challenged the validity of the proceedings invoking Article 7, TEEC, which prohibited discrimination on the basis of nationality as well as Article 59, TEEC that regulated trans-border services. The Court of First Instance issued the questions to the ECJ. In this case, the European Court of Justice dealt with two particular questions. Firstly, could this case be settled by reference to Article 128, TEEC, on vocational training? Secondly, which are the criteria to define vocational training so that it could be addressed by Article 128?[146]

The ECJ presented the following judgment: On the issue of discrimination as defined in Article 7, TEEC, the Court affirmed that it dealt with a case of unequal treatment and, thus, Article 7 prohibiting discrimination on the basis of nationality was applicable. Concerning the second issue of trans-border services, the court held that Member State nationals have the right to stay in a second country in order to use a service, given that this service is subject to remuneration. With respect to the criteria for defining vocational training, after having examined the general principles for vocational training laid down in the Council decision of April 2nd, 1963, the Court found that

---

[145] European Court of Justice 2/13/1985.
[146] European Court of Justice 2/13/1985, pp. 608–609.

any form of education which prepares for a qualification for a particular profession, trade or employment or which provides the necessary training and skills for such a profession, trade or employment is vocational training, whatever the age the level of training of the pupils or students, and even if the training program includes an element of general education.[147]

What implications did this judgment have for education policy? First of all, the most important implication was the broad definition of vocational training. The ECJ drew from the wording of the 1963 *Council Decision on principles of a vocational training policy*. This Decision proposed a policy addressing all training of young people or adults, whether employed or not, to help them acquire a comprehensive set of vocational and social competences. After the ECJ interpretation, it was possible to apply Article 128, TEEC, also in the case of higher education. The second implication was that all Member State students have gained the right to undertake vocational training – and, thus, also higher education courses – in other Member States without being charged more than these country's nationals. Finally, the third implication was that vocational training (not general education) was considered a service within the meaning of Articles 59 and 60, TEEC, and thus, subject to freedom of movement, right to establishment and freedom of service.

In consequence to the *Gravier* judgment, the Belgian government issued rules to govern conditions for the access to university programs. The following was included: migrant workers and their spouses were not required to pay fees, non-Belgian nationals were only exempt from paying the fees if following vocational training or university study, and foreign students participating in Belgian University programs were subsidized only when their total number remained under 2% of all students. Belgium argued that university studies cannot be sub-summed under vocational training and, hence, that the *Gravier* decision was not applicable to University programs.

In the so-called *Gravier II* case, the Court maintained that all education potentially leading to professional qualifications or providing skills necessary to enter certain professions falls within the scope of Article 128 and constitute a type of vocational training.[148] Consequently, the imposition of fees to foreign university students was also prohibited since they result in discrimination according to Article 7, TEEC.

---

[147] European Court of Justice 2/13/1985, p. 614.
[148] Watson 1987, pp. 91–93.

Chapter summary

The 1980s are indicative of the fact that ET politics had entered a phase of expansion and were brought closer to the political mainstream. Introducing issues of ET to the general political framework meant a major boost. First, the merger with employment and social affairs and then the recognition of education as an important part of the People's Europe strategy helped it to receive the necessary financial and institutional support. The Parliament and the ECJ were the most important supporters. While the parliamentary support made it possible to increase the budgets allocated to ET programs, judgments of the ECJ paved the way for an extension and definition of the competences of the EC. By the end of the decade, the basic framework for governance, established in the 1970s, was on the way to gaining structure: in terms of legislation, back-up existed, action programs were running, the financial situation had improved and as a result of societal changes, the topic of ET was becoming more and more important for the success of the European project.

6.5 Education and training in the 1990s

The 1990s were a particularly vibrant decade for ET politics, which finally led to the completion of the mainstreaming process. The 1980s corollary of political, economic and technological developments had connected ET more tightly with the notion of economies and societies, whose prosperity and cohesion increasingly depended on the use of knowledge. This formed the argumentative backdrop against which a pervasive policy discourse was constructed with the concept of lifelong learning at the center. The EU itself was about to undergo a meaningful transformation after the former communist countries disintegrated and the democratic legitimacy of the administration was put into question on several occasions. All this encouraged political leaders to devise a new strategy, which was eventually implemented after the Lisbon European Council in 2000.

Outline of context developments

At the turn of the 1990s, the global political system was characterized by increasing complexity and interdependence. The rigid separation of the political east and the political west was coming to an end and new trade markets were emerging. Progress in microelectronics and telecommunication was making geographical distances irrelevant. Western culture and rationality were spreading over the world and a network system was pervading previously marginalized areas.

The American political scientist James Rosenau introduced the term "post-international politics" to describe this *'new'* global system. He described five dynamics that caused turbulence:[149] (1) the shift from industrial to post-industrial order due to the dynamics of the microelectronic revolution, (2) the emergence of topics with a global scope, like air pollution, terrorism, AIDS or currency crises, (3) the reduced capability of states and governments to provide solutions to pending problems, (4) tendencies of decentralization as result of subsystems becoming more coherent and effective and (5) new orientations and skills among the population to cope with and adapt to the new situation. Rosenau stressed that "(…) none of these dynamics would have produced parametric change if adults in every country and in all walks of life had remained essentially unskilled and detached with respect to global affairs. (…)"[150]

Hans Arnold, a former German diplomat and writer, imposed the radical question: *"has Europe come to an end?"* [151] In his view, the European Communities were in the midst of a transition period, which was crucial for the survival of Europe – a transition period that was unprecedented in character and indicated the most radical shift in European and world politics since the Second World War. Arnold arrived at the conclusion that the European Communities were facing a dilemma because the original institutional blueprint was no longer appropriate. New approaches to integration were therefore expedient.

The 1990s were an intense decade for European integration. The German reunification and the collapse of the Eastern bloc caused far-reaching long-term effects. In February 1991, the Warsaw Pact was officially disbanded. In Poland, Romania, Bulgaria and Hungary, the events initiated a process of reconciliation with western markets. In March 1991, ethnic conflicts in Yugoslavia escalated and the civil war began. In August of that year, a *coup d'etat* meant the end of the Soviet Union and gave independence to the Baltic and the South Soviet countries. Czechoslovakia officially disintegrated in 1993 and divided into the Czech Republic and Slovakia.

After the ambitious 1987 Single European Act, the 1992 Maastricht Treaty was to complete the internal market and ultimately guarantee the four freedoms: freedom of movement of people, of services, of goods and of capital. In 1995, Austria, Finland and Sweden joined the EU while some of the

---

[149] Rosenau 1990, pp. 12–13.
[150] Rosenau 1990, p. 13.
[151] Arnold 1993.

Eastern European countries entered accession negotiations. The 1997 Treaty of Amsterdam targeted institutional reform and the European Monetary Union (EMU) was finally completed in 1999.

According to the Austrian adult education scholar, Werner Lenz, the 1980s had shown that ACE was becoming an instrument for governing industrial societies.[152] ACE was addressed in terms of education reform and conceived as a transversal policy field. Adult education became a universal remedy that was supposedly useful to solve all kinds of problems ranging from environmental or democratic problems to employment and even leisure time issues. Social competencies and transversal skills, such as communication, team spirit, management, organizational skills, were gaining importance and rendering subject knowledge less relevant. A de-coupling of education and the labor market contributed to the fact that high educational attainment no longer guaranteed for a job, thus, constant investment in human capital became essential for individual careers. For ACE institutions, this meant that they had to care more for their organizational performance because they had to react to new trends. At the same time, less public support, more competition from technology and media and the need for counseling services forced ACE institutions to reconsider their work in terms of marketable products in order to respond adequately to the demands of learners and stakeholders.

Lifelong learning dominated the 1990s. "Consecration of the concept," according to George Papadopoulos, a longstanding OECD official, "was a remarkable phenomenon in the international discourse on education during the decade of the 1990s."[153] The idea of learning across the lifespan had spread in the 1970s. After less intensive discussions in the 1980s, "[d]uring the 1990s, lifelong learning emerged onto the policy scene with the suddenness of a new fashion."[154] Since lifelong learning was ubiquitous and rich in connotations, "it became a convenient political shorthand for the modernization of education and training systems."[155] Criticism emerged as fast as lifelong learning was spreading.

The aforementioned shift from teaching to learning was caused by various factors such as shrinking public budgets and a stronger tendency of individuals to become self-determined in organizing their lives and careers. Rolf

---

[152] Lenz 1989a.
[153] Papadopoulos 2002, p. 37.
[154] Field 2006, p. 11.
[155] Field 2006, p. 12.

Arnold, a proponent of the constructivist paradigm of adult learning, speaks of an "autodidactic turn".[156] He argues that the focus on individual competences was seriously changing institutionalized ET and the professionalization of staff. The reason for this was that learning had become much more an aspect of everyday life and was no longer dependent on the educational institution or the teacher. The ideal ACE institution, thus, would be one that provided the best possible environment for people to become self-directed learners.

Following Ekkehard Nuissl, former Director of the German Institute for Adult Education, an adult education institution must respond to six learner interests:[157] (1) information and counseling, (2) open access, (3) quality of provision, (4) recognition of learning, (5) continuity of learning as an element of quality and (6) learning arrangements as places of social interaction. Nuissl also suggested four areas of activity for governments and public actors:[158] firstly, facilitating an environment in which the learners' interests are addressed - for instance, information systems, quality accreditation or consumer protection; secondly, forging an integrated education system through networks for cooperation and horizontal and vertical links between the education sectors; thirdly, creating synergies between education system and industries matching the supply and demand sides; fourthly, launching initiatives and new political programs particularly for basic skills, literacy or regional development.

Examination of historical developments

The analysis of the 1990s proceeds as follows: first, for the transition period from 1988 to 1992, the most challenging developments forcing the EC and the EU to rethink ET policies will be outlined. Then, the action programs established since 1986 and the developments surrounding the Task Force Human Resources and the new DG Education will be described. After that, the contents of the three most important policy documents will be summarized in the third section. For the final section, findings from the preceding summary of the documents will be combined with findings from the literature review to argue that the Commission has gone through a number of legitimacy crises and was therefore forced to change its role from a policy-

---

[156] Arnold 1999.
[157] Nuissl 1999, pp. 8–11.
[158] Nuissl 1999, pp. 13–14.

initiating actor to a policy-facilitating actor. The result of this transformation was the emergence of a new arrangement of indirect governance.

The transition period from 1988 to 1992

Three topics dominated in the late 1980s and early 1990s: employment, global competition and ICT. These topics were not entirely new to European politics; however, the quality of discourse had changed in the late 1980s. Globalization, demographic change and technological progress were putting pressure on the EC. Combining economic performance and social cohesion became increasingly important in this context. Hywel Ceri Jones emphasized, "[t]he question of the quality and standards of our education and training systems in Europe have come to the centre of the Community agenda. Europe will simply not be competitive or cohesive if we fail to put the highest premium on our skills and talents."[159] In 1989, a task force was set up in the Commission to make ET policies ready to meet these new challenges.

In the 1993 'White Paper on Growth, competitiveness and employment', ET was, for the first time, discussed extensively in a document of high political relevance. In 1995, the 'White Paper on Education and Training' was released and in 1997, the third major document the 'Commission Communication. Towards a Europe of Knowledge'. Of greatest concern was the employment situation because it determined the place of Europe within global competition. Keeping up with technological innovation was crucial to successfully compete in the global market. The EU, therefore, emphasized (1) the continuous acquisition of skills and knowledge in a lifetime perspective and (2) the broad access to continuing education. According to the White Paper on Growth, preoccupations were nurtured by three unprecedented circumstances.

- Firstly, European states had become wealthier but the potential rate of economic growth was declining during the 1980s, from around 4% to around 2.5% per anno.[160] At the same time, unemployment rates were rising constantly leading to a profound structural unemployment on top of a pronounced cyclical unemployment and a new form of technological unemployment.
- Secondly, three developments were shaping the international economic landscape. (1) Japan and the US were setting the pace for performance in global competition. (2) The end of the Cold War opened new markets and

---

[159] Jones 1992, p. 5.
[160] Commission of the European Communities 12/5/1993, p. 9.

reshaped the international trade scene. (3) Demographic change was gaining relevance to economies especially as an aging society meant an aging workforce.

- Thirdly, ICT was about to revolutionize life in an unprecedented way. Disruptive innovations such as the *World Wide Web* were made available for commercial use. Automation in production and the PC had significant impact on the organization of work in certain industries; moreover, advanced telecommunication technology and the internet concerned all forms of human interaction. The so-called information society triggered new fears concerning social exclusion from unequal access to technology.

The first generation of action programs

From 1986 to 1990, nine action programs were established. They were designed by the Commission and suggested for implementation by the Member States. Participation in the programs was not obligatory for Member States; yet, in the case of participation they had to set up administrative structures to run a program.[161] The list includes programs in higher education, basic vocational training, continuing vocational training and transversal areas such as language and non-institutional education.

Higher education

- *COMETT I – 1986.* The *Community program for Education and Training in Technology* was the first action program adopted. It promoted cooperation between universities and businesses. The term *university* referred to all types of post-secondary ET institutions offering advanced training, qualifications or diplomas.[162] COMETT had two objectives: (1) to promote education programs in technological industries through cooperation and exchange and (2) to provide additional support for highly qualified individuals.[163]
- *ERASMUS – 1987.* The *European action scheme for the mobility of university students* was the second action program adopted. The goals were (1) to increase the number of students participating in integrated student mobility schemes, (2) to foster cooperation between higher education institutions, (3) to promote staff mobility in order to raise the quality of teaching, (4) to strengthen the People's Europe through intercultural

---

[161] Fahle 1989, p. 91.
[162] Council of the European Communities 8/8/1986.
[163] Eurostat 1992, p. 98.

exchange and (5) to create a pool of graduates with experience in other Community countries.[164]

- *TEMPUS – 1990.* Aiming at an extension of the European economic area, TEMPUS helped non-community countries in Central and Eastern Europe to adapt to the demands of market economies. To this end, the existing objectives from the ERASMUS scheme were applied to trans-European cooperation enabling students and teachers to study or teach in a Community country and facilitating cooperation between institutions.[165]

Initial and continuing vocational training

- *PETRA – 1987.* It prolonged initiatives for the transition of young people from education to work and adult life. One of the goals was to give young people the chance to take up a one-year period of apprenticeship or vocational training, after having finished compulsory school. Another goal was to contribute to qualitatively improved vocational education with measures like comparability of qualifications or cooperation with social partners.[166]

- *Eurotecnet – 1989.* Eurotecnet was the program supporting innovation in the context of technological progress and changes in the professional environments of VET and CET. Support was given to prepare people for new qualifications or to help them adapt to new demands.[167]

- *IRIS – 1987/1988.* Contrary to the others, IRIS was not an actual program but a policy recommendation. The topic was the promotion of women in training for future occupations or occupations in which women were under-represented.[168]

- *FORCE – 1990.* FORCE was specifically designed for CVET. Main actions were the investment in continuing education and innovation with regard to the management and organization of continuing education provision. The main instrument was the dissemination of good practices. The overarching goal was to contribute to a framework in which institutions could work more efficiently.[169]

---

[164] Council of the European Communities 6/25/1987.
[165] Council of the European Communities 5/23/1990.
[166] Council of the European Communities 12/10/1987.
[167] Council of the European Communities 12/30/1989.
[168] Commission of the European Communities 12/4/1987.
[169] Council of the European Communities 6/21/1990.

Transversal programs

- *LINGUA – 1989.* As a transversal program, it was recommended for universities and for all other teaching and training institutions. During the first phase (1990-1994) LINGUA was limited to secondary education institutions. It had the objective to raise the quality and the participation in language courses as well as to contribute to the improvement of foreign language and communicative skills of people.[170]
- *Youth for Europe – 1988.* This program did not focus on institutionalized education, but rather on education through cultural exchange for young people between 15 and 25 years. The objective was to raise intercultural awareness and create a feeling of belonging within the same community.[171]

The new Directorate General

The transfer of competences from national to supranational level, written down in law or manifested in the institutional structure, is the most visible sign of institutional integration. Such occurred in 1971, when the first working groups were set up and in 1973, when the directorate for education was established within the DG Research, Science and Education. Institutional integration further advanced in 1981 when general education and vocational training were merged in the DG Employment and Social Affairs. Another step towards integration was taken in 1989, when the Task Force for Human Resources was created. Initiated by Jacques Delors and managed by Hywel Ceri Jones, this task force was a deliberate attempt to develop and implement a new DG for ET. In late 1995, the DG Education, Training and Youth was finally inaugurated.

According to Brad Blitz, professor of international politics and education policy at the University College London, promoting a stronger institutional base for education was among Jacques Delors' goals.[172] Since his first presidency in 1985, he wanted to have a DG for education. Blitz reports that at that time, he began preparing plans in the background and with his second term as Commission President in 1989, he spurred on the process and asked Hywel Ceri Jones to create the task force. From Pépin, one learns that this initiative was welcomed by the Community, since its goal was to help align economic and social policy for a more comprehensive form of integration.[173]

---

[170] Council of the European Communities 8/16/1989.
[171] Council of the European Communities 6/25/1988.
[172] Blitz 2003, p. 207.
[173] Pépin 2006, p. 107.

The fact that the first action programs were already running further supported Delors' plans. Moreover, the Parliament had an important role – it was actively supporting the creation of a DG for education and formally asked the Commission to do so.

Scholarly accounts suggest that education was considered far more important to the Community than it might appear within the official documents. One reason why the importance of education was recognized was that it was considered among the most effective instruments for preparing a new generation of European citizens. Blitz asserts that for the EU, education "was essential not only to produce a competitive workforce but also in the creation of a socio-psychological community."[174] It was, thus, that Member States could no longer ignore the promotion of education as an area of community policy, even though some states were still reluctant towards a supranational governance arrangement.

Controversies between the Commission and the Member States arose over the type of arrangement suited best to preserve the interests of both. The principle of subsidiarity was being discussed at the same time as one of the basic principles of the new Treaty. Blitz reports that in order to overcome the doubts of the Member States, Delors declared he wanted education to be an area of co-ownership. [175] Governance, then, would be firmly based on the principle of subsidiarity. The Member States finally accepted, even if some still feared that the Commission would penetrate national sovereignty. Other than the principle of subsidiarity, the separation of education in Article 126 and vocational training in 127 was a tranquilizer to national sentiments.

The policy papers of the 1990s
What follows now is the discussion of the three most important policy documents. These documents are in the following order (1) the *White Paper Growth, competitiveness and employment* from 1993, (short: WP Growth) (2) the *White Paper on Education and Training. Teaching and Learning: Towards the learning society* from 1995 (short: WP Learning Society) and (3) the *Communication from the Commission to the Council, the European Parliament, the Economic and Social Committee and the Committee of the Regions. Towards a Europe of Knowledge* from 1997 (short: Communication Knowledge Society). All three documents were devised and released by the Commission. Because of this, they represent the supranational point of view

---

[174] Blitz 2003, p. 208.
[175] Blitz 2003, p. 209.

and had, besides the goals stated in the documents, also the objective to reinforce integration.

Growth, competitiveness and employment

This document addressed three issues: firstly, an employment situation at the
risk of deterioration and exclusion of the non-participating shares of the population; secondly, the not yet fully utilized capacity to effectively apply
structural and fiscal resources in the creation of jobs; and thirdly, the struggle
in global competition as a consequence of lagging behind in innovation and
failing to penetrate into emerging market pockets.

Education and training were addressed in the section "action for jobs"
and in the sub-section "investment in education and training". In the section
"action for jobs", ET policies were considered part of a broader policy pack-
age together with labor contract, fiscal or social protection policies. The
overall message was: growth alone cannot eradicate unemployment; it needs
proactive concerted job creation measures. "The educational system, labour
laws, work contracts, contractual negotiation systems and the social security
system form the pillars of the various 'national employment systems' (…),"
according to the argument. "In each case, the entire system must be mobi-
lized to improve the functioning of the labour market."[176]

In the sub-section "investment in education and training", two issues were
addressed: (1) investment in and (2) access to continuing education. The
Commission had realized that changes in the individual and organizational
knowledge management made continuous learning across the lifespan inevitable. Consequently, it was demanded to set up financing schemes for lifelong learning. And so it developed that investment in human resources, in
terms of intellectual capacity and technical skills became a larger issue.
Moreover, the Commission encouraged Member States to better connect
public and private resources so that the right to initial and ongoing training
could be fully established.

The WP Growth was part of a general attempt to encourage a more integrated approach to economic development. Such an integrated approach
means that the connections and interdependencies of different policy fields
are recognized and that they are addressed through measures of a wider
scope. For instance, the Commission asserted that progress in employment
or competitiveness could only come from the interplay of different policy
fields. "There is no doubt" – says the argument – "that [education and

---

[176] Commission of the European Communities 12/5/1993, p. 16.

training] could play a significant part in the emergence of a new development model in the Community in the coming years." For this reason, it was suggested to re-examine "(...) the place of education and training in the fabric of society and their links with all economic and social activity (...)".[177]

An ET system, as desired by the Commission, should promote lifelong development of human resources. It was asserted that "[t]he main principle of the various types of measures to be taken should be to develop human resources throughout people's working lives, starting with basic education and working through initial training to continuing training."[178] To this end, it was suggested to establish closer ties between the world of education and the world of work. So-called classroom education should move closer to the offices and production plants, whether be it via apprenticeships, in-service training or business-university cooperation. The goals of future curricula should be to strengthen the learning to learn competences, communicative and management skills.

Regarding the organization of ACE, flexible and more open types of training provision, such as short cycle programs, were considered better suited to the changing demands of labor markets. Based upon this argument, public actors were asked to take care of the policy infrastructure and the policy framework. Furthermore, they were asked to take responsibility for fiscal incentive measures to encourage initiatives by private actors, or for effective funds allocation. Finally, private businesses were encouraged to strengthen human resource development and to integrate continuing education more seriously into business strategies.

The section in which Member State and Community activities were presented, indicates the first governance guidelines under the TEU provision. It was emphasized in accordance with the TEU that the Member States were to remain in charge of all activities and the EU's involvement was limited to providing financial support, encouraging discourse and coordinating programs. National governments were asked to gather public authorities, corporate actors and social partners on equal terms to devise training policies. Like in the 1980s, cooperation between public and private actors was pushed, especially concerning university business cooperation and the training of employees in SMEs.

---

[177] Commission of the European Communities 12/5/1993, p. 117.
[178] Commission of the European Communities 12/5/1993, p. 119.

Some interesting proposals were made with regard to the use of fiscal instruments.[179] According to the argument, fiscal instruments would encumber public budgets in a less restrictive way than extensive funding. One of the measures suggested to support businesses was to lower the amount of social contribution as a reward for them having ET measures in place. It was hypothesized that financial gains from using such instruments could be reallocated to the benefit of unskilled people affected by unemployment or to young people in a phase of transition from education to work.

For supranational actors, three objectives were formulated: the promotion of student and teacher exchanges or joint projects; the initiation of a debate on recognition of qualifications and diplomas as well as a debate on the implications of an emerging market for skills and training; and the creation of a database for information exchange to identify best-practice examples.

Towards the Learning Society

The document is divided into two main parts. The first part identifies and analyzes three "factors of upheaval":[180] the impact of the information society; the impact of internationalization and the impact of scientific and technological knowledge. In response to these, the focus of ET policy should be to equip people with a broad knowledge base and to strengthen individual employability. The second part sets out five objectives in order to develop a learning society. Among the five objectives were, for instance, combating exclusion and equal treatment of capital investment and investment in training.

Education and training should equip people with a broad knowledge base and assist in the development of individual employability. What did the Commission understand regarding „broad knowledge base"? They had in mind an education that equipped people with the knowledge necessary to find orientation within a constantly changing society. According to the argumentation, such education enables people to understand the complexity of society and to develop responsible citizenship. It was stated that

> the essential mission of education is to help everyone to develop their own potential and become a complete human being, as opposed to a tool at the service of the economy; the acquisition of knowledge and skill should go

---

[179] Commission of the European Communities 12/5/1993, p. 121.
[180] Commission of the European Communities 11/29/1995, pp. 5–9.

hand in hand with building up character, broadening outlook and accepting one's responsibility in society.[181]

According to the Commission, a person with a broad knowledge base would need to have a set of faculties.[182] Such a person would be aware of the richness of European culture, appreciate human values and democracy, keep up with progress in scientific knowledge or embrace literature and philosophy to immunize against indiscriminate information in the mass media. Moreover, in that respect, it was stressed that teaching should promote innovation and understanding of technological progress, avoid too much standardization, educate inventors rather than technology managers and promote links between basic education and research. Lastly, understanding society in its historical evolution, acknowledging the world as an incomplete construction, developing personal and social values and acquiring knowledge of history and geography to navigate in ever more internationalized societies were considered further elements of a broad knowledge base.

The section, in which individual employability is discussed, begins by asking what will be required in the future? According to the Commission, basic knowledge, technical knowledge and social aptitudes would be required.

Basic knowledge is the foundation on which individual employability is built. This is *par excellence* the domain of the formal education and training system. A good balance has to be struck in basic education between acquiring knowledge and methodological skills which enable a person to learn alone.[183]

Technical knowledge is knowledge which permits clear identification with an occupation. It is acquired partly within the vocational education and training system and partly on the job. (...) However, acquiring technical knowledge should not be restricted to leading-edge or newly-emerged sectors.[184]

Social aptitudes concern interpersonal skills, i.e. behavior at work and a whole range of skills corresponding to the level of responsibility held, such as the ability to cooperate and work as part of a team, creativeness and the quest for quality. Full mastery of these skills can be acquired only in a working environment and therefore mainly on the job.[185]

---

[181] Commission of the European Communities 11/29/1995, p. 10.
[182] Commission of the European Communities 11/29/1995, pp. 10–13.
[183] Commission of the European Communities 11/29/1995, p. 13.
[184] Commission of the European Communities 11/29/1995, pp. 13–14.
[185] Commission of the European Communities 11/29/1995, p. 14.

It was contended that employability results from the combination of the three: basic knowledge, technical knowledge and social aptitudes. To construct one's own employability, knowledge and skills from different educational and learning pathways, such as institutional, occupational and personal training, should be combined. "By diversifying education provision, building bridges between various channels, increasing preoccupational [sic] experience and by opening up the potential for mobility"[186] learners should be enabled to take charge of their own employability and career.

The interrelationship and interdependency of employment and education were used as the main argument to encourage the integration of general education and vocational training in the comprehensive lifelong learning. It was stated, "[t]he crucial problem of employment in a permanently changing economy compels the education and training system to change."[187] Some tendencies had been observed in the Member States according to which general education and vocational training, as well as the education system and the business sector were no longer considered incompatible with one another and teaching approaches were slowly adapting to the new reality that emerged from technological progress. From these observations the Commission concluded that previously discouraging debates on educational principles, such as whether general or vocational education is to be preferred or whether education should serve economic or democratic purposes, were slowly coming to an end.

Concerning the promotion of a learning society, five proposals were formulated: (1) encourage the acquisition of new knowledge, (2) bring schools and businesses closer together, (3) combat exclusion, (4) promote proficiency in three community languages and (5) treat capital investment and investment in training on an equal basis.

With regard to objective number one "encourage the acquisition of new knowledge", none of the three proposed actions actually dealt with the acquisition of knowledge. Neither methods for recognition of skills, nor support for mobility, nor the use of new technology are directly associated with acquisition of knowledge. Upon a closer look, it appears as if these three actions formed an attempt to encourage the creation of new services. For instance: one idea was to establish accreditation systems where people receive a certificate for having submitted an individual portfolio of their skills

---

[186] Commission of the European Communities 11/29/1995, p. 14.
[187] Commission of the European Communities 11/29/1995, p. 23.

and knowledge. It was argued that this could motivate especially those who had fallen out of the formal system.

Objective number five "treat capital investment and investment in training on an equal basis" addressed some unusual issues.[188] The Commission suggested accounting and fiscal solutions be reconsidered by the Member States to encourage greater corporate education spending. It was argued that when a recession aggravates the market situation, budgetary cut backs are unavoidable for corporations. In such circumstances, it is very likely that their education spending will suffer, primarily because it could be perceived that it is not vital to business. The question, therefore, was if public tax policy can encourage education spending. It was put forward that Member States devise policies that make it possible to shift expenditure for education from the passive to the active side of the corporate balance sheet. Then, these expenditures could be considered an asset rather than operating costs and could be depreciated, which in turn could encourage corporations to increase their investment in education.

Further, the Commission formulated three reasons why governance had to be reconsidered.[189] Firstly, quality of ET was becoming crucial. Competitiveness and the European social model depended on the management of quality. Secondly, both sides of the education market were on the move. Learners' demands were growing while, because of better technology, institutions had new instruments at their disposal to improve educational provision. Thirdly, widening the gap between well-educated and less educated parts of the population had to be avoided at any cost.

The *European Year of Lifelong Learning* (EYLLL), announced for 1996, was to initiate a debate within the ET community. Its aim was to find clarity, get a better division of labor and define "action to be carried out at local and national level (…) action to be carried out at European level (…) cooperation and support between the EU and its Member States." The principle of subsidiarity was firmly emphasized in this regard since "the highest political level, thus, the furthest away from the area of application, should only act when individuals, families, and political authorities at all other levels cannot. (…) the move to the learning society must be centred on the individual."[190]

---

[188] Commission of the European Communities 11/29/1995, pp. 50–52.
[189] Commission of the European Communities 11/29/1995, p. 30.
[190] All part in Commission of the European Communities 11/29/1995, p. 31.

Towards a Europe of Knowledge
The Commission's Communication Knowledge Society was far more distilled than the two preceding documents. It was much more direct and succinct. Limiting objectives, focusing actions and streamlining approaches, were key in order to set the tone. Consequently, the problematic areas addressed were narrowed down to two major issues. The first concerned so-called "knowledge policies" and the second concerned the contribution of education and training to employment.

The concept of "knowledge policies" was introduced to connect those policy areas, which presumably make society a knowledge-based society. According to the argument these areas were innovation, research, education and training. Already in 1997, the Commission had begun planning to make knowledge policies "one of the four fundamental pillars of the Union's internal policies."[191] It was acknowledged that knowledge policies were paramount because, in the future, wealth creation would come from the production and dissemination of knowledge rather than the production of physical goods. Property and hard work as sources of a satisfactory life would be replaced by flexibility and knowledge work.

Promoting employment was still a concern. To keep employment high, any kind of policy "must be able to build on an in-depth medium-term strategy to enhance the knowledge and skills of European citizen's [sic]."[192] The need for developing both vocational skills and social skills was diagnosed. The three dimensions considered important in the formation of the European educational area were: *knowledge* in order to participate actively in the process of change, European *citizenship* as a prerequisite of solidarity among the peoples of Europe, and *competencies* – particularly the ability of learning to learn – "in order to overcome the now rapid obsolescence of skills."[193] Moreover, a new approach to connect ET and the world of work was considered necessary; namely, one that would be adequate for tackling youth unemployment, early school leaving, continuing training or apprenticeship schemes.

The three objectives of the Communication Knowledge Society mark the departure from the rather passive and general approach. The number of objectives was downsized to three. The attempt to set up a governance arrangement based on monitoring instruments was made. While the WP Learning

---

[191] Commission of the European Communities 11/12/1997, p. 1.
[192] Commission of the European Communities 11/12/1997, p. 1.
[193] Commission of the European Communities 11/12/1997, p. 3.

Society had stressed subsidiarity, the Communication Knowledge Society did not even mention it. Instead, the idea was to develop a framework of action and a European area of education. Six major types of actions were proposed to create a European education area.[194]

1. Physical mobility as continuation of the existing exchange programs for students, apprentices, teachers, trainers or education managers, and mutual recognition to facilitate such exchanges.
2. Virtual mobility in the sense of infrastructure enabling people to make use of new technology. The provision of multi-media educational material with content specified to promote European identity.
3. Cooperation networks forming the basis for exchange of good practice and experience with policies. Forming the expertise necessary to work on education and training for future demands.
4. Knowledge of languages and intercultural competencies must connect all the other activities especially those concerned with citizenship, exchange and creating the European education area.
5. Establishing partnerships to come up with innovative approaches and instruments for the accreditation of skills or the production of educational products.
6. Community databases to collect information about the education and training systems in the Member States as sources for reference.

To implement the idea of a European area of education, the Commission set out to reform their governance approach. Instead of provision and administration of programs in a top-down manner, the new approach was to build a framework for activities. The basic principle was that of shared responsibilities by all the actors involved. Responsibilities were defined for the Community, the Member States, the social partners, economic partners, regional and local partners and partners in the voluntary sector. This approach emerged from the YELL and the amendments made in the Amsterdam Treaty.

Governance included elements of peer learning, coordination and deliberation. The EU institutions had the task of disseminating and communicating good practice. Better organized consultation and cooperation with educational institutions, social partners, regional actors in the public sector and businesses was envisaged. With regard to the business sector, it was stated that "[t]he dividing line between the world of education and that of

---

[194] Commission of the European Communities 11/12/1997, pp. 4–5.

information society is increasingly fluid, and connections need to be established in both directions to improve the quality of education products."[195] What was said about the regional actors and third sector actors is significant. "The organization of Community activities must take account of the trend towards decentralization of responsibilities (...)"and "Community activities must attract the support of associations and foundations involved in actions of tangible solidarity (...)".[196]

The role of the European Commission

Next, the 1990s developments will be discussed using academic literature. In the first part of the discussion, the focus is on policy change. This will be exemplified by the change in the concept of lifelong learning. The second part deals with governance change and takes a look at how the role of the Commission has changed during the 1990s. Finally, the last part of the discussion looks at both changes from the perspective of institutional learning and argues in accordance with Lee, Thayer and Madyun that the 1996 European Year of Lifelong Learning was a turning point in European educational governance.[197]

Policy change

Since the late 1960s, IGOs have been promoting concepts of learning and education across the lifespan. The Council of Europe started with *education permanente*, followed by the UNESCO with *lifelong education*. In the 1970s, OECD promoted *recurrent education*. When the EU launched *lifelong learning* in the 1990s, it could build on existing ideas. Education scholars have paid much attention to the EU's strategic move to come up with lifelong learning. They argue that the EU has massively contributed to a conceptual shift from the social emancipatory *lifelong education* to the economic human resource based *lifelong learning*.[198] The shift in the international discourse from lifelong education to lifelong learning, therefore, represents a prime case example of long-term policy change.

In the 1980s, the EEC was pushing forward a merger of vocational training and general education. This had proven a viable way to erect institutional structures and implement action programs. Having gained new competences, the 1990s were devoted to all-encompassing concepts like lifelong learning,

---

[195] Commission of the European Communities 11/12/1997, p. 6.
[196] Commission of the European Communities 11/12/1997, pp. 6–7.
[197] Lee et al. 2008.
[198] Lima and Guimarães 2011.

learning society and knowledge society. These concepts promoted ET as transversal issues relevant across several policy areas. It can be agreed with Alexandra Dehmel when she states that the 1990s were a second boom period in the discourse on learning and education across the lifespan, in which the economic and human resource rationale was fine-tuned.[199] Especially the OECD and the Commission were pushing their own agenda. However, the 1990s also meant a period of trial and error. The Commission had to learn from its own failure, as it faced considerable opposition and legitimacy problems. By the end of the decade, the EU had elaborated a politically viable conception of lifelong learning, which was eventually disseminated by the 2000 *Commission Staff Working Paper: A Memorandum on Lifelong Learning*.

Until 1992, the EC vocabulary hardly included the term '*lifelong learning*'. The Commission had utilized terms like *continuing and recurrent education, lifelong education, continuing training* or *professional and vocational retraining*. This changed with the WP Growth, which introduced the term *lifelong learning* to high politics. Thinking strategically, the EU policy work responded to the challenges of increasing competition on the global markets, which forced policymakers to think of new ways of connecting education with economic concerns. Lifelong learning was to be implemented in the Member States as a means of forming a highly competitive and innovative marketplace that would make Europe stand against the rise of Asian and American economies. Japan, for instance, had already passed a national law on lifelong learning in 1990.[200] The *WP Growth* proposed: "Permanent recomposition and redevelopment of knowledge and know how. The establishment of more flexible and more open systems of training and the development of individuals' ability to adapt (...)"[201] are vital. The overall sentiments of the WP Growth, thus, were tuned towards developing human resources throughout the whole working life of a person.

In 1995, the WP Learning Society was prepared for public consultation. It was groundbreaking for a number of reasons. One reason was the focus on learning society; another one was the advancement of lifelong learning. According to Pépin, the *WP Learning Society* was the first document to really break up the division between general education and vocational training

---

[199] Dehmel 2006.
[200] Hake 1999, pp. 54; 59.
[201] Commission of the European Communities 12/5/1993, p. 120.

since it proposed to set up integrated education systems.[202] However, even though lifelong learning and the learning society were concepts that would have allowed opening up for a more integrated approach to education, the documents' line was almost exclusively built around initial education and with disregard for adult education.

Pépin adds that it was the *WP Learning Society*, which was shaping actions in the late 1990s, that had greatly influenced the Lisbon declarations in 2000.[203] As pointed out by George Papadopoulos from the OECD, the 1997 *Communication Europe of Knowledge*, having integrated findings from the EYLLL and the Member States' responses to the *WP Learning Society* public consultation, put a greater emphasis on social and civic education.[204]

Two more changes linked with the critical response to the *WP Learning Society* can be identified in the *Communication Europe of Knowledge*. The first concerns the social dimension. Emphasis was put on citizenship education. Common values, a sense of belonging to a common social and cultural area, active solidarity and mutual understanding had become relevant categories.[205] The second significant change concerned the parties involved in ET policy. While the *WP Learning Society* stressed education business cooperation, the *Communication Knowledge Society* noticed the critique from the European Trade Union and the Committee of the Regions. Social partners, regional and local partners and the voluntary sector were included as important partners. Also, in 1997, lifelong learning was made a guiding principle of EU policy in the Treaty of Amsterdam, where the role of regional actors (e.g. Committee of the Regions) was also strengthened.

The Lisbon European Council of March 2000 set the ambitious strategic goal for Europe "to become the most competitive and dynamic knowledge-based economy in the world capable of sustainable economic growth with more and better jobs and greater social cohesion."[206] Even if the knowledge-based economy had prime character, the social dimension was not forgotten. ET was regarded integral to the European social model with the main goals of investing in people and developing an active welfare state. Moreover, the Lisbon Council officially introduced the Open Method of Coordination as a

---

[202] Pépin 2007, p. 126.
[203] Pépin 2006, p. 160.
[204] Papadopoulos 2002, p. 47.
[205] Commission of the European Communities 11/12/1997, p. 3.
[206] European Council 3/23/2000.

regulating instrument "to ensure more coherent strategic direction and effective monitoring of progress."[207]

Also, in 2000, the '*Memorandum on Lifelong Learning*' was released.[208] It reaffirmed that lifelong learning must become the guiding principle of all ET policy. It further extended the boundaries of lifelong learning emphasizing the life-wide aspects, like the different forms of learning: formal, non-formal and informal learning. Employability and active citizenship were defined as equally important pillars of lifelong learning. What finally emerged was an all-embracing conception intended to enable interconnectedness between previously disconnected structures of educational provision.

The *WP Learning Society* was criticized – for instance – by Hans Schuetze for being overly economically oriented and paying too little attention to matters of social exclusion.[209] Throughout the EYLLL and the follow up processes on a political level, the Commission as well as the Council learned from the critical feedback so that the subsequent documents presented a more social outlook. The *Memorandum* with its all-embracing view of lifelong learning, then, was criticized by Carmel Borg and Peter Mayo for "seeking to provide a humanistic façade to what is, in effect, a neo-liberal inspired set of guidelines."[210] Most of the academic post-2000 literature argues that the all-embracing lifelong learning concept is characterized by its universal appeal and flexible application in various contexts. Alexandra Dehmel called it a "chameleon"[211] and a "plastic term"; Claudia Dellori referred to it as "absolute metaphor"[212] and George Zarifis and Maria Gravani spoke of it as a "dubious terminology".[213]

Governance change

Throughout the 1990s, the Commission shifted its approach from a rather top-down imposed to a rather bottom-up informed policy formation process. This shift is visible in two regards: the role the Commission took in the course of the 1996 EYLLL and the introduction of the OMC as the preferred governance instrument at the Lisbon European Council in 2000.

---

[207] European Council 3/23/2000.
[208] Commission of the European Communities 10/30/2000.
[209] Schuetze 2006, p. 293.
[210] Borg and Mayo 2005, p. 218.
[211] Dehmel 2006.
[212] Dellori 2016.
[213] Zarifis and Gravani 2014.

According to Lee, Thayer and Madyun, the Commission found itself confronted with three latent crises of legitimacy. [214] The legitimacy crises occurred partly before Maastricht 1992 and partly throughout the 1990s, which forced the Commission to invest in new strategies of policy-making. These authors argue that the Commission invested in institutional learning as a means to regain legitimacy and to succeed with its policy proposals. Learning, in this respect, refers to the use of information from various sources and the use of interaction with other policy-making institutions (e.g. the OECD, the UNESCO or the Roundtable of Industrialists), resulting in an instrumental change of policy as well as in a change in the political strategy.

In the previous two chapters (1970s and 1980s), it was pointed out that with regard to education and training, the Commission was not very powerful. The first administrative structures were established in the early 1970s and could only implement rudimentary programs. During the crisis years from 1978 to 1980, no meeting of the Education Ministers took place because Member States were opposing Community action. Transferring education to the DG for Employment and Social Affairs placed the Commission policy work in a new context and helped raise its status. However, as the 1980s proved, there was still massive opposition so that eventually the ECJ had to intervene as a mediator, allotting formal competences to the Commission against considerations of Member States. In line with Lee, Thayer and Madyun, these events can be understood as indicators of a first crisis of legitimacy.[215] The established British adult education scholar John Field seems to be of a similar opinion. He even calls the first mobility programs a failure. Field remarks that "rather than disheartening the Commission, that failure has been used to justify a more radical approach, which has involved the Commission in pursuing educational and training policies across a number of discrete policy areas (...)".[216]

In 1992, the TEU redefined the relationship between EU and Member States. Education and vocational training became subject to the principle of subsidiarity, which defined the Commission's competences. Some scholars consider it an extension of the Commission's competences; others – like the Dutch adult education scholar Barry Hake – did not see any significant change as far as formal competences were concerned.[217]

---

[214] Lee et al. 2008.
[215] Lee et al. 2008, p. 452.
[216] Field 1997, p. 74.
[217] Hake 1999, p. 56.

The 1993 *WP Growth* initiated a discourse in which ET was understood as an important factor in global economic competition. As stated in the preamble: "Looking at the traditional bases of prosperity and competitiveness, Europe has preserved its chances. It possesses assets that it has only to exploit – assets such as its abundant non-physical capital (education skills, capacity for innovation, traditions) (...)".[218]

While the *WP Growth* only indirectly addressed education, the *WP Learning Society* put forward guidelines for action in the field of ET. The Member States' commitment to the guidelines was to be supported and complemented by the Community, who had to make best use of the competences conferred upon it by the TEU. Sustaining the economic rationale behind ET, the *WP Learning Society* argued that because of (1) radical changes from information technology, (2) the impact of scientific knowledge and (3) the internationalization of the economies, the society of the future would have to be a learning society.

The reactions to the *WP Learning Society* were critical or in the words of John Field: "Within the Union, the White Paper's reception was at best lukewarm."[219] At this stage, a second crisis of legitimacy can be identified. Criticism came from outside the Community (e.g. German Adult Education Association/Deutscher Volkshochschulverband, European Trade Union) and from inside the Community (Council of Education Ministers, Committee of the Regions). Irritations were caused by the preponderance of the economic argument and consequently the disregard of social issues, the ambiguous use of terminology in relation to the learning society and lifelong learning and the broad interpretation of the EU's competences tending to trespass the principle of subsidiarity.[220]

The Committee of the Regions (CoR) pointed out positive and negative aspects in its Opinion of March 21st, 1996. It welcomed the emphasis on lifelong learning and cooperation and appreciated the Commission's initiative, but added, "[t]he objective of the EU is not to set up a European Planning Authority for training and education".[221] The CoR was a strong proponent of the principle of subsidiarity and, therefore, promoted regional actors such as libraries and regional learning centers and local actors. Moreover, it clearly expressed concerns about the merely economically oriented conception of

---

[218] Commission of the European Communities 12/5/1993, Preamble.
[219] Field 1997, p. 81.
[220] Field 1997; Schuetze 2006.
[221] Committee of the Regions 6/24/1996, p. 16.

lifelong learning saying that "[t]he COR envisages a new learning society in which human values take precedence over the acquisition of knowledge per se (...)".[222] Also, the German Adult Education Association was not satisfied with the WP Learning Society. Especially since "in the White Paper, general continuing education is primarily justified on grounds of its occupational benefits for individuals and its economic benefits for society."[223] In this regard, the German Adult Education Association joined the critique of the CoR.

The third crisis of legitimacy started when, in 1998, some high ranked Commission officials were accused of mismanagement and fraud. After the scandal had spread and evidence grew against the Commission members and officials, the Parliament supported an investigation that culminated in late 1999 in the official resignation of the entire Commission College. It was the case of Commissioner Edith Cresson, who was in charge of the heatedly discussed education portfolio. Cresson, among others, had mismanaged several funding programs, submitted documents with fake signatures and had commissioned acquaintances to complete policy tasks. When, in 2000, the new Commission under the Italian Romano Prodi was accepted, they had to recover legitimacy and come up with new modes for dealing with policy formation. The OMC was introduced as the new governance instrument addressing in particular the legitimacy issue and the democratic deficit.[224]

Institutional learning
The Commission had great problems maintaining its technocratic legitimacy. First, they did not have the formal competences to set up proper policy programs. Then, they experienced broad opposition from within EU organs and from civil society organizations and finally, a political scandal forced the Commission to reconsider its own methods. Moreover, changes with regard to policy were completed. Lifelong learning was introduced as an all-encompassing approach to connect education with other policy fields and the Commission reacted to the critique on the *WP Learning Society* and added a social dimension to the prevailing economic dimension in subsequent policy documents.

Lee, Thayer and Madyun explain these developments as a result of institutional learning. They refer to the Belgian political scientist Liesbet

---

[222] Committee of the Regions 6/24/1996, p. 21.
[223] quoted in Field 1997, p. 90.
[224] Lee et al. 2008, p. 456.

Hooghe[225] applying "[a]n 'institutional learning' perspective, (...) [which] refers to the process by which an organization is exposed to, learns, and then adopts the norms and values that are predominated and practiced by particular social systems."[226] Lee, Thayer and Madyun argue that the Commission had learned from other actors – particularly other IGOs – in order to regain the loss in legitimacy and to justify their actions. The term Lee et al. use is "hybridization",[227] indicating that the Commission had not fully adopted, but rather deliberately chosen viable policy goals and even ideologies in order to create their own concepts. In the following, the year 1996 will be looked at in more detail in order to follow up on what Lee, Thayer and Madyun observed.

First, the roots of the *European Year of Lifelong Learning* will be uncovered. In the *WP Growth*, the organization of a European Year of Education was proposed for the first time. Such was considered capable of raising awareness of the importance of education, training and culture among the European population.[228] Behind the idea of a European Year of Education stood the assumption that it would be easier to achieve long-term goals when the public not only supported but also understood the contribution ET could make to economic wellbeing. The Commission immediately started to elaborate on this idea.

On September 29th, 1994, the Commission submitted a proposal for establishing the European Year of Lifelong Learning in 1996 to the Council and the Parliament. In its joint decision of October 23rd, 1995, the Council and the Parliament eventually established the EYLLL. The objective was to promote "personal development and sense of initiative of individuals, their integration into working life and society, their participation in the democratic decision-making process and their ability to adjust to economic, technological and social change."[229] Activities were divided into three categories: (1) the EU budget should be used to fully finance the organization of meetings at European level as well as within the Member States, information and promotional campaigns, presentation of surveys and studies; (2) the budget should also be used to co-finance national and regional events, dissemination of good practice examples and competitions at national or regional level; (3)

---

[225] Hooghe 1999.
[226] Lee et al. 2008, p. 450.
[227] Lee et al. 2008, p. 451.
[228] Commission of the European Communities 12/5/1993, p. 122.
[229] European Parliament; Council of the European Union 10/26/1995, Article 1.

actions that needed no financial support were left to the initiative of private actors.[230]

In a Commission background paper from 1996, Commissioner Edith Cresson reported that a survey on attitudes towards education, training and lifelong learning, as well as studies on investment and economic returns on investment in lifelong learning had already been conducted. In the same introduction, Cresson states that "(…) an institutional debate is being stimulated in order to help identify how each participating country's education and training system can develop these opportunities and make lifelong learning more of a reality."[231] In the course of the EYLL, more than 500 events took place. From the previously mentioned information as well as other information on the internal policy formulation processes and the external policy formulation and dissemination processes, it seems as if the Commission added new facets to its role. Lee, Thayer and Madyun consider the EYLLL a decisive moment, when they say, "the Commission found its role changed, from that of a policy laboratory to a policy clearinghouse".[232]

Two other evidences indicate that a new approach to policy-making was developed around 1996. John Field informs that the 1995 *WP Learning Society* did not originate in the usual procedures. It was not preceded by a consultative Green Paper, as is normally the case. Drawing from interviews with Commission officials, Field reports that the White Paper "was largely written by a group of advisers (mainly academics) who reported directly to Commissioner Edith Cresson."[233]

It was mentioned earlier; the 1997 *Communication Knowledge Society* integrated the critique that had been raised after the *WP Learning Society*. For instance, the section entitled "parties involved" starts off by saying "Community action is not limited to actions initiated and piloted directly by the Commission."[234] The section continues by enumerating the parties wished to be involved, while ascribing certain tasks to each of them. Consultation was extended to actors from education (schools, universities, training organizations, third sector), business (particularly small and medium enterprises), regional and local partners and the voluntary actors.

Other than the EYLLL, the time around 1996 provides evidence helpful for discussing institutional learning as the result of activities of other

---

[230] European Parliament; Council of the European Union 10/26/1995, Annex.
[231] Gass 1996, p. 5.
[232] Lee et al. 2008, p. 454.
[233] Field 1997, p. 79.
[234] Commission of the European Communities 11/12/1997, p. 6.

international organizations. In February 1995, the *Round Table of Industrialist* published a report entitled *Education for Europeans Towards the Learning Society*.[235] There was UNESCO's *Learning the Treasure within*,[236] a report written by a commission that was chaired by Jacques Delors, who shortly before had ended his 10-year tenure as the President of the Commission. There was also OECD's *Lifelong Learning for All*,[237] a report written in preparation for the Meeting of Education Ministers in January 1996.

On this OECD report, Hans Schuetze notes, "Education ministers adopted the report and the goals of aiming for Lifelong Learning for all, marrying the economic rationale with wider societal objectives."[238] Lee, Thayer and Madyun add that it is very likely that the 24 education ministers who attended the OECD meeting were the same ministers who attended EU education minister meetings in the same years.[239] One can certainly claim that the education ministers contributed the same ideas to the OECD meeting as to the EU meeting. The similarities between the policies of the two IGOs, therefore, come as no surprise. It is, moreover, a longstanding practice that the Commission uses all kinds of interaction with other policy actors, particularly since the cooperation with other IGOs has been a key aspect of its work since the mid-1970s and even adopted as a necessary action by the Council in the 1976 action program.

Chapter summary

Since the articles on general education and vocational training in the TEU eventually defined the competences of the institutions in all fields of ET, the 1990s provided the EU with much more power. The analyses of the three most important policy documents and the role of the Commission have produced findings that confirm the EU's attempt to introduce a new governance arrangement. The concept of lifelong learning was used to establish a discourse going far beyond discussions of education systems, subjects or teaching methods. Two implications of this discourse come to the foreground. The first is the shift from collective responsibility to individual responsibility; in other words, the shift from teaching to learning and the stronger focus on the individual learner. The second is the even stronger emphasis, compared to

---

[235] ERT 1995.
[236] UNESCO 1996.
[237] OECD 1996.
[238] Schuetze 2006, p. 292.
[239] Lee et al. 2008, p. 458.

the 1980s, on cooperation between all relevant stakeholders like educational institutions, public authorities, private enterprises, social partners, civil society organizations or international organizations. In this context, the Commission turned into a political clearinghouse coordinating the Member States' actions through best practice examples and country reports.

6.6 Education and training after 2000

All that has happened in the last eighteen years since 2000 suggests that beyond the mainstreaming, ET has become a political priority of the EU. Under the circumstances of a massive enlargement integrating twelve new Member States up until 2007, much hope was set on ET and its contribution to innovation, labor market stability, economic competitiveness as well as social cohesion and democratization. Since the economic crises in 2010, ET has lost some of its status but is still firmly settled as a main concern in the Europe 2020 strategy. The new OMC governance approach, which was introduced in 2001, reorganized the cooperation among the Member States and the EU institutions and brought about the so-called European area of ET.

From the early 1960s on, ACE was marginalized in European ET politics and discussed mostly in relation to vocational training. Since the creation of the Grundtvig action, the ACE policy sub-area slowly began to emerge. The focus on lifelong learning helped to increase the importance of ACE. The Communication on adult learning from 2006[240] and the Action Plan on adult learning from 2007[241] as well as the renewed European agenda for adult learning from 2011[242] eventually outlined the contours of this policy sub-area.

Outline of context developments

At the European Council meeting in Lisbon, in March 2000, the EU heads of state started ambitiously on a plan to make the EU fit for global economic competition in the age of the knowledge-based economy. In 2002, the Euro became the official currency in twelve of the fifteen Member States. After lengthy negotiations, in 2004, the first step towards opening up the EU to the east was completed. Eight countries from Central and Eastern Europe and

---

[240] Commission of the European Communities 11/23/2006.
[241] Commission of the European Communities 9/27/2007.
[242] Council of the European Union 12/20/2011.

two from the Mediterranean area joined the EU: the Czech Republic, Estonia, Latvia, Lithuania, Hungary, Poland, Slovenia, Slovakia, Malta and Cyprus.

Also, in 2004, all 25 Member States signed a draft for a European Constitution aiming to make the EU more democratic and less bureaucratic. European citizens did not fully support the proposal and the French and the Dutch voted against the Constitution. The rebuilding of the Union, however, was not finished yet. In 2007, the second step of the eastern enlargement was completed with the accession of Bulgaria and Romania making the EU 27 members strong. On December 13th, 2007, the Treaties of Lisbon amending the Treaty on the European Union (TEU) and the Treaty on the functioning of the European Union (TFEU) were signed and went into force on December 1st, 2009.

In 2008/2009, the economic crisis swept over from the US and caused considerable damage also in Europe. National public budgets were affected to such an extent that the EU had to intervene. More pleasurable was the awarding of the 2012 Nobel Peace Prize for the EU's sixty-year contribution to peace and stability in Europe. The last member to join the EU was Croatia in 2013.

In 2014, the civil war in the Ukraine and the following Russian annexation of the Crimea peninsula aggravated the relations between Russia and the EU resulting, among others, in sanctions against Russian products. Still suffering from the economic crisis and bureaucratic misconduct, Greece almost went bankrupt and had to be supported with EU money. Again, the discussions following the Greek problems did not do well to further political cooperation in Europe. The Syrian civil war caused a migration movement that brought new challenges to all Member States. During the whole of 2015, roughly one million people reached Europe from the Middle Eastern regions. Lastly, in 2017, for the first time in history, a Member State decided to leave. In an official vote, the British people decided on Great Britain leaving the EU. Until the end of 2019, however, the so-called Brexit has not been not completed and it seems unclear as to when or if Great Britain will eventually leave. Obviously, this added to the fact that today the EU still remains under pressure.

The people seem ambivalent: on the one hand, many consider the EU an insufficient bureaucracy that causes more damage than it does good; on the other hand, people still believe that the only way to maintain peace and stability is through European cooperation and integration.

A concept that rose in importance in the academic and political discourses on ET at the end of the 1990s was that of knowledge-based economy. With globalization and technological innovation, new forms for organizing work and economies have become expedient. The concept of knowledge economy was constructed to address these new forms. It indicates a form of organizing economic activity and growth on investment into knowledge and human resources. In this regard, politics referred to the *Endogenous Growth Model*, which argues that economic growth is generated within an organization or within a country under particular circumstances where investments in human capital, research and development and knowledge exchange in international networks are most beneficial. The 2018 winner of the Nobel Prize for economics, Paul Romer asserts, "[W]hat is important for growth is integration not into an economy with a large number of people but rather into one with a large amount of human capital."[243] *Knowledge-based economy* and *endogenous growth* imply that if knowledge is the key to innovation and economic growth, ET must then refer to a much broader frame of reference. The emphasis on lifelong learning and continuing education was regarded as a logical consequence.

The derestriction of existing boundaries of institutionalized ACE was taking up speed, meaning the expansion of spatial, temporal and interpersonal borders that defined ACE practice was a much-discussed fact. For instance, the German adult education scholar Joachim Knoll argues that traditionally, the type of education was closely linked with the institution that provided it: those institutions specializing in liberal arts education, provided liberal arts courses; those specializing in vocational education, provided vocational courses and so on. Courses offered, thus, were limited to a small number of topics, according to Knoll.[244] With the derestriction of boundaries, topics have multiplied since they have become subject to the market and respond to the demands of customers. ACE organizations no longer stick with the traditional program because they are demanded to provide, for instance, counseling or validation of learning outcomes in addition to educational courses.

Quality assurance was another important topic with broad implications. Contrary to the institutionalization and professionalization of ACE – two other topics of great relevance – quality assurance does not originate in the educational practice and discourse. Coming from industrial production, quality assurance was prominent in the late 1990s and closely connected with the commercialization of education. Josef Schrader, Director of the German Institute for Adult Education, argues, while professionalization is about

---

[243] Romer 1990, p. 98.
[244] Knoll 2015.

improving pedagogical elements of didactics and methods, quality assurance is about the business model of ACE.[245] The function of quality assurance is manifold: it helps to adapt programs more adequately to the demands of learners and stakeholders and helps establish efficient and effective processes. In addition to that, when quality accreditation schemes are in place, they serve the customers and the public authorities since they allow for transparency, consumer protection or funds allocation.

Examination of historical developments

The major policy documents of the 1990s brought ET closer to EU mainstream politics. Action programs were consolidated and re-launched under the umbrella of the Socrates and the Leonardo Programs. They were attracting increasingly more students, apprentices and adult learners. In this section, it will be shown how the mainstreaming was reinforced at the Lisbon European Council and how a European area of ET was formed through common objectives and new governance arrangements like the ones in the Rolling Agenda or the OMC. Moreover, changes in the understanding of quality and the *European Qualifications Framework* (EQF), which has been one of the most important sector-spanning policy instruments, will be discussed.

The second generation of action programs

After the first action programs had expired, the Commission proposed to reorganize them and bring them together under new framework programs. The two new framework programs, Leonardo and Socrates, ran from 1995 to 1999. Socrates was allocated 850 million ECU and Leonardo 620 million ECU.[246] In the Socrates program, higher education (ERASMUS) and school education (COMENIUS) were joined with horizontal areas like language education, open and distance education and exchange of information. Adult education was mentioned in the section on exchange of information in that "[t]he European dimension is to be reinforced in all areas of adult education (general, cultural and social), by means of transnational cooperation and exchange of experience between adult education organizations and institutions."[247] The Leonardo program concentrated on vocational training as well

---

[245] Schrader 2011, p. 84.

[246] European Parliament; Council of the European Union 4/20/1995, Art. 7; Council of the European Union 12/29/1994, Art. 5.

[247] European Parliament; Council of the European Union 4/20/1995, 24.

as continuing vocational training, lifelong learning, vocational guidance, and the transition from education to work.

At the end of 1999, it was decided to continue Socrates and Leonardo with a slightly different structure and a much higher budget of EUR 1.850 million for Socrates II and EUR 1.150 million for Leonardo II. This period ran from 2000 until 2006.[248]

Within Socrates II, ACE occupied more space with the Grundtvig action. Grundtvig addressed adult education, lifelong learning and other educational pathways and in particular "people who, at whatever stage of their life, seek access to knowledge and competences within the framework of formal or non-formal education or by means of autonomous learning, (…)".[249] The objective of Grundtvig was fourfold: increasing intercultural learning, employability, participation in society and broad access to all kinds of education.

The goals of the Leonardo program were to raise skill levels through vocational training and apprenticeships, to improve quality of and access to continuing vocational training, to contribute to innovation and competitiveness and to intensify the cooperation between educational organizations and private businesses. Participation was intended for vocational training organizations of public and private character including higher education institutions, research organizations, small and medium-sized enterprises, social partners, or NGOs.

In their textbook on adult education in the European Union from 2005, Bechtel, Nuissl and Lattke report that within Socrates II, ACE was intended to address transnational cooperation rather than learner mobility.[250] In comparison, in ERASMUS 90% and in Leonardo 40% of the budget was made available for learner and teacher mobility. In the Grundtvig action of Socrates, mobility accounted for only 5% of the budget. These authors assert that, implementing Grundtvig, the Commission hoped that transnational cooperation would lead to the creation of new educational products and contribute to the improvement of quality in ACE. For instance, within Grundtvig, in 2003, roughly 40% of the budget was dedicated to projects of transnational cooperation. Individuals and organizations benefited strongly from these projects, but the lack of sustainability of the created products was unsatisfactory, Bechtel et al. claim.

---

[248] European Parliament; Council of the European Union 2/3/2000, Art. 10; Council of the European Union 6/11/1999, Art. 12.

[249] European Parliament; Council of the European Union 2/3/2000, 9.

[250] Bechtel et al. 2005, pp. 98–100.

The Lisbon Agenda

The Lisbon Agenda continued the competitiveness strategy of the 1990s.[251] It was an attempt to keep up in global economic competition within the context of increasingly more knowledge-based economies. According to Pépin, in the "Lisbon spirit", it was intended to "mobilise forces in key fields where the Union does not have specific competences or where these are limited in order to advance alongside an economy-based and a social Europe."[252] The Conclusions of the Lisbon Council Meeting proposed the strategic goal "to become the most competitive and dynamic knowledge-based economy in the world, capable of sustainable economic growth with more and better jobs and greater social cohesion."[253] One of the instruments considered suitable to reach this goal was the Open Method of Coordination (OMC), referred to by Pépin as the engine of the Lisbon Strategy.[254] It was expected that through dissemination of best-practice examples, the OMC would be a softer solution to achieve convergence of national policies in the direction of the new goal.

In the Lisbon Conclusions, under the headline "education and training for living and working in the knowledge society" three main components of a new approach were defined: "the development of local learning centers, the promotion of new basic skills, in particular in the information technologies, and increased transparency of qualifications."[255] Member States agreed to meet six targets. Among those were: increasing per capita investment in human resources, raising the number of young adults with a higher-level education than secondary education, transforming training centers into multipurpose learning centers, or defining key competences for lifelong learning.[256]

One knows by now that the Lisbon strategy was far too ambitious and that, already by 2005, EU leaders had concluded that it was bound to fail. After that, in the second half of the decade, the rhetoric of EU leaders became much more severe and threatening concerning the dangers of falling behind in global competition.[257] Notwithstanding the failure, which was admitted by the 2009 launch of the Europe 2020 Strategy, the Lisbon agenda had far-reaching implications. It confirmed the high-level commitment to and

---

[251] Jones 2005, p. 247.
[252] Pépin 2011, p. 26.
[253] European Council 3/23/2000, p. 2.
[254] Pépin 2011, p. 25.
[255] European Council 3/23/2000, p. 7.
[256] European Council 3/23/2000, pp. 7–8.
[257] Nordin 2011, p. 14.

indicated a direction for ET, while documents that followed in the years 2000 and 2001 defined the topics to be worked on.

Important policy documents

In 2000, Commission staff published the working paper *A Memorandum on Lifelong Learning.*[258] The aim of the *Memorandum* was to launch a European-wide debate on a comprehensive strategy for lifelong learning. Actions in six areas were proposed: (1) basic skills development, (2) investment in human resources, (3) innovation in teaching and learning, (4) validation of learning outcomes, (5) guidance and counseling and (6) local learning initiatives facilitated by the use of ICT. Moreover, objectives defined were to strengthen social cohesion, human resource development and active citizenship and to raise awareness for formal, non-formal and informal learning.

Shortly after the *Memorandum* had been published, the Commission released a report on concrete future objectives of education systems.[259] Subject to the report was not only general education but also vocational training. Because of this, the future of ACE was also taken into consideration. In the first part of the report, results from a Member State consultation and EU actions were presented. The five issues Member States were concerned with were: (1) quality of national ET systems, (2) access and attractiveness of ET, (3) contents such as values of society (democracy, citizenship, community) or ICT, (4) openness of ET systems to external interests from the business world, to the local environment, or the wider world and (5) effectiveness of investment and quality assurance.

In the Annex, the Commission presented an analysis of the status quo in the Member States and also made some remarks on ACE.[260] It was stated that next to secondary education, adult education was the field in which a better management of financial resources would be most necessary, especially as concerned the per capita spending. Addressing the organization of vocational training and ACE, the Commission was of the opinion that the systems needed to undergo major changes. Measures such as the modularization of course offers or the introduction of new courses, better evaluation mechanisms for learner outcomes, cooperation with the business world or personalized training would be necessary to make the systems more responsive to the needs of the labor market and employers.

---

[258] Commission of the European Communities 10/30/2000.
[259] Commission of the European Communities 1/31/2001.
[260] Commission of the European Communities 1/31/2001, pp. 17–18.

In November 2001, the Commission Communication *Making Lifelong Learning a Reality* was released.[261] One finds in this Communication the results of a wide-ranging consultation having taken place in response to the Memorandum. The Commission received roughly three thousand individual submissions and, furthermore, twelve thousand people from Member States, states of the *European Economic Area* (EEA) and candidate countries participated in meetings accompanying the consultation process. Also, the social partners, civil society organizations and IGOs were involved in the process. One of the most significant results of this consultation was a broad agreement on the fact that national learning systems must change to allow for better access to all kinds of quality learning.

New methods of cooperation

The TEU limited the competence of the EU and established the principle of subsidiarity as the guiding principle of ET politics. The policy decision process as stipulated in the Treaty, however, was soon supplemented by initiatives of a different kind, or as Anders Hingel, a former official of the European Commission asserted, there was a "manifest will and political demand to go beyond [what was] presented by the Member States and reinforced by the European Parliament, the Social and Economic Committee as well as by the Committee of regions."[262] In fact, the Rolling Agenda and the Open Method of Coordination reorganized the procedures in the Council and reorganized cooperation among the various stakeholders. These two arrangements are subject to analysis on the next pages.

Since 1974, decisions were discussed and made by the Education Committee. As previously mentioned, the Education Committee was comprised of representatives from the Member States, usually senior officials from the education ministries and officials of the Member States' permanent representations, joined by officials from the Commission. Pépin points out that the Education Committee was unique in that it has hardly ever been the case that Council members and Commission members have cooperated with one another in the policy process. Behind this cooperation was the intention to protect the national prerogative in ET against attempts to harmonize ET systems.[263]

As defined by the Council Resolution of 1976, the chair of the Education Committee had to be held by a Member of the country providing the

[261] Commission of the European Communities 11/21/2001.
[262] Hingel 2001, p. 7.
[263] Pépin 2006, pp. 88–89.

presidency of the Council.[264] Since the Council presidency rotates every six months, obviously, the chair of the Education Committee has rotated accordingly. This led to a constant change of priorities and topics to be discussed in the Education Committee. Therefore, continuity in the discussions was difficult to maintain. When the Rolling Agenda was proposed at the Education Council meeting in September 1999, this changed.

The Rolling Agenda should guarantee that the Education Committee agreed on a limited number of topics to be discussed in cycles. Hingel argues, "[a]s well as creating greater continuity, the implementation of the Rolling Agenda would enable a more effective exchange of information, experience and good practice between the Member States."[265] The 1999 *Resolution developing new working procedures for European cooperation in the field of education and training* defined the following flexible steps in the Rolling Agenda.

> the Council discusses priority themes of common interest - submitted either by Member States or the Commission - and agrees, if appropriate, how to take forward individual themes,

> the Member States are invited to inform the Commission of relevant political initiatives and examples of best practice at national level in relation to the agreed priority themes,

> the Commission provides a summary analysis of the information supplied by Member States to the Council. This should also cover relevant Community action,

> the Council considers the Commission's analysis and, where appropriate, decides on future initiatives[266]

The 1999 Resolution not only established the Rolling Agenda but also suggested three topics to which it should be applied. The first topic was the role of ET in employment policies. The second topic was the development of quality education in all sectors and at all levels and the third topic was mobility and recognition of qualifications.

Even though one might expect that the Commission introduced the Rolling Agenda, Anders Hingel holds that it was rather the Member States' initiative. According to Hingel, what distinguishes pre-Lisbon from post-Lisbon governance is that "[s]ince the very beginning of European co-operation

---

[264] Council of the European Communities 2/19/1976, 1.
[265] Hingel 2001, p. 9.
[266] Council of the European Union 1/12/2000.

in the field of education, Ministers of Education have underlined the diversity of their systems of education (…). The Lisbon Conclusions break with this by asking the Ministers to concentrate their reflection on what is common."[267] The Lisbon Conclusions established common ground by defining clear benchmarks and asking the Education Council to agree on common objectives. On that basis, according to Hingel, everything was prepared for the OMC to be activated.[268] In June 2001, the Commission released the *White Paper on European governance* in which the use of the OMC was reinforced.[269]

Ase Gornitzka, a Norwegian political scientist, reports that one of the problems that occurred in the OMC inception phase was that the DG Employment demanded the lifelong learning agenda so that education ministers could be disregarded and instead the respective ministers for employment and labor market could be consulted. "The 'collision' that contributed to creating new political space in the case of OMC education was between the cognitive and normative understanding of 'education and learning' as part of labour market policy, rather than framed as an education policy issue."[270] The prominent position that was conferred upon ET in the Lisbon Council Conclusions, however, was an incentive for DG Education and Culture (DG EAC). Gornitzka quotes a staff member: "It was immediately in the education field understood that this concerned us – 'this is a method for us'"[271]

The first years after the 2000 Lisbon Council, DG EAC was presented with the chance to create "a platform for profiling the sector in the wider context of the EU" and thereby raise awareness for its major contribution to European integration going beyond the already existing mobility programs. "DG EAC's will and capacity to download the concept of OMC and translate it into practical terms are essential for understanding what the education sector did with the OMC template."[272] On the grounds of the accounts presented, it seems reasonable to agree with both Hingel and Gornitzka that that the dynamics of change in the area of education and training have not only been imposed by external forces, but have been shaped by national education ministers and by actors within the Commission's education divisions.

---

[267] Hingel 2001, p. 12.

[268] Hingel 2001, p. 13.

[269] Commission of the European Communities 7/25/2001, pp. 21–22.

[270] Gornitzka 2006a, p. 15.

[271] Gornitzka 2006b, p. 10.

[272] Both quotations in Gornitzka 2006a, p. 49

The European Qualifications Framework

One of the most discussed ET policies of recent years is the *European Qualifications Framework* (EQF). The EQF was discussed for the first time in 2002, in the context of the Copenhagen Process, which aimed at intensifying cooperation in the field of VET. In 2008, a Recommendation of the Council and the Parliament established the EQF.[273] The EQF is a central element in the promotion of free movement of people, i.e. transnational mobility of workers and learners, and in supporting the supply and demand within the European labor market. Comparability of qualifications across all Member States as well as output orientation in all education sectors should be guaranteed. According to the EQF Recommendation, the "objective (...) is to create a common reference framework which should serve as a translation device between different qualifications systems and their levels, whether for general and higher education or for vocational education and training."[274]

In May 2017, a new Council Recommendation repealed and consolidated the one from 2008.[275] While the framework has not changed much, the Recommendation was extended to include a more elaborated list of definitions of key terms, a much clearer description of the purpose and the context of usage. The new EQF Recommendation is unequivocal in the fact that the implementation of national equivalents requires the involvement and compliance of a broad range of stakeholders. Moreover, reacting to the migrant crisis of 2015, validation and recognition of learning outcomes is also an important instrument supporting integration in society and in the labor market. Member States are now asked to refer all new qualifications to the EQF levels and to make sure they are indicated on the respective certificates or diplomas.

The EQF is the manifestation of the shift towards outcome-oriented ET. In general, the shift has much to do with the increasing importance of useful and applicable knowledge and the simultaneously decreasing importance of the ways by which knowledge is acquired. Whenever one proves that he/she has obtained a certain reference level, it should, theoretically, no longer be important how it was reached. As Ekkehard Nuissl et al. point out, the EU has played a key role in institutionalizing outcome orientation, most of all because it corresponds well with the overall ET policy direction.[276]

---

[273] European Parliament; Council of the European Union 5/6/2008.

[274] European Parliament; Council of the European Union 5/6/2008, 2.

[275] Council of the European Union 6/15/2017.

[276] Nuissl et al. 2010, p. 77.

Because the EQF tries to integrate diversity of learners into one standard framework, it is very well suited as a governance instrument that reduces complexity and makes behavior, therefore, controllable. This has been stressed by many ET academics. Rudolf Egger, an Austrian education scholar, argued that the use of a framework idea serves the EU to control the dynamisms of advanced knowledge-based societies.[277] Among the goals of the EQF are comparability, transparency and portability of qualifications. Pia Cort, a Danish adult education scholar, is very critical of these. She holds that looking at empirical evidence, "it appears that there is no substantial evidence that qualifications frameworks achieve their objectives of transparency, comparability and portability. Indeed, they seem to promote a higher degree of intransparency."[278]

Problems arise especially when the various stakeholders of worker and employer organizations and of vocational and non-vocational ET institutions meet to discuss the matching of reference levels. As Carmen Baumeler and Sonja Engelage from the Swiss Federal Institute for Vocational Education and Training have shown in research on the implementation of national qualifications frameworks (NQF) in Germany, Austria and Switzerland, the interests of the stakeholders involved in the translation of the EQF at the national level are often contradictory or non-commensurable.[279]

Quality in adult and continuing education
In the analysis of the TEU, it was stressed that one of the responsibilities assigned to the EU is to contribute to the development of quality in education. Respective provision, thus, made quality one of the most important policy subjects. The Lisbon agenda and the Memorandum on lifelong learning reinforced the discourse on quality in education. As far as ACE was concerned in the practice field, the issue of quality has been intensively discussed and, since the beginning of the 1990s, the use of Quality Management Systems (QMS) in ACE organizations has become widespread. On a European level, the 2006 *Communication on adult learning* and the 2007 *Action Plan on adult learning* are important references because the proposals therein connect quality with efficiency and effectiveness at the system level and not just with organizational performance. The *renewed European agenda for adult learning* from 2011 eventually provided a list with five priority areas Member States should consider in terms of quality assurance.

---

[277] Egger 2009, p. 62.
[278] Cort 2010, p. 310.
[279] Baumeler and Engelage 2017.

The following discussion draws from a book chapter by Bert-Jan Buiskool and Simon Broek, two researchers and consultants from the Netherlands, and continues on their findings concerning a paradigm shift in the EU's understanding of quality in ACE.[280]

In the Memorandum, quality was not limited to one area of ET, rather it was presented throughout the document as a topic that touches upon the whole spectrum of lifelong learning and concerns all ET sectors. Even if no section was specifically dedicated to quality, in the context of the six key messages, quality was mentioned in relation to a large number of issues such as high quality of information, high quality basic education, adequate public funding, high-quality teaching, learning methods and materials, recognition of learning outcomes or counseling and guidance.

This broad range of issues proves that quality was important in terms of three types of services: services necessary in the development of ET programs such as public funds, services necessary to inform learners about ET programs such as good public relations measures and services that supplement or even substitute traditional ET programs such as recognition of learning outcomes. The more traditional understanding of quality in ET is implicit only in issues like quality of teaching and learning methods. As Buiskool and Broek point out, in summary, two aspects are termed particularly important for the quality: broad access to ET and skills acquisition responding to the demands of society.[281]

The 2006 *Commission Communication on adult learning 'It Is Never Too Late To Learn'* wanted to position adult learning against the backdrop of the Lisbon goals and the three challenges of competitiveness, demographic change and social inclusion. In this context – according to the summarized argument of the Commission – contributing to the acquisition and maintenance of key competences, adult learning facilitated the employability, mobility in labor markets and social inclusion. The second of five key messages addressed the issue of quality of adult learning.

The argumentation began with a very direct statement: "Poor quality provision of adult learning leads to poor quality learning outcomes."[282] It was admitted that quality must take account for aspects like socially and economically relevant and useful learning content; information, guidance and learning support; assessment and needs analysis; or recognition of prior learning.

---

[280] Buiskool and Broek 2014.
[281] Buiskool and Broek 2014.
[282] Commission of the European Communities 11/23/2006, p. 6.

With a view on quality, four topics were discussed: teaching methods, quality of staff, quality of providers, and quality of delivery.[283] The Commission's view on quality in ACE as in the 2006 Communication is summarized below.

> In order to foster a culture of quality in adult learning, Member States should invest in improving teaching methods and materials adapted to adult learners and put in place initial and continuing professional development measures to qualify and up-skill people working in adult learning. They should introduce quality assurance mechanisms, and improve delivery.[284]

Following a wide-ranging consultation after the 2006 Communication, the *Action Plan on Adult Learning* with the evocative title *It Is Always A Good Time To Learn* was published in 2007. As far as quality was concerned, the Action Plan was very clear: "[The Action Plan] starts from the premise that the need for a high quality and accessible adult learning system is no longer a point of discussion, given the challenges Europe has to meet in the coming years (…)."[285] In the passages on quality in adult learning, it is discernible that the Commission considered the quality of staff of utmost importance when it emphasized that the "[q]uality of provision is affected by policy, resources, accommodation and a host of other factors, but the key factor is the quality of the staff involved in delivery." Moreover, it was affirmed, "[a]dult learning staff in this context is not limited to teachers and trainers but includes management, guidance personnel, mentors and administration."[286] The Commission considered staff important because it assumed that the quality of staff is vital for the motivation of the learners, which again corresponds positively with the learning outcomes.

In its Conclusions of May 22nd, 2008, the European Council welcomed the provision of the Communication and the Action Plan and endorsed the importance of adult learning. Among others, the Council called on the Member States to "to remove barriers to participation, to increase overall quality and efficiency in adult learning, to speed up the process of validation and recognition and to ensure sufficient investment in and monitoring of the field."[287] Quality was linked with the need for demand-driven provision and with the need for better ICT provision.

---

[283] Commission of the European Communities 11/23/2006, pp. 6–7.

[284] Commission of the European Communities 11/23/2006, p. 7.

[285] Commission of the European Communities 9/27/2007, p. 3.

[286] Both quotations in Commission of the European Communities 9/27/2007, p. 8.

[287] Council of the European Union 6/6/2008, p. 10.

Three years later, in 2011, the *Council Resolution on a renewed European agenda for adult learning* provided the most refined and distilled approach with a focus on quality and efficiency. In the renewed agenda, the Council welcomed the fact that Member States had done much to raise the quality of ACE systems. Especially the progress that had been achieved regarding qualification profiles for staff or accreditation schemes for providers was mentioned benevolently.

This time, the part dedicated to quality was more elaborate compared to the Action Plan. Among the five priority areas of the renewed agenda was also improvement of quality and efficiency of ET.[288] The link to the issue of efficiency had not been made so prominent in previous documents. The Council invited the Member States to focus on the following five areas, which can be summarized briefly as below.[289]

1. a system for the accreditation of ACE organizations
2. a system for the professional education and development of ACE staff
3. a funding system that caters for broad access to ACE
4. measures to make ACE provision responsive to the changing labor market
5. a governance arrangement integrating all relevant stakeholders

Working Group on quality in adult learning

In October 2011, in line with the ET 2020 framework and the renewed agenda for adult learning, two *Thematic Working Groups* (TWG) were formed as part of the OMC. The first TWG dealt with issues of financing in adult learning and the second dealt with issues of quality in adult learning. This second TWG on quality will be examined on the next pages. Before presenting the outcomes, the organization of the TWG will be presented.

According to the official mandate, the working group comprised representatives from 19 EU Member States and two non-Member States (Croatia and Norway).[290] In addition, it included representatives from the European social partners (European Trade Union Confederation – ETUC, European trade union committee for education – ETUCE) and from other relevant

---

[288] The other four priority areas were: (1) Making lifelong learning and mobility a reality (2) Promoting equity, social cohesion and active citizenship through adult learning (3) Enhancing the creativity and innovation of adults and their learning environments (4) Improving the knowledge base on adult learning and monitoring the adult-learning sector. Council of the European Union 12/20/2011, Annex.

[289] Council of the European Union 12/20/2011, Annex.

[290] European Commission no year.

stakeholders like CEDEFOP, EURYDICE, the European Association for the Education of Adults (EAEA), the European Lifelong Guidance Policy Network, the European Basic Skill Network, and VOX – the Norwegian LLL agency. The TWG was coordinated by policy officers from the Commission and was supported and facilitated by three non-partisan researchers.

The task was to develop a quality framework that should help providers and policymakers define criteria for quality in in ACE. The goal was to explore to what extent it was possible to link quality initiatives in vocational education and training, adult learning and higher education. In the TWG, three subgroups were built on indicators, accreditation/governance and staff competences, while guidance and validation were integrated as transversal topics. All of these topics had been derived from policy documents like the Action Plan and the renewed agenda.[291]

The TWG met in ten plenary sessions, discussed online and convened for three Peer Learning Activities (PLAs) concerning accreditation of providers in Austria, concerning staff professionalization in Romania and concerning guidance, validation and indicators in Malta.[292] The work of the TWG resulted in a quality framework, policy guidelines with good practice examples, a tool kit for Member States and a joint conference with the TWG on financing.[293] The results were published in a final report.

The final report informs that the TWG started from the ISO definition of quality. The ISO defines quality as "'all characteristics of an entity that bear on its ability to satisfy stated and implied needs' or 'the degree to which a set of inherent characteristics fulfills requirements.'"[294] Moreover, the TWG took inspiration from the CEDEFOP definition. This definition emphasizes the importance of all measures of planning, evaluation or reporting, performed by ACE organizations to meet the requirements of stakeholders. Furthermore, it was asserted that quality is more than a technical issue and that it is strongly integrated in the societal dimension since it helps to achieve economic or social policies. With regard to the quality approach, reference was also made to the UNESCO. The UNESCO approach distinguishes four elements of quality: equity of access and participation, efficiency of investment and resource allocation, effectiveness of input-outcome relations and

---

[291] European Commission no year.
[292] Thematic Working Group on Quality in Adult Learning 2013, p. 64.
[293] European Commission no year.
[294] Thematic Working Group on Quality in Adult Learning 2013, p. 13.

relevance of provision.[295] The results were presented in the format of three key messages.[296]

- The first key message is concerned with the fact that ACE has a "cross-sectoral nature" and includes innately within its structures and provision the diversity of stakeholder and learners' interests. It was there that it was requested to set up a comprehensive system of cross-sector measures breaking down rigid separations between vocational and non-vocational types of ACE.
- The second key message considered the lack of evidence and the lack of knowledge as concerns the effects and impact of quality assurance or quality management. To solve this problem, it was suggested to concentrate on proper evaluation mechanisms helping to further develop the quality of provision.
- The last key message admitted the difficulties of the comprehensive approach requested in the first key message. Especially the problem of time was mentioned, since a comprehensive system cannot be established quickly. Therefore, it was stressed to make use of existing resources in the various sectors of education and to integrate them into a framework based on principles, criteria and guidelines.

Education and training and the Europe 2020 Strategy

In 2010, the Commission released a Communication in which the *Europe 2020 Strategy* was presented as the successor to the *Lisbon Strategy*. This new strategy put forward a vision indicating objectives and plans for the next ten years.[297] In the introductory part of this book, the three priorities of the EU 2020 strategy were already mentioned and it must be stressed that ET was of paramount importance to the handling of these priorities and, therefore, became itself somewhat of a priority for the EU. The three priorities of the *Europe 2020 Strategy* are: firstly, smart growth deriving from investment in the knowledge-based economy and in innovation of all kinds; secondly, sustainable growth through the promotion of an ecologically more efficient economy; and thirdly, inclusive growth signifying the strive for an economy with high employment rates and a positive social cohesion.

So-called headline targets were set in order to operationalize these priorities and make them quantifiable. Two of the five headline targets are

[295] Thematic Working Group on Quality in Adult Learning 2013, pp. 14–15.
[296] Thematic Working Group on Quality in Adult Learning 2013, pp. 6–9.
[297] European Commission 3/3/2010.

dependent on the performance of ET: target number one is the stabilization of the employment rate of the population aged 20 to 64 at 75% and target number four is to lower the early school leavers rate to under 10% and raise the percentage of people with a tertiary education degree to 40%.

Lastly, two out of seven so-called flagship initiatives were directly linked with the almost simultaneously devised *Strategic Framework for Cooperation in Education and Training* (ET 2020), namely the "youth on the move" and the "agenda for new skills and jobs" initiatives.

Already one year before the Europe 2020 Strategy, in 2009, cooperation in ET had been reorganized in accordance with the so-called ET 2020 framework. Being an umbrella structure, ET 2020 incorporates several educational sectors, transversal topics and objectives pertaining to the lifelong learning approach.

The education and training framework 2020

Corresponding to the Lisbon Agenda in 2001, a program was established after a Communication by the Commission, which was going to be the historically first solid framework for political cooperation in ET.[298] This program was later known as the *Education and Training 2010 Program* (ET 2010). It was established to assure that the proposals from the 2001 *Commission Report on future objectives of education systems* were put into practice.

In 2009, the successor, the ET 2020 framework, was established with the primary goal being to organize cooperation in a manner that would make it possible to further develop national education systems. According to the Council Conclusion that established ET 2020, such development of national education system should ensure the personal, social and professional fulfillment of all European citizens, plus, on one side, sustainable economic prosperity and individual employability, and on the other side, social cohesion, active citizenship and intercultural dialogue.[299] The following four strategic objectives have been pursued in the ET 2020 framework by means of multilateral cooperation in the period from 2010 to 2020.[300]

- First, the objective of "making lifelong learning and mobility a reality" has been concerned with the integration of the various ET sectors into the approach of lifelong learning. Moreover, it has also been concerned with horizontal and vertical mobility achieved by means of the recognition of

---

[298] Commission of the European Communities 2001.
[299] Council of the European Union 5/28/2009, p. 2.
[300] Council of the European Union 5/28/2009, pp. 3–4.

competences and qualifications and with transnational mobility. Altogether, by this, it is hoped to achieve greater adaptability and employability of individuals on European labor markets.

- Second, the objective of "improving the quality and efficiency of education and training" has been concerned with the improvement of basic skills such as literacy and numeracy as well as with supporting excellence in sciences, technology and languages, Moreover, teacher training, educational leadership and governance, but also the development of quality assurance systems and the efficient use of resources have been addressed in the pursuit of the second objective.

- Third, the objective of "promoting equity, social cohesion and active citizenship" has been concerned with early childhood and inclusive education trying to help all people acquire job-specific and life skills. Other issues dealt with are cultural and intercultural values and competences, the integration of migrants and minority groups and the promotion of second chance or third chance schools.

- Fourth, the objective of "enhancing creativity and innovation, including entrepreneurship at all levels of education and training" has been concerned with the acquisition of transversal skills, learning-to-learn skills and technological skills as well as with cultural awareness and personal fulfillment, and with the creation of an environment in which various stakeholders can innovate.

In order to monitor the Member States' performance in the cooperative pursuit of the four strategic objectives and the further development of national education systems, benchmarks were agreed upon. Originally, five such benchmarks were defined, however, meanwhile, two more benchmarks were added to the list concerned with mobility and employed tertiary education graduates.

Adult participation in lifelong learning
With a view to increasing the participation of adults in lifelong learning, particularly that of the low-skilled:
— By 2020, an average of at least 15 % of adults should participate in lifelong learning.

Low achievers in basic skills
With a view to ensuring that all learners attain an adequate level of basic skills, especially in reading, mathematics and science:
— By 2020, the share of low-achieving 15-years olds in reading, mathematics and science should be less than 15 %.

Tertiary level attainment

Given the increasing demand for higher education attainment, and whilst acknowledging the equal importance of vocational education and training:

— By 2020, the share of 30-34 year olds with tertiary educational attainment should be at least 40 %.

Early leavers from education and training

As a contribution to ensuring that a maximum number of learners complete their education and training:

— By 2020, the share of early leavers from education and training should be less than 10 %.

Early childhood education

With a view to increasing participation in early childhood education as a foundation for later educational success, especially in the case of those from disadvantaged backgrounds:

— By 2020, at least 95 % of children between 4 years old and the age for starting compulsory primary education should participate in early childhood education.[301]

[Later added benchmarks]

at least 20% of higher education graduates and 6% of 18-34 year-olds with an initial vocational qualification should have spent some time studying or training abroad.

the share of employed graduates (aged 20-34 with at least upper secondary education attainment and having left education 1-3 years ago) should be at least 82%.[302]

The ET 2020 policy dimension comprises five institutionalized areas of ET: early childhood education, schools, higher education, vocational education and training, and adult learning. Moreover, it includes four other policy areas, namely that of international cooperation and policy dialogue, innovation in education, multilingualism and migrants and education. Topics that are addressed under the umbrella of a European education area are quality in early childhood education and care, mutual recognition of diplomas, language learning, key competences, digital education and common values. In line with the ET 2020 Conclusion, the governance approach is constructed on the basis of a number of elements.

---

[301] Council of the European Union 5/28/2009, Annex 1.

[302] European Commission. European Policy Cooperation [website]

- First, the ten-year ET 2020 work program is structured, just as the Rolling Agenda, in cycles with every cycle concentrating on priority areas proposed by the Commission and adopted by the Council. Priority areas ought to be flexible as to allow for an optimal cooperation between Member States.
- Second, progress reports, process monitoring and the dissemination of results ought to guarantee visible and transparent performance assessment, the possibility to constantly adapt measures to new priorities and mutual learning.
- Third, mutual learning is relevant for the interaction with expert groups, in reviewing studies, or when engaging in peer activities and online platforms.[303] Altogether, evidence-based policy making and evidence-based policy learning are the core of the governance approach of the OMC.

International cooperation and policy dialogue are used to implement the ET 2020 work program. To this end several soft governance instruments are used, all of which together pertain to the OMC logic of mutual learning and policy transfer. Among those instruments are "Working Groups, composed of experts nominated by Member States and key stakeholders (…) [and] Peer Learning Activities (PLAs), hosted by a Member State to showcase existing good practice at the national level or to explore a particular issue with other Member States (…)". Other, even softer instruments are peer reviews and peer counseling. "Peer Reviews involve a group of Member States providing guidance to another Member State on a specific national challenge [...] Peer counselling brings together experienced peers from a small number of national administrations to provide advice (at the request of a Member State) on designing or implementing a policy as a response to a specific national challenge".[304]

What is so particular about the ET 2020 is that it is a real framework program that brings together two DG's, the Member States governments and public service, and various of stakeholders to work on issues of ET. It is interesting to note that in 2019, there exists a shared responsibility for the management and administration of the ET 2020 between the *DG for Education, Youth, Sports and Culture* and the *DG for Employment, Social Affairs and Inclusion*. Because of the frequent changes of the DG's portfolios in consequence of political decisions, a brief overview of the portfolio allocation in 2019 will be provided.

---

[303] Council of the European Union 5/28/2009, p. 5.
[304] European Commission. European Policy Cooperation [website]

For nearly twenty years, the *DG for Education and Culture* (DG EAC) was responsible for all matters of ET – compulsory school, higher education as well as vocational education and training and adult learning. At the end of 2014, when the Commission of Jean Claude Juncker took office, however, VET and the labor market-oriented parts of adult learning and higher education were transferred to the *DG for Employment, Social Affairs and Inclusion* (DG EMPL) and integrated in the umbrella name of skills and qualifications. The former DG EAC was slightly reformed and is now in charge of what in the past would have been general education, while DG EMPL is now in charge of all the areas that in the past would have been classified as vocational training.

The flagship policy programs administered by the current DG EAC are the ERASMUS+, the Horizon 2020 or the Creative Europe funding schemes, which aim to provide young people with the possibility to move across Europe and improve their skills and employability.[305]

The DG EMPL currently administrates under shared responsibility, for instance, the European Social Fund (ESF), including the Youth Employment Initiative (YEI), the European Globalisation Adjustment Fund (EGF), and under its own direct responsibility the EU Programme for Employment and Social Innovation (EaSI). Moreover, DG EMPL is in charge of the CEDEFOP and the ETF agencies. These programs and agencies focus altogether on the issues of free movement of workers particularly pursued by means of initiatives for the validation and recognition of competences but also the issue of entrepreneurship education and digital skills in terms responding to the changing labor markets.[306]

A new skills agenda for Europe

The most recent policy document of great significance is the Commission Communication entitled *A New Skills Agenda for Europe* released in June 2016. Its purpose is to "streamline existing initiatives to better assist Member States in their national reforms (…) It seeks a shared commitment to reform in a number of areas where Union action brings most added value."[307]

Most important in this regard is that the proposals are related to three areas: improving the quality and relevance of skills formation; making skills and qualifications more visible and comparable; and improving skills

---

[305] European Commission 2016a.
[306] European Commission 2016b.
[307] European Commission 6/10/2016, p. 3.

intelligence and information for better career choices.[308] In these areas, lines of action were defined to organize the policy work of the Commission and to structure the discourse.

Below the ten actions that have been worked on in the context of the new skills agenda are listed. They can be found in the Commission Communication[309] and on the Commission website.[310]

- *Upskilling Pathways: New Opportunities for Adults:* Literacy, numeracy and digital skills for low-skilled adults and second chance education to acquire qualifications.
- *European Qualifications Framework:* Comparability of qualifications, recognition of learning outcomes to allow for workers' and learners' mobility and for labor market supply and demand.
- *Digital Skills and Jobs Coalition:* Improving digital skills of the population and cooperation among actors from education, industries and public contexts.
- *Blueprint for Sectoral Cooperation on Skills:* Framework to identify skill gaps in selected industries and to develop measures for cooperation to close these gaps.
- *EU Skills Profile Tool Kit for Third-Country Nationals:* Tools to support the identification of skills of migrants, refugees and asylum seekers from non-EU countries.
- *Vocational education and training (VET):* Measures to bring forward the modernization of VET systems.
- *Key competences:* Release a revision of the key competences for lifelong learning focusing on entrepreneurial competences and competences needed for innovation.
- *Europass:* Revision of the existing Europass framework to make the presentation of skills and competences easier.
- *Graduate Tracking:* Measures to help identify the competences and performance of higher education graduates.
- *Analyzing and sharing of best practice on brain flows:* Instruments to organize information flows on the movement of people within Europe and to better manage their potential.

[308] European Commission 6/10/2016, p. 3.
[309] European Commission 6/10/2016, Annex.
[310] Employment, Social Affairs and Inclusion. New Skills Agenda for Europe. [website]

Chapter summary

Since 2000, ET has been among the EU's priority topics. The Conclusions of the Lisbon European Council reinforced ET based on the assumption that it would contribute to making the EU the most advanced and most socially cohesive knowledge-based economy in the world. To this end, the Council defined indicators, benchmarks, and common objectives to monitor the Member States' progress. The Rolling Agenda and the OMC were devised and implemented to govern the policymaking process in the Council as well as to structure cooperation between various stakeholders.

In the first few years, lifelong learning was the predominant discourse. A number of policy documents were released with regard to lifelong learning which introduced a new vocabulary including the *trias* of formal, non-formal, and informal learning; the distinction between lifelong and life wide learning; or the topics of validation and learning outcomes.

Among the most discussed measures is the *European Qualifications Framework* (EQF), which was proposed in 2008 and serves as a translation device for qualifications between Member States. Its main objective is in line with earlier attempts to the recognition of qualifications, namely to make learning outcomes transparent and comparable across Europe and to facilitate workers and learner mobility. Whether the EQF meets this objective, cannot yet be assessed satisfactorily.

For adult and continuing education, the last twenty years have proven beneficial. The evolution of the topic of quality in ACE was discussed and it was pointed out that over the years, quality was more and more linked to issues like governance or professionalization. The key messages presented by the Thematic Working Group on quality in adult learning indicate the situation of ACE in Europe, which is characterized by national idiosyncrasies on one hand and an insidious convergence of practice and politics on the other hand.

Since 2010, the ET 2020 Framework has organized ET politics in line with the Europe 2020 Strategy. This framework, including its policy focus and its governance methods, clearly indicates that the EU has effectively managed to reduce political tensions of the past by focusing on commonalities instead of differences and by opening up the policy formation process to networks and non-political stakeholders. Member States, therefore, can comply with supranational initiatives without fearing that they will have to give up their core political or cultural standpoints and values; a fear that has impeded ET policy for many decades.

7. Closing remarks

This study recounted the historical development of *education and training* (ET) in the *European Communities* (EC) and the *European Union* (EU) from a side issue to a topic of political priority. The focus was on the formation of policies and governance, in particular with regard to the ET policy sub-area of *adult and continuing education* (ACE).

The historical study sought to answer the following two research questions: which historical developments have shaped the current EU policy and the current EU governance in the field of education and training? In what way have the EC and the EU addressed adult and continuing education in the history of education and training? As a means to seek answers, four historical phases were derived from the relevant academic literature and a fifth chapter was added in which primary law, vocational training and general education were discussed.

The starting point of the first historical phase was fixed at the turn of the 1960s to the 1970s when political leaders recognized that general education was relevant in the pursuit of the EC's goals. The Council resolution on education from 1976 marked the end of this first phase. After a transition period of five years, the beginning of the second phase was set with the meeting of education ministers in June 1981 and concluded with a discussion of the most important judgments of the *European Court of Justice* (ECJ) and its implications for the implementation of the action programs COMETT and ERAMSUS.

Phase three continued with the 1993 *White Paper on growth, competitiveness and employment*, covered the rise of *lifelong learning* (LLL) and looked at how the role of the Commission changed within this context. In the fourth and last phase, various developments that occurred after 2000 were addressed, whereby the focus was on the policy proposals concerning quality in ACE and on the *European framework for cooperation in education and training* – ET 2020.

The *timeline* in the Annex of this book summarizes the main findings of the historical study. It is an attempt to comprehend key historical moments and turning points, policy discourses, and the role of adult and continuing education in one single illustration. The key at the center right of the diagram explains the composition of the timeline. In short, from top to bottom: (1) key moments/turning points concerning the accretion of competences of the EC/EU, (2) the phases of the historical study, (3) the policy and governance focus and key topics, (4) the development of adult learning/adult and continuing education.

Final assessment of the history of education and training

In 1979, the editors of the *European Journal of Education* were preparing an issue on the topic of European education policy. According to the chief editor, Gabriel Fragniere, the group was asking researchers and academics all over Europe for contributions so that a debate could be started concerning the potential and future directions of a common policy.

> The time seemed ripe for (...) a debate about the particular problem which European integration has to face. In the mind of many Europeans, the problem of education is indeed a key element in political integration. The success of the education action programme (...) was a convincing factor in thinking that after three years, at a moment when a new programme of action was being prepared, we would be able to develop an interesting debate.[1]

As it turned out, the editors seriously struggled to arrange the issue because all they received were some comments on recent initiatives, but they received not enough contributions to initiate a serious debate. These troubles led Fragniere to gain the impression that European education policy had not yet developed into a subject appropriate for academic treatment. After some further inquiry, Fragniere realized that indeed there was not even a proper vocabulary constituting a European education policy and that could consequently serve as a point of reference for researchers, a reason for criticism or bear a potential for future development.

In the first chapter of the historical study, it was stressed that the fact that insufficient provision for vocational training and no provision at all for general education were included in EC primary law, was impeding the creation of an education policy on a formal level. Education was too sensitive of a topic as to be considered a topic of mutual concern. Only direct, hierarchical governing intervention by means of primary law provision concerning the four fundamental freedoms was it possible to eventually break up the barriers and encourage the adoption of proper education policies by the Member States in the mid-1980s. Only in 1992, when the EU was formed, did the Treaty define the responsibilities with regard to ET and, therefore, also the an indirect, more coordinating governance approach; however, the fact that the two areas of general education and vocational training are still separate,

---

[1] Fragniére 1979, p. 311.

though, leaves room for discussion as it suggests that there is a difference in the way the EU is supposed to treat general education as opposed to vocational training.

As was indicated in the second chapter, ambitiously acting individuals based in the Commission were trying to advance education politics by implicit competences. People like Ralf Dahrendorf, Hywel Ceri Jones or Alan Smith were able to make substantial gains through strategic political thinking and a clear vision of what ET and ET politics should be and how they should develop. By 1979, when Gabriel Fragniere wrote the just mentioned article, a small but advancing supranational institutional structure had already been established in the Commission. Moreover, the Education Committee was set up as a unique intergovernmental governance arrangement, in the supranational Parliament a committee concerned with the question of education was created and the first measures had already been adopted in the intergovernmental Council and were starting to gain impetus.

Considering these ambivalent developments – the impasse on a formal level and the improvement on the institutional level – one was to expect that enough material would have been available to start a debate about European education policy. In fact, that was apparently not the case and somewhat disappointed, Fragniere stated,

> [w]e wanted to discuss the future policy in education not the achievements of the past [...] Indeed, it appears that a European policy in education is in many respects still to be invented. [...] Not only are the issues not yet well defined, but they are not mature enough for constituting the object of thorough analysis or constructive developments.[2]

At the beginning of the third chapter, it was speculated that in the late 1970s, the political climate outside the inner circles of the Commission and the Directorate General for Science, Research and Education appeared to not be in favor of a common European education policy. An institutional crisis paralyzed the Council of education ministers over a period of almost three years from 1978 to 1980. The crisis could only be resolved when it was decided to direct the future of education away from the traditional issues of education, firmly rooted within national contexts, towards more labor market-oriented issues, subjected to the increasing speed of economic globalization and, thus, affecting all Member States on equal terms.

In 1981, after durable negotiations, the education division that had been located in the DG Science, Research and Education was transferred to the

---

[2] Fragniére 1979, p. 311.

DG Employment and Social Affairs where it merged the vocational training division. This transfer was positive for general education and had a tremendous impact on the general advancement of ET. For instance, it became suddenly possible to allocate higher shares of the budget to ET simply because it was much more related with issues of employment and labor market – topics, which had been high on the political agenda in the early 1980s.

ACE policies of the 1980s reflected very clearly the changes concerning the organization of work that were taking place during that decade. The rise of service occupations and the globalization of labor markets did not go unnoticed by the European politicians who utilized ACE and VET to further strengthen the construction of a European single market. Progress in ICT, the search for flexibility and mobility and the connection between the world of work and the world of education drove ET forward on the 1980s political agenda. The action programs COMETT, Eurotecnet and FORCE were the manifest proof of this policy focus.

The 1990s marked a formative period in which developments with far-reaching implications for ET politics occurred, even though from a long-term perspective the 1990s were only the final phase of the mainstreaming that had started in the early 1970s and culminated with the Lisbon Council in 2000. The documents consulted in the fourth chapter confirm that through a pervasive policy discourse based on the concept of lifelong learning, the driving forces in the EU continued to bring ET into the mainstream economic politics; however, there was hardly enough space to fully accommodate the social claims attached to the idea of lifelong learning.

From an analytical point of view, perhaps it was to a lesser extent the idea of learning across a person's lifespan that was so intriguing to politicians and civil servants but rather more intriguing that the concept of lifelong learning could be used as a "coalition magnet"[3] to attract and assemble heterogeneous claims, particularly in combination with the fears triggered by an increasingly knowledge-based economy and society. At the same time, these "coalitions magnets" were part of the formation of an indirect governance arrangement based on commonalities between the Member States.

According to Anja Jakobi, "the idea of a knowledge society has helped countries to increasingly perceive themselves as similar with respect to necessary educational changes." This had a significant impact on the governance of ET since the Member States started to "exchange policies which, some decades ago, would have been assumed to be bound to and determined by

---

[3] Béland and Cox 2016.

specific national traditions."[4] Also Anders Hingel, pointed out that at the turn from the 1990s to the 2000s, a new governance approach was taking shape out of the Member States' willingness to find common goals instead of arguing differences.[5]

In the fifth chapter, it was argued that in the first decade of the new millennium, the new indirect, coordinating governance approach, whose topics were agreed in the Rolling Agenda in 1999 and whose organization has become manifest in the *Open Method of Coordination*, reinforced a type of governance that Martin Lawn and Sotiria Grek call 'governing at a distance'.[6] By governing at a distance, Lawn refers to the specific practice by which the EU abstains from direct intervention and legislative measures and instead organizes a policy discourse, coordinates the formation of common goals and monitors the performance of Member States in the pursuit of these goals. All this happens on the grounds of indicators and benchmarks commonly agreed upon by the Member States supported by so-called policy learning methods such as best-practice examples, peer-learning activities, peer-review or peer-consultation.

One of the topics that is perfectly suited for such an approach is the topic of quality, which was discussed in relation to *adult and continuing education* (ACE) in the fifth chapter. Concerning quality within ACE, by the beginning of the decade, quality was a rather weakly operationalized concept that was used to indicate almost anything. The Communication and the Action Plan on adult learning from 2006 and 2007, then, stressed the contribution of staff professionalization to quality and the renewed agenda on adult learning from 2011 eventually shifted attention to issues such as accreditation of providers, competence profiles, financing schemes, matching skills supply and skills demand or cooperation between all stakeholders.

Contributing to the quality of education and training systems has since the Maastricht Treaty been the overarching responsibility of the EU. In the pursuit of education systems with a good quality, it is possible to control and govern the performance rather easily, since the basic ideas to which quality assurance refers are those of standardization, output assessment and customer satisfaction. Defining what would satisfy the potential beneficiaries of highly educated people in terms of standard outcomes and measuring the achievement of these standard outcomes has become the prime approach to

---

[4] Jakobi 2007, p. 40.
[5] Hingel 2001.
[6] Lawn and Grek 2012.

the politics of quality in education and is, in fact, nothing more than the logic on which *New Public Management* (NPM) in general and the OMC in particular operate.

Taking seventy years into account, it can be said that the history of *education and training* (ET) in the *European Communities* (EC) and the *European Union* (EU) by and large reflects the ever-increasing importance of ET in Europe that effectively took off during the late 1970s when it was realized that the progress of technology and its implications for the society in general and for the economy in particular demand highly educated and well-trained citizens. In fact, the transformation of the societal context has been regulating the recognition of ET in the political sphere. The more the economic, social and cultural circumstances have demanded well-educated and well-trained individuals, the more European politics have embraced cooperation with regard to ET. The history, therefore, shows no coherent development of ET politics on the basis of pedagogical considerations. In the long run, it seems, an instrumental character of an economic rationale has prevailed over concerns related to the actual learning and education of individuals. The question of *what is best for the learning and education of individuals* has less often been posed compared to the question *how can learning contribute to economic prosperity and social cohesion.*

The primary motive for political actors for a stronger commitment to ET has been the creation, first, of a common market and then the competitive advantage in global economic competition. Organizing ET in a way that facilitates people moving across borders for professional or educational reasons or promoting European identity and languages have been essential elements of European education politics in the first phases. Later, high quality ET necessary to remain competitive and innovative in international trade markets and to keep up to date with technological progress and to lower the unemployment rates has become the main concern. Lastly, broad access to ET and, in particular, to continuing education and training has been and remains essential to a socially, and overarchingly, cohesive Europe.

Considering the history of the EC and the EU as a whole, with all its ups and downs, it can be said that the history of education and training is one of the best-practice examples of how to construct, develop and manage a policy field moving from no political cooperation at all to an impressive compliance of Member States with supranational governance. Compared with other political areas, perhaps, if some more policy measures were as successful and as much appreciated as for example ERASMUS, the "concrete achievements which first create a de facto solidarity" Robert Schuman aspired to in 1951,[7] would most likely prevail in the academic and public perception over much of the perennial negative sentiments towards European politics.

Implications for future research

The narrative that was unfolded and the findings that were presented in this book are the results of more than four years of intensive research and writing. The line of action arose out of the personal conviction that it is necessary to understand the history of ET politics in order to critically reflect upon, and discuss the current ET politics. The purpose of this study, thus, was to process historical data and rearrange it so that the results may help other scholars with their research, education and training practitioners with the comprehension of discourse and policy makers with their reform choices.

To this end, extensive desk research and an in-depth examination of legislative and political documents released by the EC and EU institutions and related actors over the course of the last seventy years was conducted. In order to contextualize the historical study, the relevant academic literature concerning ACE in Europe and ET in the EU was discussed, important concepts were defined for a conceptual framework and the political system as well as the governance of the EU was described.

Since this book gives a broad overview of the history, some occurrences and debates could not be problematized. For future research, therefore, it is not only desirable to engage in empirical research on European ET and ACE politics, but it is also valuable to deepen the historical knowledge base. Some the issues (among many) considered worthy of further investigation are the following:

- The years from 1951 to 1970 and what impact the provisions in the TECSC on re-training of industrial workers and on the ESF scheme in the TEEC had on ACE in selected Member States.
- The individual actors that shaped ET in the early years (Spinelli, Dahrendorf, Delors), how their biography formed their approach to ET and what implications this had for the politics they promoted.
- The court cases of the 1980s and the question inasmuch the judgments are consistent with the legislation in selected Member States in particular as concerns the broad definition of vocational training and its implications for the practice and politics of ACE.

---

[7] Fondation Robert Schuman 2011, p. 1.

- The development of the European labor market in a long-term perspective from 1950 to 2020 and how ET politics in the EC and the EU has responded to the developments.
- Selected examples of the cyclic process of politics (e.g. from the first action programs to ERASMUS+, or the quality discourse since 2000) and how political actors have learned from the outcome and impact evaluation to adapt, improve or change policy proposals or political output.

Whether it be historical or contemporary research, examination should take into consideration the fact that even the most valuable pedagogical ideal or the best concept or reform strategy can only become as effective as the circumstances allow it to. Especially research should, therefore, sharpen its senses and conceive ET as a phenomenon that has implications on many areas of individual, community and political life and is equally dependent on the developments in these areas.

Appendix: Illustrated summarized results

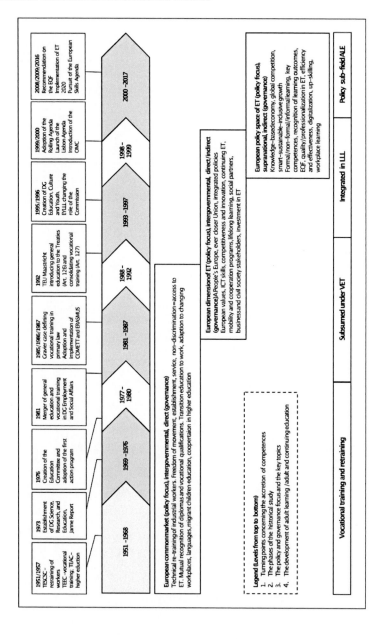

Publication bibliography

Alexiadou, Nafsika (2007): The Europeanisation of Education Policy: researching changing governance and 'new' modes of coordination. In *Research in Comparative and International Education* 2 (2), pp. 102–116. DOI: 10.2304/rcie.2007.2.2.102.

Arnold, Hans (1993): Europa am Ende? Die Auflösung von EG und NATO. München: Piper.

Arnold, Rolf (1999): Vom autodidactic zum facilitative turn - Weiterbildung auf dem Weg ins 21. Jahrhundert´. In Rolf Arnold, Wiltrud Gieseke (Eds.): Die Weiterbildungsgesellschaft. Band 1. Bildungstheoretische Grundlagen und Perspektiven. Neuwied: Luchterhand, pp. 3–14.

Aschemann, Birgit (2015): "Adult Learning" und Europäische Koordination: Wohin geht die Reise? Schlussfolgerungen aus einer aktuellen ET 2020-Arbeitsgruppe. In *Magazin erwachsenenbildung.at* (25), 06-01 - 06-13. Available online at https://erwachsenenbildung.at/magazin/15-25/06_aschemann.pdf, checked on 11/28/2017.

Aust, Kirsten; Schmidt-Hertha, Bernhard (2012): Qualitätsmanagement als Steuerungsinstrument im Weiterbildungsbereich. In *REPORT - Zeitschrift für Weiterbildungsforschung* 35 (2), pp. 43–55. DOI: 10.3278/REP1202W043.

Barnard, Catherine (1992): The Maastricht agreement and education: one step forward, two steps back. In *Education and the Law* 4 (3), pp. 123–134. DOI: 10.1080/0953996920040302.

Barnard, Catherine (1995): The Treaty on European Union, Education and Vocational Training. In David Philips (Ed.): Aspects of Education and the European Union. Oxford: Triangle Books, pp. 13–28.

Baumeler, Carmen; Engelage, Sonja (2017): Neue Steuerung durch Klassifikationssysteme: Nationale Qualifikationsrahmen in der Schweiz, Österreich und Deutschland. In Axel Bolder, Helmut Bremer, Rudolf Epping (Eds.): Bildung für Arbeit unter neuer Steuerung. Wiesbaden: Springer VS, pp. 223–246.

Bechtel, Mark; Lattke, Susanne; Nuissl, Ekkehard (2005): Porträt Weiterbildung Europäische Union. Bielefeld: W. Bertelsmann.

Bektchieva, Jana (2004): Die Europäische Bildungspolitik nach Maastricht. Münster: LIT.

Béland, Daniel; Cox, Robert Henry (2016): Ideas as coalition magnets: coalition building, policy entrepreneurs, and power relations. In *Journal of European Public Policy* 23 (3), pp. 428–445. DOI: 10.1080/13501763.2015.1115533.

Bell, Daniel (1979): Die nachindustrielle Gesellschaft. Reinbeck bei Hamburg: Rowohlt.

Blitz, Brad K. (2003): From Monnet to Delors: Educational Co-operation in the European Union. In *Contemporary European History* 12 (2), pp. 197–212. DOI: 10.1017/S0960777303001140.

Blum, Sonja; Schubert, Klaus (2009): Politikfeldanalyse. Wiesbaden: VS Verlag für Sozialwissenschaften.

Blumenthal, Julia von (2014): Governance im und durch den Staat. Politikwissenschaftliche Perspektiven der Governance-Forschung. In Katarina Maag Merki, Roman Langer, Herbert Altrichter (Eds.): Educational Governance als Forschungsperspektive. Wiesbaden: VS Verlag für Sozialwissenschaften, pp. 87–110.

Bolder, Axel; Bremer, Helmut; Epping, Rudolf (Eds.) (2017): Bildung für Arbeit unter neuer Steuerung. Wiesbaden: Springer VS.

Borchardt, Klaus-Dieter (2010): The ABC of European Union Law. Luxembourg: Publications Office of the European Union. Available online at DOI: 10.2830/13717.

Borg, Carmel; Mayo, Peter (2005): The EU Memorandum on lifelong learning. Old wine in new bottles? In *Globalisation, Societies and Education* 3 (2), pp. 203–225. DOI: 10.1080/14767720500167082.

Botkin, James W.; Elmandjra, Mahdi; Malitza, Mircea (1979): Das Menschliche Dilemma. Zukunft und Lernen. Herausgegeben und eingeleitet von Aurelio Peccei Präsident des Club of Rome. München: Molden.

Brine, Jacky (1995): Educational and Vocational Policy and Construction of the European Union. In *International Studies in Sociology of Education* 5 (2), pp. 145–163. DOI: 10.1080/0962021950050202.

Bruno, Isabelle; Jacquot, Sophie; Mandin, Lou (2006): Europeanization through its instrumentation. Benchmarking, mainstreaming and the open method of co-ordination … toolbox or Pandora's box? In *Journal of European Public Policy* 13 (4), pp. 519–536. DOI: 10.1080/13501760600693895.

Brüsemeister, Thomas (2011): Educational governance: Aufriss von Perspektiven für die empirische Bildungsforschung. In Christiane Hof, Joachim Ludwig, Burkhard Schäffer (Eds.): Steuerung - Regulation - Gestaltung. Governance-Prozesse in der Erwachsenenbildung zwischen Struktur und Handlung ; Dokumentation der Jahrestagung der Sektion Erwachsenenbildung der Deutschen Gesellschaft für Erziehungswissenschaft vom 23. - 25. September 2010 an der TU Chemnitz. Baltmannsweiler: Schneider, pp. 7–16.

Buiskool, Bert-Jan; Broek, Simon (2014): Quality in Adult Learning: EU Policies and Shifting Paradigms? In George K. Zarifis, Maria N. Gravani (Eds.): Challenging the 'European Area of Lifelong Learning'. A Critical Response. Dordrecht: Springer, pp. 189–202.

Clement, Ute (2015): Politische Steuerungslogik berfulicher Bildung. Zentrifugale und zentripetale Kräfte in der Governance beruflicher Bildung. In Sandra Bohlinger, Andreas Fischer (Eds.): Lehrbuch europäische Berufsbildungspolitik. Grundlagen, Herausforderungen und Perspektiven. Bielefeld: W. Bertelsmann, pp. 25–56.

Commission of the European Communities (2001): Draft Detailed Work Programme for the Follow-up of the Report on the Concrete Objectives of Education and Training Systems. COM (2001) 501 final. Available online at http://aei.pitt.edu/63037/1/COM_(2001)_501_final.pdf.

Coombs, Philip H. (1968): The World Educational Crisis. A Systems Analysis. New York: Oxford University Press. Available online at http://www.unesco.org/education/nfsunesco/pdf/COOMBS_E.PDF, checked on 6/8/2018.

Corbett, Anne (2003): Ideas, Institutions and Policy Entrepreneurs: towards a new history of higher education in the European Community. In *European Journal of Education* 38 (3), pp. 315–330. DOI: 10.1111/1467-3435.00150.

Corbett, Anne (2005): Universities and the Europe of knowledge: ideas, institutions and policy entrepreneurship in European Community higher education policy, 1955-2005. Basingstoke: Palgrave Macmillan [could not be accessed].

Cort, Pia (2010): Stating the Obvious: the European Qualifications Framework is not a neutral evidence-based policy tool. In *European Educational Research Journal* 9 (3), pp. 304–316. DOI: 10.2304/eerj.2010.9.3.304.

Dahrendorf, Ralf (1965): Bildung ist Bürgerrecht. Plädoyer für eine aktive Bildungspolitik: Nannen Verlag.

Dahrendorf, Ralf (1978): Wenn uns die Arbeit ausgeht. Die Zukunft verlangt neue Gestaltung des sozialne Lebens. Zeit Online (Nr. 39/1978). Available online at https://www.zeit.de/1978/39/wenn-uns-die-arbeit-ausgeht, updated on 11/21/2012, checked on 4/29/2018.

Dehmel, Alexandra (2006): Making a European Area of Lifelong Learning a Reality? Some Critical Reflections on the European Union's Lifelong Learning Policies. In *Comparative Education* 42 (1), pp. 49–62. DOI: 10.1080/03050060500515744.

Dellori, Claudia (2016): Die absolute Metapher 'lebenslanges Lernen'. Eine Argumentationsanalyse. Mit einem Geleitwort von Jochen Kade. Wiesbaden: Springer VS.

Dinan, Desmond (2012): How Did We Get Here? In Elizabeth Bomberg, John Peterson, Richard Corbett (Eds.): The European Union: How does it work. 3rd edition. Oxford: Oxford University Press, pp. 23–46.

Egger, Rudolf (2009): Die Bedeutung und die Konsequenzen des Europäischen und des Nationalen Qualifikationsrahmens für die Entwicklung der Volkshochschule. Wien: LIT.

Eggers, Philipp; Hablitzel, Hans (2002): Schranken einer Europäisierung des Weiterbildungsrechts - Bemerkungen zu Art. 149 (ex-Art. 126) und 150 (ex-Art. 127) EGV. In Björn Pappe, Karl Pütz (Eds.): Die Zukunft des lebenslangen Lernens. The Future of Lifelong Learning. Festschrift zum 75. Geburtstag von Franz Pöggeler. Frankfurt: Peter Lang, pp. 167–184.

ERT (1995): Education for European. Towards the Learning Society. A Report from the European Round Table of Industrialists. Brussles: The European Round Table of Industrialists.

Ertl, Hubert (2006): European Union Policies in Education and Training: The Lisbon Agenda as a Turning Point? In *Comparative Education* 42 (1), pp. 5–27. DOI: 10.1080/03050060500515652.

European Commission (2016a): Strategic Plan 2016-2020. DG Education and Culture. Available online at https://ec.europa.eu/info/sites/info/files/strategic-plan-2016-2020-dg-eac_march2016_en.pdf, checked on 11/23/2019.

European Commission (2016b): Strategic Plan 2016-2020. Employment, Social Affairs and Inclusion DG. Available online at https://ec.europa.eu/info/sites/info/files/strategic-plan-2016-2020-dg-empl_march2016_en.pdf, checked on 11/23/2019.

European Commission. European Policy Cooperation. Available online at https://ec.europa.eu/education/policies/european-policy-cooperation/et2020-framework_en, checked on 9/17/2019.

Fahle, Klaus (1989): Die Politik der Europäischen Gemeinschaften in den Bereichen Erziehung, Bildung und Wissenschaft. Frankfurt am Main: Max-Träger Stiftung der GEW.

Faulstich, Peter (1985): Arbeitslosigkeit als Aufgabe für die Erwachsenenbildung? In Peter Faulstich, Hermann G. Ebner (Eds.): Erwachsenenbildung und Arbeitslosigkeit. Zur Praxis eines schwierigen Verhältnisses. München: Hueber, pp. 12–44.

Faure, Edgar; Herrera, Felipe; Abdul-Razzak, Kaddoura; Lopes, Henri; Petrovsky, Arthur V.; Rahnema, Majid; Champion Ward, Frederick (1972): Learning to be. The world of education today and tomorrow. Paris: UNESCO Publishing. Available online at http://www.unesco.org/education/pdf/15_60.pdf, checked on 6/8/2018.

Federighi, Paolo (1999): Introduction. In Paolo Federighi (Ed.): Glossary of Adult Learning in Europe. With assistance of Willem Bax, Lucien Bosselaers. Hamburg: The European Association for the Education of Adults; Unesco Institute for Education, pp. 3–11.

Field, John (1997): The learning Society and the European Union: A Critical Assessment of Supranational Education Policy Formation. In *Journal of Studies in International Education*, pp. 73–92. DOI: 10.1177/102831539700100205.

Field, John (2006): Lifelong learning and the new educational order. 2nd, revised ed. Stoke-on-Trent: Trentham.

Filla, Wilhelm; Gruber, Elke; Jug, Jurij (Eds.) (2002): Von Zeitenwende zu Zeitenwende. Erwachsenenbildung von 1939 bis 1989. Innsbruck: Studien Verlag.

Flynn, James (1988): Vocational Training in Community Law and Practice. In *Yearbook of European Law* 8, pp. 59–85. DOI: 10.1093/yel/8.1.59.

Fondation Robert Schuman (2011): Declaration of 9th May 1950 delivered b Robert Schuman. European Issue, No. 204, 10th May 2011. Fondation Robert Schuman. Available online at https://www.robert-schuman.eu/en/doc/questions-d-europe/qe-204-en.pdf, updated on 7/22/2018.

Fragniére, Gabriel (1979): Editorial: Is It too Early for a European Education Policy? In *European Journal of Education* 14 (4), pp. 311–312. Available online at http://www.jstor.org/stable/1503281.

Fritsch, Anke (1998): Europäische Bildungspolitik nach Maastricht - Zwischen Kontinuität und neuen Dimensionen. Eine Untersuchung am Beispiel der Programme ERASMUS/SOKRTES und LEONARDO. Frankfurt am Main: Peter Lang.

Gaio, Ana (2015): Policy formation in the European Community - the case of culture: [unpublished doctoral thesis, City University London]. Available online at http://openaccess.city.ac.uk/13689/1/Gaio%2C%20Ana.pdf, checked on 6/28/2018.

Geiss, Michael (2017): Die Politik des lebenslangen Lernens in Europa nach dem Boom. In *ZfW* 40 (2), pp. 211–228. DOI: 10.1007/s40955-017-0093-1.

Gornitzka, Ase (2006a): The Open Method of Coordination as practice - A watershed in European education policy? Working Paper No. 16, December 2006. Centre for European Studies, University of Oslo. Available online at http://www.sv.uio.no/arena/english/research/publications/arena-working-papers/2001-2010/2006/wp06_16.pdf, checked on 11/28/2017.

Gornitzka, Ase (2006b): The Open Method of Coordination in European Education and Research Policy: Animating a Label. Paper presented at European Union Center of Excellence and School of Education University of Wisconsin, October 2006.

Gruber, Elke; Lenz, Werner (2016): Erwachsenen- und Weiterbildung Österreich. 3., überarb. Auflage. Bielefeld: W. Bertelsmann.

Hake, Barry J. (1999): Lifelong Learning Policies in the European Union: developments and issues. In *Compare* 29 (1), pp. 53–69. DOI: 10.1080/0305792990290105.

Hatzopoulos, Vassilis (2007): Why the Open Method of Coordination Is Bad For You. A Letter to the EU. In *European Law Journal* 13 (3), pp. 309–342. DOI: 10.1111/j.1468-0386.2007.00368.x.

Hausmann, Gottfried (1972): Einleitung. In Paul Lengrand (Ed.): Permanente Erziehung. Eine Einführung. München: Dokumentation, pp. 9–20.

Holford, John; Milana, Marcella (2014): Introduction. European Adult Education Policy in Question. In Marcella Milana, John Holford (Eds.): Adult education policy and the European Union. Theoretical and methodological perspectives. Rotterdam: Sense, pp. 1–13.

Holford, John; Milana, Marcella; Mohorčič Špolar, Vida (2014): Adult and lifelong education. The European Union, its member states and the world. In *International Journal of Lifelong Education* 33 (3), pp. 267–274. DOI: 10.1080/02601370.2014.911518.

Holzer, Boris (2015): Politische Soziologie. Baden-Baden: Nomos; UTB.

Hooghe, Liesbet (1999): Supranational Activists or Intergovernmental Agents? Explaining the Orientations of Senior Commission Officials Toward European Integration. In *Comparative Political Studies* 32 (4), pp. 435–463. DOI: 10.1177/0010414099032004002.

Humburg, Martin (2008): The Open Method of Coordination and European Integration. The Example of European Education Policy. Berlin Working Paper on European Integration No. 8. Available online at http://www.pol-soz.fu-berlin.de/polwiss/forschung/international/europa/Partner-und-Online-Ressourcen/arbeitspapiere/2008-8_Humburg_OpenMethodofCoordination.pdf, checked on 6/24/2018.

Ioannidou, Alexandra (2010): Steuerung im transnationalen Bildungsraum. Internationales Bildungsmonitoring zum Lebenslangen Lernen. Bielefeld: W. Bertelsmann.

Ioannidou, Alexandra (2014): The Adoption of an International Education Policy Agenda at National Level: Conceptual and Governance Issues. In George K. Zarifis (Ed.): Challenging the 'European area of lifelong learning'. A critical response. Dordrecht: Springer (19), pp. 203–215.

Jacobsson, Kerstin (2004): Soft regulation and the subtle transformation of states. The case of EU employment policy. In *Journal of European Social Policy* 14 (4), pp. 355–370.

Jakobi, Anja P. (2007): The Knowledge Society and Global Dynamics in Education Politics. In *European Educational Research Journal* 6 (1), pp. 39–51. DOI: 10.2304/eerj.2007.6.1.39.

Jarvis, Peter (2010): Adult education and lifelong learning. Theory and practice. 4th. ed. London: Routledge.

Käpplinger, Bernd (2015): Adult education research between field and rhizome - a bibliometrical analysis of conference programs of ESREA. In *RELA* 6 (2), pp. 139–157. DOI: 10.3384/rela.2000-7426.rela9061.

Keogh, Helen (2009): The state and development of adult learning and education in Europe, North America and Israel. Regional synthesis report. Hamburg: UNESCO Institute for Lifelong Learning. Available online at https://unesdoc.unesco.org/ark:/48223/pf0000182946, checked on 9/6/2017.

Knoepfel, Peter; Larrue, Corinne; Varone, Frédéric; Veit, Sylvia (2011): Politikanalyse. Opladen: Budrich; UTB.

Knoll, Joachim H. (1996): Internationale Weiterbildung und Erwachsenenbildung. Konzepte, Institutionen, Methoden. Darmstadt: Wissenschaftliche Buchgesellschaft.

Knoll, Joachim H. (2015): Horizontal and vertical derestriction of "adult education" - the historical German example and the contemporary view of education policy. In Uwe Gartenschlaeger, Esther Hirsch (Eds.): Adult education in an interconnected world. Cooperation in lifelong learning for sustainable development: Festschrift in honour of Heribert Hinzen. Bonn: DVV International, pp. 77–86.

Kopp-Malek, Tanja; Lindenthal, Alexandra; Koch, Martin (2009): Die Europäische Kommission als lernende Organisation? Die Umsetzung des umweltpolitischen Integrationsprinzips in ausgewählten Generaldirektionen der Europäischen Kommission. Wiesbaden: VS Verlag für Sozialwissenschaften.

La Porte, Caroline de (2011): Principal–agent theory and the Open Method of Co-ordination. The case of the European Employment Strategy. In

Journal of European Public Policy 18 (4), pp. 485–503. DOI: 10.1080/13501763.2011.560071.

Lange, Bettina; Alexiadou, Nafsika (2007): New Forms of European Governance in the Education Sector? A Preliminary Analysis of the Open Method of Coordination. In *European Educational Research Journal* 6 (4), pp. 321–334. DOI: 10.2304/eerj.2007.6.4.321.

Lawn, Martin (2011): Standardizing the European Education Policy Space. In *European Educational Research Journal* 10 (2), pp. 259–272. DOI: 10.2304/eerj.2011.10.2.259.

Lawn, Martin; Grek, Sotiria (2012): Europeanizing Education: governing a new policy space. Oxford: Symposium Books.

Lee, Moosung; Thayer, Tryggvi; Madyun, Na'im (2008): The Evolution of the European Union's Lifelong Learning Policies: An Institutional Learning Perspective. In *Comparative Education* 44 (4), pp. 445–463. DOI: 10.1080/03050060802481496.

Lengrand, Paul (Ed.) (1972): Permanente Erziehung. Eine Einführung. München: Dokumentation.

Lenz, Werner (1989a): Einleitung - Zur Lage der Erwachsenenbildung. 1989. In Werner Lenz (Ed.): Emanzipatorische Erwachsenenbildung. Bildung für Arbeit und Demokratie. Versammelte Aufsätze. München: Profil, pp. 9–16.

Lenz, Werner (1989b): Sucht die Erwachsenenbildung ein neues Selbstverständnis? Original erschienen als: Von der Volksbildung zur Weiterbildung. In: Die Österreichische Volkshochschule, Nr. 108, März 1978, 2-8. In Werner Lenz (Ed.): Emanzipatorische Erwachsenenbildung. Bildung für Arbeit und Demokratie. Versammelte Aufsätze. München: Profil, pp. 25–36.

Lima, Licínio C.; Guimarães, Paula (2011): European strategies in lifelong learning. A critical introduction. Opladen: Budrich.

Maurer, Andreas (2012): Parlamente in der EU. Stuttgart: Facultas; UTB.

May, Peter (1992): Policy Learning and Failure. In *Journal of Public Policy* 12 (4), pp. 331–354. Available online at http://www.jstor.org/stable/pdf/4007550.pdf.

Mayntz, Renate (2008): Von der Steuerungstheorie zu Global Governance. In Gunnar F. Schuppert, Michael Zürn (Eds.): Governance in einer sich wandelnden Welt. Wiesbaden: VS Verlag für Sozialwissenschaften (Politische Vierteljahresschrift, Sonderheft (41)), pp. 43–60.

Milana, Marcella (2012): Political globalization and the shift from adult education to lifelong learning. In *European Journal for Research on the Education and Learning of Adults* 3 (2), pp. 103–117. DOI: 10.3384/rela.2000-7426.rela0070.

Milana, Marcella (2014): Europeanisation and the changing nature of the (European) state. Implicatins for studying adult and lifelong education. In Marcella Milana, John Holford (Eds.): Adult education policy and the European Union. Theoretical and methodological perspectives. Rotterdam: Sense, pp. 73–90.

Mohorčič Špolar, Vida; Holford, John (2014): Adult Learning: From the Margins to the Mainstream. In Marcella Milana, John Holford (Eds.): Adult education policy and the European Union. Theoretical and methodological perspectives. Rotterdam: Sense, pp. 35–52.

Nationalrat der Bundesrepublik Österreich (3/21/2016): Bundesgesetz über den Nationalen Qualifikationsrahmen (NQR-Gesetz). BGBl. I Nr. 14/2016. Available online at https://www.ris.bka.gv.at/Dokumente/BgblAuth/BGBLA_2016_I_14/BGBLA_2016_I_14.pdfsig, checked on 7/21/2018.

Németh, Balázs (2016): Changes in the roles and functions of adult learning and education policies in Europe in the last twenty-five years. In Simona Sava, Petr Novotny (Eds.): Researches in Adult Learning and Education: the European Dimension. Florence: Firenze University Press, pp. 27–42.

Nordin, Andreas (2011): Making the Lisbon Strategy Happen: a new phase of lifelong learning discourse in European policy? In *European Educational Research Journal* 10 (1), pp. 11–20. DOI: 10.2304/eerj.2011.10.1.11.

Nourse, Victoria; Schaffer, Gregory (2009): Varieties of New Legal Realism: Can a New Legal Order Prompt a New Legal Theory? In *Cornell Law Review* 95 (61), pp. 61–138. Available online at http://www.lawschool.cornell.edu/research/cornell-law-review/upload/Nourse-Shaffer-final.pdf, checked on 9/1/2017.

Nuissl, Ekkehard (1999): Bildungsinstitutionen, Staat und selbstorganisiertes Lernen. In Rolf Arnold, Wiltrud Gieseke (Eds.): Die Weiterbildungsgesellschaft. Band 2. Bildungspolitische Konsequenzen. Neuwied: Luchterhand, pp. 3–15.

Nuissl, Ekkehard (2010): Internationale Erwachsenenbildung. In Rolf Arnold, Ekkehard Nuissl, Sigrid Nolda (Eds.): Wörterbuch Erwachsenenbildung. 2., überarb. Aufl. Bad Heilbrunn: Klinkhardt.

Nuissl, Ekkehard (2011): Ordnungsgrundsätze der Erwachsenenbildung in Deutschland. In Rudolf Tippelt, Aiga von Hippel (Eds.): Handbuch Erwachsenenbildung/Weiterbildung. 5. Auflage. Wiesbaden: VS Verlag für Sozialwissenschaften, pp. 329–346.

Nuissl, Ekkehard; Lattke, Susanne; Pätzold, Henning (2010): Europäische Perspektiven der Erwachsenenbildung. Bielefeld: wbv.

OECD (1996): Lifelong Learning for All. Meeting of the Education Committee at Ministerial Level, 16-17 January 1996. Paris: OECD Publications. Available online at http://www.voced.edu.au/content/ngv%3A25305, checked on 7/21/2018.

Offe, Claus (2008): Governance – „Empty signifier" oder sozialwissenschaftliches Forschungsprogramm? In Gunnar F. Schuppert, Michael Zürn (Eds.): Governance in einer sich wandelnden Welt. Wiesbaden: VS Verlag für Sozialwissenschaften (Politische Vierteljahresschrift, Sonderheft (41)), pp. 61–76.

O'Leary, Zina (2010): The essential guide to doing your research project. London: Sage.

Papadopoulos, George (2002): Policies for lifelong learning: an overview of international trends. In UNESCO (Ed.): Learning throughout life: challenges for thetwenty-first century. Paris: UNESCO Publishing, pp. 37–62.

Parreira do Amaral, Marcelo (2017): Educational Governance: International vergleichende Perspektiven auf Neue Steuerung im Bildungsbereich. In Axel Bolder, Helmut Bremer, Rudolf Epping (Eds.): Bildung für Arbeit unter neuer Steuerung. Wiesbaden: Springer VS, pp. 201–221.

Peters, Guy B.; Pierre, John (1998): Governance without Government? Rethinking Public Administration. In *Journal of Public Administration Research and Theory* 8 (2), pp. 223–243. Available online at https://www.jstor.org/stable/1181557.

Picht, Georg (1964): Die deutsche Bildungskatastrophe. Analyse und Dokumentation. Freiburg im Breisgau.

Pollak, Johannes; Slominski, Peter (2006): Das politische System der EU. Wien: WUV; UTB.

Preunkert, Jenny (2009): Chancen für ein soziales Europa? Die Offene Methode der Koordinierung als neue Regulierungsform. Wiesbaden: VS Research.

Punch, Keith F. (2009): Introduction to Research Methods in Education. London: Sage.

Radaelli, Claudio M. (2003): The Open Method of Coordination: A New Governance Architecture for the European Union? Stockholm: Swedish Institute for European Policy Studies (Report no. 1). Available online at http://www.eurosfaire.prd.fr/7pc/doc/1168434892_cr20031.pdf.

Ranacher, Christian; Staudigl, Fritz (2010): Einführung in das EU-Recht. Institutionen, Recht und Politiken der Europäischen Union. 2., Auflage. Wien: Facultas; UTB.

Rasmussen, Palle (2014): Adult Learning Policy in the European Commission. In Marcella Milana, John Holford (Eds.): Adult education policy and the European Union. Theoretical and methodological perspectives. Rotterdam: Sense, pp. 17–34.

Rasmussen, Palle; Larson, Anne; Rönnber, Linda; Tsatsaroni, Anna (2015): Policies of 'modernisation' in European education: Enactments and consequences. In European Educational Research Journal 14 (6), pp. 479–486. DOI: 10.1177/1474904115610783.

Romer, Paul M. (1990): Endogenous Technological Change. In Journal of Political Economy 98 (5, Part 2), S71-S102. Available online at http//www.jstor.org/stable/2937632.

Rosamund, Ben (2009): Supranational Governance. In Chris Rumford (Ed.): The SAGE handbook of European studies. Los Angeles: Sage, pp. 89–109.

Rosenau, James N. (1990): Turbulence in World Politics. A Theory of Change and Continuity. Princeton, NJ: Princeton University Press.

Sabel, Charles F.; Zeitlin, Jonathan (2008): Learning from Difference. The New Architecture of Experimentalist Governance in the EU. In *Eur Law J* 14 (3), pp. 271–327. DOI: 10.1111/j.1468-0386.2008.00415.x.

Sava, Simona; Nuissl, Ekkehard; Lustrea, Anca (2016): Adult Learning and Education: Current European Perspectives. In Simona Sava, Petr Novotny (Eds.): Researches in Adult Learning and Education: the European Dimension. Florence: Firenze University Press, pp. 3–26.

Schemmann, Michael (2007): Internationale Weiterbildungspolitik und Globalisierung. Orientierungen und Aktivitäten von OECD, EU, UNESCO und Weltbank. Bielefeld: wbv.

Schmidt-Lauff, Sabine; Egetenmeyer, Regina (2015): Internationalisierung. In Jörg Dinkelaker, Aiga von Hippel (Eds.): Erwachsenenbildung in Grundbegriffen. 1. Aufl. Stuttgart: Kohlhammer, pp. 272–279.

Schneider, Volker; Janning, Frank (2006): Politikfeldanalyse. Akteure, Diskurse und Netzwerke in der öffentlichen Politik. Wiesbaden: VS Verlag für Sozialwissenschaften.

Schrader, Josef (2010): Governance in Adult and Further Education. Unified Germany as a Case Study. In *European Education* 41 (4), pp. 41–64. DOI: 10.2753/EUE1056-4934410403.

Schrader, Josef (2011): Struktur und Wandel der Weiterbildung. Bielefeld: W. Bertelsmann.

Schroeder, Werner (2015): Grundkurs Europarecht. 4., überarb. Auflage. München: Beck.

Schuetze, Hans G. (2006): International concepts and agendas of Lifelong Learning. In *Compare* 36 (3), pp. 289–306. DOI: 10.1080/03057920600872381.

Senden, Linda (2005): Soft Law, Self-Regulation and Co-Regulation in European Law: Where Do They Meet? In *Electronic Journal of Comparative Law* 9 (1). Available online at https://www.ejcl.org/91/art91-3.PDF, checked on 9/4/2017.

Shaw, Josephine (1991): Education and the European Community. In *Education and the Law* 3 (1), pp. 1–18. DOI: 10.1080/0953996910030101.

Szyszczak, Erika (2006): Experimental Governance: The Open Method of Coordination. In *European Law Journal* 12 (4), pp. 486–502. DOI: 10.1111/j.1468-0386.2006.00329.x.

UNESCO (1996): Learning: the treasure within. Report to UNESCO of the International Commission on Education for the Twenty-first Century. With assistance of Jacques Delors, In'am Al Mufti, Isao Amagi, Roberto Carneiro, Fay Chung. Paris: UNESCO Publishing. Available online at http://unesdoc.unesco.org/images/0010/001095/109590eo.pdf, checked on 6/28/2018.

van Kersbergen, Kees; Verbeek, Bertjan (1994): The Politics of Subsidiarity in the European Union. In *Journal of Common Market Studies* 32 (2), pp. 215–236. DOI: 10.1111/j.1468-5965.1994.tb00494.x.

Volles, Nina (2016): Lifelong learning in the EU: changing conceptualisations, actors, and policies. In *Studies in Higher Education* 41 (2), pp. 343–363. DOI: 10.1080/03075079.2014.927852.

Waterstone, Michael (2007): A New Vision of Public Enforcement. Loyola-LA Legal Studies Paper No. 2007-22. In *Minessota Law Review* 92. Available online at http://www.minnesotalawreview.org/wp-content/uploads/2012/01/Waterstone_final.pdf, checked on 9/1/2017.

Watson, Philippa (1987): Case 293/83, Gravier v. City of Liège, Judgement of 13 February 1985. Reference to the Court by the Tribunal de Première Instance, Liège, for a preliminary ruling on the interpretation of Articles 7 and 59 of the EEC Treaty. Case 293/85R, Commission of the European Communities v. Kingdom of Belgium: Order of the President of the Court of 25 October 1985. In *Common Market Law Review* 24 (1), pp. 89–97.

Wildemeersch, Danny; Salling Olesen, Henning (2012): Editorial: The effects of policies for the education and learning of adults - from 'adult education' to 'lifelong learning', from 'emancipation' to 'empowerment'. In *European Journal for Research on the Education and Learning of Adults* 3 (2), pp. 97–101. DOI: 10.3384/rela.2000-7426.relae5.

Williamson, Oliver (2009): Transaction Cost Economic: The Natural Progression. Prize Lecture, December 8, 2009. Available online at https://www.nobelprize.org/nobel_prizes/economic-sciences/laureates/2009/williamson-lecture.html, checked on 9/1/2017.

Zarifis, George K.; Gravani, Maria N. (Eds.) (2014): Challenging the 'European Area of Lifelong Learning'. A Critical Response. Dordrecht: Springer.

Archives and Databanks

EurLex. Access to European Union Law. Available online at http://eurlex.europa.eu/homepage.html?locale=en., checked on 25/11/2019.

Official Journal of the European Union. Available online at https://eurlex.europa.eu/oj/direct-access.html, checked on 25/11/2019.

Official website of the European Union. Available online at https://europa.eu/european-union/index_en, checked on 25/11/2019.

University of Luxembourg. CVCE.eu. Available online at https://www.cvce.eu/de, checked on 25/11/2019.

University of Pittsburgh. European Studies Center. Available online at https://www.ucis.pitt.edu/esc/, checked on 25/11/2019.

Treaties

TECSC (4/18/1951): Treaty constituting the European Coal and Steel Community. Available online at https://www.cvce.eu/en/obj/treaty_establishing_the_european_coal_and_steel_community_paris_18_april_1951-en-11a21305-941e-49d7-a171-ed5be548cd58.html, checked on 6/7/2018.

TEAC (3/25/1957): Treaty establishing the European Atomic Energy Community (EURATOM). Available online at https://www.ab.gov.tr/files/ardb/evt/1_avrupa_birligi/1_3_antlasmalar/1_3_1_kurucu_antlasmalar/1957_treaty_establishing_euratom.pdf, checked on 6/7/2018.

TEEC (3/25/1957): Treaty establishing the European Economic Community. Available online at https://www.cvce.eu/de/collections/unit-content/-/unit/en/d5906df5-4f83-4603-85f7-0cabc24b9fe1/11ef151e-c7b0-46ae-86c9-bc195addc07d/Resources#cca6ba28-0bf3-4ce6-8a76-6b0b3252696e_en&overlay, checked on 7/22/2018.

TEU (2/7/1992): Treaty on European Union. In *Official Journal of the European Communities* (C 191/01). Available online at http://www.ecb.europa.eu/ecb/legal/pdf/maastricht_en.pdf, checked on 6/7/2018.

Treaty of Amsterdam (6/18/1997): Treaty of Amsterdam amending the Treaty on European Union, the treaties establishing the European

Communities and certain related acts. Available online at http://www.europarl.europa.eu/topics/treaty/pdf/amst-en.pdf, checked on 7/22/2018.

EU Charter (6/7/2016): Charter of Fundamental Rights of the European Union. In *Official Journal of the European Communities* (2016/C 202/02), pp. 389–405. Available online at https://eur-lex.europa.eu/legal-content/EN/TXT/PDF/?uri=OJ:C:2016:202:FULL&from=EN, checked on 6/27/2018.

TEU consolidated (6/7/2016): Consolidated version of the Treaty on European Union. In *Official Journal of the European Union* (2016/C 202/01), pp. 13–46. Available online at https://eur-lex.europa.eu/legal-content/EN/TXT/PDF/?uri=OJ:C:2016:202:FULL&from=EN, checked on 6/27/2018.

TFEU consolidated (6/7/2016): Consolidated version of the Treaty on the Functioning of the European Union. In *Official Journal of the European Union* (2016/C 202/01), 47-388. Available online at https://eur-lex.europa.eu/legal-content/EN/TXT/PDF/?uri=OJ:C:2016:202:FULL&from=EN, checked on 6/27/2018.

European Council

European Council (6/19/1983): Solemn Declaration on European Union (Stuttgart, 19 June 1983). In *Bulletin of the European Communities* (6), pp. 24–29. Available online at http://www.cvce.eu/obj/solemn_declaration_on_european_union_stuttgart_19_june_1983-en-a2e74239-a12b-4efc-b4ce-cd3dee9cf71d.html, checked on 6/8/2018.

European Council (6/25/1984): Conclusions of the Fontainebleau European Council (Fontainebleau, 25 and 26 June 1984). In *Bulletin of the European Communities* (6), pp. 11–12. Available online at http://www.cvce.eu/obj/conclusions_of_the_fontainebleau_european_council_25_an d_26_june_1984-en-ba12c4fa-48d1-4e00-96cc-a19e4fa5c704.html, checked on 6/8/2018.

European Council (3/23/2000): Conclusions of the Lisbon Extraordinary European Council (Lisbon, 23 and 24 March 2000). Available online at https://www.cvce.eu/content/publication/2007/6/8/5ad9ce9c-c7ff-42fa-b00b-e70a97061fe1/publishable_en.pdf, checked on 6/8/2018.

Council of the European Union

Council of the European Communities (4/20/1963): Council Decision of 2 April 1963 laying down general principles for implementing a common vocational training policy. 63/266/EEC. In *Official Journal of the European Communities* (1338/63), pp. 25–28. Available online at https://eur-lex.europa.eu/legal-content/EN/TXT/PDF/?uri=CELEX:31963D0266&from=FR, checked on 7/22/2018.

Council of the European Communities (10/19/1968): Regulation (EEC) No 1612/68 of the Council of 15 October 1968 on freedom of movement for workers within the Community. 1612/68/EEC. In *Official Journal of the European Communities* (L 257/2). Available online at https://eur-lex.europa.eu/legal-content/EN/TXT/PDF/?uri=CELEX:31968R1612&from=en, checked on 7/22/2018.

Council of the European Communities (8/12/1971): General guidelines for drawing up a Community programme on vocational training (adopted at the 162nd session of the Council held on 26 July 1971). In *Official Journal of the European Communities* (C 81/5). Available online at https://eur-lex.europa.eu/legal-content/EN/TXT/PDF/?uri=CELEX:31971Y0812&from=FR, checked on 7/22/2018.

Council of the European Communities (2/13/1975): Regulation (EEC) No 337/75 of the Council of 10 February 1975 establishing a European Centre for the Development of Vocational Training. 337/75. In *Official Journal of the European Communities* (L 39/1). Available online at https://eur-lex.europa.eu/legal-content/EN/TXT/PDF/?uri=CELEX:31975R0337&from=FRF, checked on 7/22/2018.

Council of the European Communities (2/19/1976): Resolution of the Council and of the Ministers of Education, meeting within the Council, of 9 February 1976 comprising an action programme in the field of education. 76/C 38/01. In *Official Journal of the European Communities* (C 38/1). Available online at https://eur-lex.europa.eu/legal-content/EN/TXT/PDF/?uri=CELEX:41976X0219&from=EN, checked on 7/22/2018.

Council of the European Communities (7/28/1982): Council Resolution of the Council and the Ministers for Education, meeting within the Council of 12 July 1982 concerning measures to be taken to improve the preparation of young people for work and to facilitate their transition from education to working life. 82/C 193/01. In *Official Journal of the European Communities* (C 193/1). Available online at https://eur-lex.europa.eu/legal-content/EN/TXT/PDF/?uri=CELEX:41982X0728&from=EN, checked on 7/22/2018.

Council of the European Communities (6/25/1983): Council Resolution of 2 June 1983 concerning vocational measures relating to new information technologies. 83/C 166/01. In *Official Journal of the European Communities* (C 166/1). Available online at https://eur-lex.europa.eu/legal-content/EN/TXT/PDF/?uri=CELEX:31983Y0625(01)&from=EN, checked on 7/22/2018.

Council of the European Communities (7/20/1983): Council Resolution of 11 July 1983 concerning vocational policies in the European Community in the 1980s. 83/C 193/02. In *Official Journal of the European Communities* (C 193/2). Available online at https://eur-lex.europa.eu/legal-content/EN/TXT/PDF/?uri=CELEX:31983Y0720(02)&from=EN, checked on 7/22/2018.

Council of the European Communities (8/8/1986): Council Decision of 24 July 1986 adopting the programme on cooperation between universities and enterprises regarding training in the field of technology (COMETT). 86/365/EEC. In *Official Journal of the European Communities* (L 222/17). Available online at https://eur-lex.europa.eu/legal-content/EN/TXT/PDF/?uri=CELEX:31986D0365&from=EN, checked on 7/22/2018.

Council of the European Communities (1987): Conclusions of the Council and of the Ministers for Education meeting within the Council of 4 June 1984. In Council of the European Communities General Secretariat (Ed.): European educational policy Statements. 3rd edition, June 1987. Luxembourg: Office for Official Publications of the European Communities, pp. 113–126.

Council of the European Communities (1987): Conclusions of the joint session of the Council (Labour and Social Affairs)/Council and the Ministers for Education meeting within the Council of 3 June 1983 on the transition of young people from education to adult and working life. In Council of the European Communities General Secretariat (Ed.): European educational policy Statements. 3rd edition, June 1987. Luxembourg: Office for Official Publications of the European Communities, pp. 93–96.

Council of the European Communities (1987): Summary by the President of the arguments put forward during the meeting of the Council and the Ministers for Education meeting within the Council of 22 June 1981. In Council of the European Communities General Secretariat (Ed.): European educational policy Statements. 3rd edition, June 1987. Luxembourg: Office for Official Publications of the European Communities, pp. 73–76.

Council of the European Communities (6/25/1987): Council Decision of 15 June 1987 adopting the European Community Action Scheme for the Mobility of University Students (ERASMUS). 87/327/EEC. In *Official Journal of the European Communities* (L 166/20). Available online at https://eur-lex.europa.eu/legal-content/EN/TXT/PDF/?uri=CELEX:31987D0327&from=EN, checked on 7/22/2018.

Council of the European Communities (12/10/1987): Council Decision of 1 December 1987 concerning an action programme for the vocational training of young people and their preparation for adult and working life. 87/569/EEC. In *Official Journal of the European Communities* (L 346/31). Available online at https://eur-lex.europa.eu/legal-content/EN/TXT/PDF/?uri=CELEX:31987D0569&from=EN, checked on 7/22/2018.

Council of the European Communities (6/25/1988): Council Decision of 16 June 1988 adopting an action programme for the promotion of youth exchanges in the Community - 'Youth for Europe' programme. 88/348/EEC. In *Official Journal of the European Communities* (L 158/42). Available online at https://eur-lex.europa.eu/legal-content/EN/TXT/PDF/?uri=CELEX:31988D0348&from=EN, checked on 7/22/2018.

Council of the European Communities (1/21/1989): Council Directive of 21 December 1989 on a general system for the recognition of higher-education diplomas awarded on completion of professional education and training of at least three years' duration. 89/48/EEC. In *Official Journal of the European Communities* (L 19/16). Available online at https://eur-lex.europa.eu/legal-content/EN/TXT/PDF/?uri=CELEX:31989L0048&from=EN, checked on 7/22/2018.

Council of the European Communities (8/16/1989): Council Decision of 28 July 1989 establishing an action programme to promote foreign language competence in the European Community (Lingua). 89/489/EEC. In *Official*

Journal of the European Communities (L 239/24). Available online at https://eur-lex.europa.eu/legal-content/EN/TXT/PDF/?uri=CELEX:31989D0489&from=EN, checked on 7/22/2018.

Council of the European Communities (12/30/1989): Council Decision of 18 December 1989 establishing an action programme to promote innovation in the field of vocational training resulting from technological change in the European Community (Eurotecnet). 89/657/EEC. In *Official Journal of the European Communities* (L 393/29). Available online at https://eur-lex.europa.eu/legal-content/EN/TXT/PDF/?uri=CELEX:31989D0657&from=EN, checked on 7/22/2018.

Council of the European Communities (5/23/1990): Council Decision of 7 May 1990 establishing a trans-European mobility scheme for university studies (Tempus). 90/233/EEC. In *Official Journal of the European Communities* (L 131/21). Available online at https://eur-lex.europa.eu/legal-content/EN/TXT/PDF/?uri=CELEX:31990D0233&from=EN, checked on 7/22/2018.

Council of the European Communities (6/21/1990): Council Decision of 29 May 1990 establishing an action programme for the development of continuing vocational training in the European Community (Force). 90/267/EEC. In *Official Journal of the European Communities* (L 156/1). Available online at https://eur-lex.europa.eu/legal-content/EN/TXT/PDF/?uri=CELEX:31990D0267&from=EN, checked on 7/22/2018.

Council of the European Communities General Secretariat (Ed.) (1987): European educational policy Statements. 3rd edition, June 1987. Luxembourg: Office for Official Publications of the European Communities.

Council of the European Union (12/29/1994): Council Decision of 6 December 1994 establishing an action programme for the implementation of a European Community vocational training policy. 97/819/EC. In *Official Journal of the European Communities* (L 340/8). Available online at https://eur-lex.europa.eu/legal-content/EN/TXT/PDF/?uri=CELEX:31994D0819&from=EN, checked on 6/15/2018.

Council of the European Union (6/11/1999): Council Decision of 26 April 1999 establishing the second phase of the Community vocational training action programme 'Leonardo da Vinci'. 1999/382/EC. In *Official Journal of the European Communities* (L 146/33). Available online at https://eur-lex.europa.eu/legal-content/EN/TXT/PDF/?uri=CELEX:31999D0382&from=EN, checked on 6/15/2018.

Council of the European Union (1/12/2000): Council Resolution of 17 December 1999 on 'into the new millenium': developing new working procedures for European cooperation in the field of education and training. 2000/C 8/04. In *Official Journal of the European Communities* (C 8/6). Available online at https://eur-lex.europa.eu/legal-content/EN/TXT/PDF/?uri=CELEX:32000Y0112(03)&from=EN, checked on 6/13/2018.

Council of the European Union (6/6/2008): Council conclusions of 22 May 2008 on adult learning. 2008/C 140/09. In *Official Journal of the European Union* (C 140/10). Available online at https://eur-lex.europa.eu/legal-content/EN/TXT/PDF/?uri=CELEX:52008XG0606(02)&from=EN, checked on 6/8/2018.

Council of the European Union (5/28/2009): Council conclusions of 12 May 2009 on a strategic framework for European cooperation in education and training ('ET 2020'). 2009/C 119/02. In *Official Journal of the European Union* (C 119/2). Available online at https://eur-lex.europa.eu/legal-content/EN/TXT/PDF/?uri=CELEX:52009XG0528(01)&from=EN, checked on 6/15/2018.

Council of the European Union (12/20/2011): Council Resolution on a renewed European agenda for adult learning. 2011/C 372/01. In *Official Journal of the European Union* (C 372/1). Available online at https://eur-lex.europa.eu/legal-content/EN/TXT/PDF/?uri=CELEX:32011G1220(01)&from=EN, checked on 6/8/2018.

Council of the European Union (6/15/2017): Council recommendation of 22 May 2017 on the European Qualifications Framework for lifelong learning and repealing the recommendation of the European Parliament and of the Council of 23 April 2008 on the establishment of the European Qualifications Framework for lifelong learning. 2017/C 189/03. In *Official Journal of the European Union* (C 189/15). Available online at https://eur-lex.europa.eu/legal-content/EN/TXT/PDF/?uri=CELEX:32017H0615(01)&from=EN, checked on 6/24/2018.

Council of the European Union; European Commission (12/15/2015): 2015 Joint Report of the Council and the Commission on the implementation of the strategic framework for European cooperation in education and training (ET 2020) - New priorities for European cooperation in education and training. 2015/C 417/04. In *Official Journal of the European Union* (C 417/25). Available online at https://eur-lex.europa.eu/legal-content/EN/TXT/PDF/?uri=CELEX:52015XG1215(02)&from=EN, checked on 6/17/2018.

Ministers for Education (8/20/1974): Resolution of the ministers of education, meeting within the Council, of 6 June 1974 on cooperation in the field of education. In *Official Journal of the European Communities* (C 98/2). Available online at https://eur-lex.europa.eu/legal-content/EN/TXT/PDF/?uri=CELEX:41974X0820&from=EN, checked on 6/28/2018.

Ministers for Education (1987): Resolution of the Ministers for Education meeting within the Council of 16 November 1971 on cooperation in the field of education. In Council of the European Communities General Secretariat (Ed.): European educational policy Statements. 3rd edition, June 1987. Luxembourg: Office for Official Publications of the European Communities, pp. 9–11.

European Parliament and Council of the European Union

European Parliament; Council of the European Union (4/20/1995): Decision No 819/95/EC of the European Parliament and of the Council of 14 March 1995 establishing the Community action programme 'Socrates'. 819/95/EC. In *Official Journal of the European Communities* (L 87/10). Available online at https://eur-lex.europa.eu/legal-content/EN/TXT/PDF/?uri=CELEX:31995D0819&from=EN, checked on 6/15/2018.

European Parliament; Council of the European Union (10/26/1995): Decision No 2493/95/EC of the European Parliament and of the Council of 23 October 1995 establishing 1996 as the 'European year of lifelong learning'. 2493/95/EC. In *Official Journal of the European Communities* (L 256/45). Available online at https://eur-lex.europa.eu/legal-content/EN/TXT/PDF/?uri=CELEX:31995D2493&from=EN, checked on 6/15/2018.

European Parliament; Council of the European Union (2/3/2000): Decision No 253/2000/EC of the European Parliament and of the Council of 24 January 2000 establishing the second phase of the Community action programme in the field of education 'Socrates'. 253/2000/EC. In *Official Journal of the European Communities* (L 28/1). Available online at https://eur-lex.europa.eu/legal-content/EN/TXT/PDF/?uri=CELEX:32000D0253&from=EN, checked on 6/15/2018.

European Parliament; Council of the European Union (5/6/2008): Recommendation of the European Parliament and of the Council of 23 April 2008 on the establishment of the European Qualifications Framework for lifelong learning. 2008/C 111/01. In *Official Journal of the European Union* (C 111/1). Available online at https://eur-lex.europa.eu/legal-content/EN/TXT/PDF/?uri=CELEX:32008H0506(01)&from=EN, checked on 6/15/2018.

European Parliament

European Parliament (4/16/1984): Minutes of the sitting of Tuesday, 13 March 1984. Regulation on higher education and the development of cooperation between higher education establishments. 84/C 104/02. In *Official Journal of the European Communities* (C 104), pp. 48–55. Available online at https://eur-lex.europa.eu/legal-content/EN/TXT/PDF/?uri=OJ:JOC_1984_104_R_0032_01&from=EN, checked on 6/15/2018.

European Parliament (5/20/1985): Resolution on the recognition of national university degrees and professional qualifications at European level. 85/C 122/04. In *Official Journal of the European Communities* (C 122), pp. 121–122. Available online at https://eur-lex.europa.eu/legal-content/EN/TXT/PDF/?uri=OJ:JOC_1985_122_R_0099_01&from=EN, checked on 6/15/2018.

European Commission

Commission of the European Communities (01.1970): The Hague Summit. Final communiqué of the conference (2.12.1969). In *Bulletin of the*

European Communities 3 (1). Available online at
http://aei.pitt.edu/58651/1/BUL154.pdf, checked on 7/22/2018.

Commission of the European Communities (1973): Information Brochure
showing the principal activities of the various services of the Commission
of the European Communities. Commission of the European Communities,
General Directorate Personell and Administration. Available online at
http://aei.pitt.edu/41805/1/A5948.pdf, checked on 6/7/2018.

Commission of the European Communities (5/23/1973): Working Program
in the Field of "Research, Science and Education" (personal statement by
Mr. Dahrendorf). SEC (73) 2000/2. Available online at
http://aei.pitt.edu/5452/1/5452.pdf, checked on 6/7/2018.

Commission of the European Communities (3/17/1974): Education in the
European Community. Communication from the Commission to the Council presented on 11 March 1974. COM (74) 253 final/2. In *Bulletin of the
European Communities* (Supplement 3/74). Available online at
http://aei.pitt.edu/5593/1/5593.pdf, checked on 6/7/2018.

Commission of the European Communities (12/4/1987): Commission Recommendation of 24 November on vocational training for women.
87/567/EEC. In *Official Journal of the European Communities* (L 342/35).
Available online at https://eur-lex.europa.eu/legal-con-
tent/EN/TXT/PDF/?uri=CELEX:31987H0567&from=EN, checked on
6/7/2018.

Commission of the European Communities (6/2/1989): Communication
from the Commission to the Council. Education and Training in the European Community Guidelines for the Medium Term: 1989-1992. COM (89)
236 final. Available online at http://aei.pitt.edu/5697/1/5697.pdf, checked
on 6/7/2018.

Commission of the European Communities (12/5/1993): Growth, competitiveness, employment. The challenges and ways forward into the 21st century. White Paper. COM (93) 700. In *Bulletin of the European Communities* (Supplement 6/93). Available online at
http://aei.pitt.edu/1139/1/growth_wp_COM_93_700_Parts_A_B.pdf,
checked on 6/7/2018.

Commission of the European Communities (11/29/1995): White Paper on
Education and Training. Teachning and Learning towards the Learning

Society. COM (95) 590 final. Available online at
http://aei.pitt.edu/1132/1/education_train_wp_COM_95_590.pdf, checked
on 6/7/2018.

Commission of the European Communities (11/12/1997): Communication
from the Commission to the Council, the European Parliament, the Economic and Social Committee and the Committee of the Regions. Towards a
Europe of Knowledge. COM (97) 563 final. Available online at
http://aei.pitt.edu/5546/1/5546.pdf, checked on 6/7/2018.

Commission of the European Communities (10/30/2000): Commission
Staff Working Paper. A Memorandum on Lifelong Learning. SEC (2000)
1832. Available online at http://uil.unesco.org/i/doc/lifelong-learning/poli-
cies/european-communities-a-memorandum-on-lifelong-learning.pdf,
checked on 6/7/2018.

Commission of the European Communities (2001): Draft Detailed Work
Programme for the Follow-up of the Report on the Concrete Objectives of
Education and Training Systems. COM (2001) 501 final. Available online
at http://aei.pitt.edu/63037/1/COM_(2001)_501_final.pdf, checked on
6/7/2018.

Commission of the European Communities (1/31/2001): Report from the
Commission. The Concrete Future Objectives of Education Systems. COM
(2001) 59 final. Available online at
http://aei.pitt.edu/42877/1/com2001_0059.pdf, checked on 6/7/2018.

Commission of the European Communities (7/25/2001): European Governance. A White Paper. COM (2001) 428 final. Available online at
http://aei.pitt.edu/1188/1/european_governance_wp_COM_2001_428.pdf,
checked on 6/7/2018.

Commission of the European Communities (11/21/2001): Communication
from the Commission. Making a European Area of Lifelong Learning a Reality. COM (2001) 678 final. Available online at
http://aei.pitt.edu/42878/1/com2001_0678.pdf, checked on 6/7/2018.

Commission of the European Communities (11/23/2006): Communication
from the Commission. Adult learning: It is never too late to learn. COM
(2006) 614 final. Available online at https://eur-lex.europa.eu/legal-con-
tent/EN/TXT/PDF/?uri=CELEX:52006DC0614&from=EN, checked on
6/8/2018.

Commission of the European Communities (9/27/2007): Communication from the Commission to the Council, the European Parliament, the European Economic and Social Committee and the Committee of the Regions. Action Plan on Adult learning. It is always a good time to learn. COM (2007) 558 final. Available online at https://eur-lex.europa.eu/legal-content/EN/TXT/PDF/?uri=CELEX:52007DC0558&from=EN, checked on 6/7/2018.

European Commission (no year): Mandate Thematic Working Group on Quality in Adult Learning. October 2011 - October 2013. Available online at http://ec.europa.eu/dgs/education_culture/repository/education/policy/strategic-framework/doc/quality_en.pdf, checked on 6/12/2018.

European Commission (1998): The European Social Fund: an overview of the programming period 1994-1999. Luxemburg: Office for Official Publications of the European Communities. Available online at http://aei.pitt.edu/33298/1/A6.pdf, checked on 6/27/2018.

European Commission (3/3/2010): Communication from the Commission. Europe 2020. A strategy for smart, sustainable and inclusive growth. COM (2010) 2020. Available online at http://ec.europa.eu/eu2020/pdf/COMPLET%20EN%20BARROSO%20%20%20007%20-%20Europe%202020%20-%20EN%20version.pdf, checked on 6/16/2018.

European Commission (2016): Strategic Plan 2016-2020. Employment, Social Affairs and Inclusion DG. Available online at https://ec.europa.eu/info/sites/info/files/strategic-plan-2016-2020-dg-empl_march2016_en.pdf, checked on 11/23/2019.

European Commission (2016): Strategic Plan 2016-2020. DG Education and Culture. Available online at https://ec.europa.eu/info/sites/info/files/strategic-plan-2016-2020-dg-eac_march2016_en.pdf, checked on 11/23/2019.

European Commission (6/10/2016): Communication from the Commission to the European Parliament, the Council, the European Economic and Social Committee and the Committee of the Regions. A new skills agenda for Europe. Working together to strengthen human capital, employability and competitiveness. COM (2016) 381 final. Available online at https://eur-lex.europa.eu/legal-content/EN/TXT/PDF/?uri=CELEX:52016DC0381&from=EN, checked on 6/8/2018.

European Court of Justice

European Court of Justice (7/3/1974): Judgment of 3.7.1974 - Case 9/74. Casagrande vs. City of Munich. Case 9/74. In *European Court Reports* 1974, pp. 774–780. Available online at https://eur-lex.europa.eu/legal-content/EN/TXT/PDF/?uri=CELEX:61974CJ0009&rid=1, checked on 7/22/2018.

European Court of Justice (1/31/1984): Judgment of 31.01.1984 - Joined Cases 286/82 and 26/83. Luisi and Carbone vs. Ministero del Tesoro. Joined Cases 286/82 and 26/83. In *European Court Reports* 1984, pp. 379–409. Available online at https://eur-lex.europa.eu/legal-content/EN/TXT/PDF/?uri=CELEX:61982CJ0286&from=LT, checked on 7/22/2018.

European Court of Justice (3/15/1984): Judgment of 13.7.1983 - Case 152/82. Forcheri vs. Belgium. Case 152/82. In *European Court Reports* 1984, pp. 2324–2338. Available online at https://eur-lex.europa.eu/legal-content/EN/TXT/PDF/?uri=CELEX:61983CJ0028&rid=1, checked on 7/22/2018.

European Court of Justice (2/13/1985): Judgment of 13.02.1985 - case 293/83. Gravier vs. City of Liège. Case 293/83. In *European Court Reports* 1985, pp. 606–614. Available online at https://eur-lex.europa.eu/legal-content/EN/TXT/PDF/?uri=CELEX:61983CJ0293&rid=2, checked on 22.07.2ß18.

Committee of the Regions

Committee of the Regions (6/24/1996): Opinion of the Committee of the Regions on 'The White Paper on Education and Training - Teaching and learning towards the learning society'. 96/C 182/04. In *Official Journal of the European Communities* (C 182/15). Available online at https://eur-lex.europa.eu/legal-content/EN/TXT/PDF/?uri=CELEX:51996AR0115&from=EN, checked on 6/27/2018.

Reports, Glossaries, Speeches, Opinions

Adonnino, Pietro (1985): A People's Europe. Report from the ad hoc Committee. In *Bulletin of the European Communities* (Supplement 7/85). Available online at http://aei.pitt.edu/992/1/andonnino_report_peoples_europe.pdf, checked on 6/17/2018.

Broek, Simon (2017): ET 2020 Adult Learning Working Group. Report. Policies promoting medium skills in the workplace. Peer Learning Activity. Available online at https://ec.europa.eu/education/sites/education/files/adult-pla-reims_en.pdf, checked on 6/17/2018.

Broek, Simon; Buiskool, Bert-Jan; Hake, Barry J. (2010): Impact of ongoing reforms in education and training on the adult learning sector. (2nd phase) Final report. Available online at https://www.ab.gov.tr/files/ardb/evt/1_avrupa_birligi/1_9_politikalar/1_9_4_egitim_politikasi/adultreport_en.pdf, checked on 6/24/2018.

Cedefop (2014): Terminology of European education and training policy. A selection of 130 key terms. A selection of 130 key terms. 2nd edition. Luxembourg: Publications Office of the European Union. Available online at DOI: 10.2801/15877.

ERASMUS+ UK (2017): Origins of the Erasmus programme - interview with Hywel Ceri Jones. Available online at https://erasmusplus.org.uk/blog/origins-of-the-erasmus-programme-%E2%80%93-interview-with-hywel-ceri-jones, updated on 2/22/2017, checked on 7/22/2018.

Europe Documents (Ed.) (1981): Address given by Emilio Colombo (Florence, 28 January 1981). 03.02.1981, n° 1136. With assistance of Dir. of publi. Riccardi, Lodovico, Emanuele Gazzo. Available online at http://www.cvce.eu/obj/address_given_by_emilio_colombo_florence_28_january_1981-en-d2f67c9c-715c-44dbabef-c9240193a8a3.html, checked on 7/22/2018.

European Community Information Service (1972): European Community. Education in Europe. March 1972, No. 154. Available online at http://aei.pitt.edu/43885/1/A7539.pdf, checked on 7/22/2018.

Eurostat (1992): Europa in Zahlen. Dritte Ausgabe. Luxemburg: Amt für amtliche Veröffentlichungen der Europäischen Gemeinschaften.

Fondation Robert Schuman (2011): Declaration of 9th May 1950 delivered b Robert Schuman. European Issue, No. 204, 10th May 2011. Fondation Robert Schuman. Available online at https://www.robert-schuman.eu/en/doc/questions-d-europe/qe-204-en.pdf, updated on 7/22/2018.

Freie Demokratische Korrespondenz (Ed.) (1981): Rede von Hans-Dietrich Genscher (Stuttgart, 6. Januar 1981). 06.01.1981, Nr. 2. Bonn: Pressedienst der Freien Domokratischen Partei. Available online at http://www.cvce.eu/obj/rede_von_hans_dietrich_genscher_stuttgart_6_januar_1981-de-73cd40b0-7dce-479b-8c7c-8404afe7c69e.html, updated on 7/22/2018.

Gass, J. R. (1996): European Year of Lifelong Learning 1996. The Goals, Architecture and Means of Lifelong Learning. Background paper issued by the European Commission. Luxembourg: Office for Official Publications of the European Communities. Available online at http://aei.pitt.edu/43219/1/A7181.pdf, checked on 6/27/2018.

Guichard, Olivier (1972): L'éducation et l'Europe. [Originally published in Le Monde, 19 July 1971]. In *Rivista di Studi Politici Internazionali* 39, pp. 119–124. Available online at https://www.jstor.org/stable/42733619.

Janne, Henri (1973): For a Community policy on education. Report by Henri Janne. In *Bulletin of the European Communities* (Supplement 10/73). Available online at http://aei.pitt.edu/5588/1/5588.pdf, checked on 6/27/2018.

Thematic Working Group on Quality in Adult Learning (2013): Final Report. Available online at https://www.hm.ee/sites/default/files/thematic_wg_quality_report.pdf, checked on 6/11/2018.

Publications by European Commission Officials

Fogg, Karen; Jones, Hywell (1985): Educating the European Community: Ten Years on. In *European Journal of Education* 20 (2/3), pp. 293–300. DOI: 10.2307/1502956.

Hingel, Anders J. (2001): Education policies and European governance - contribution to the interservice groups on European governance. In *European Journal for Education Law and Policy* 5 (7), pp. 7–16. DOI: 10.1023/B:EELP.0000006722.94222.78.

Jones, Hywel Ceri (1992): Education in a Changing Europe. Charles Gittins Memorial Lecture presented at the University College of Wales, March 16, 1992. Available online at https://files.eric.ed.gov/fulltext/ED354373.pdf, checked on 6/28/2018.

Jones, Hywel Ceri (2005): Lifelong Learning in the European Union: whither the Lisbon Strategy? In *European Journal of Education* 40 (3), pp. 247–260. DOI: 10.1111/j.1465-3435.2005.00224.x.

Pépin, Luce (2006): The history of European cooperation in education and training. Europe in the making - an example. Brussels: Office for Official Publications of the European Communities. Available online at http://biblioteka-krk.ibe.edu.pl/opac_css/doc_num.php?explnum_id=301, checked on 6/28/2018.

Pépin, Luce (2007): The History of EU Cooperation in the Field of Education and Training: how lifelong learning became a strategic objective. In *European Journal of Education* 42 (1), pp. 121–132. DOI: 10.1111/j.1465-3435.2007.00288.x.

Pépin, Luce (2011): Education in the Lisbon Strategy: assessment and prospects. In *European Journal of Education* 46 (1, Part 1), pp. 25–35. DOI: 10.1111/j.1465-3435.2010.01459.x.

Smith, Alan (1980): From 'Europhoria' to Pragmatism: Towards a New Start for Higher Education Co-operation in Europe? In *European Journal of Education* 15 (1), pp. 77–95. DOI: 10.2307/1503275.

Smith, Alan (1985): Higher Education Co-operation 1975-1985: creating a basis for growth in an adverse economic climate. In *European Journal of Education* 20 (2/3), pp. 267–292. DOI: 10.2307/1502955.

Websites

Council of the European Union. Council preparatory bodies. Available online at http://www.consilium.europa.eu/de/council-eu/preparatory-bodies/, checked on 25/11/2019.

Employment, Social Affairs and Inclusion. New Skills Agenda for Europe. Available online at http://ec.europa.eu/social/main.jsp?catId=1223, checked on 25/11/2019.

European Commission. European Policy Cooperation. Available online at https://ec.europa.eu/education/policies/european-policy-cooperation/et2020-framework_en, checked on 25/11/2019.

European Commission. The Commissioners. Available online at https://ec.europa.eu/commission/commissioners/2014-2019_en, checked on 25/11/2019.

European Parliament. Committees. Available online at http://www.europarl.europa.eu/committees/en/home.html, checked on 25/11/2019.

European Union. The history of the European Union. Available online at https://europa.eu/european-union/about-eu/history_en, checked on 25/11/2019.

Studies on Education

Torill Strand; Richard Smith; Anne Pirrie; Zelia Gregoriou;
Marianna Papastephanou (Eds.)
Philosophy as Interplay and Dialogue
Viewing landscapes within philosophy of education
Philosophy as Interplay and Dialogue is an original and stimulating collection of essays. It covers
conceptual and critical works relevant to current theoretical developments and debates.
Imagine an international group of philosophers of education coming together each summer on a
Greek island. All texts are product of their diligent philosophical analysis and extended dialogues. To
deploy their arguments, the authors draw on classical thinkers and contemporary prominent theorists,
such as Badiou and Malabou, with fresh and critical perspectives. This book thus makes an original
contribution to the field.
Bd. 5, 2017, 516 S., 34,90 €, br., ISBN 3-643-90956-5

Isabelle Duquesne
Schools as Zones of Peace in Nepal
The Impact of Peace Education on Social Equity, Good Governance and Sustainable Economic Development in Post-Conflict Societies. Applying the PACE formula $B3.i3^2$
The four-year long action research in far-eastern Nepal blends peace education, social studies and
local (ethnic) politics within national, post-conflict and state-building efforts. The outcomes of these
studies and programs suggest a recipe for peaceability that could be included in the country's educational curricula. A formula – PEACE $B3.i3^2$ – synthesizes how educationalists may transform
teaching into laboratories to develop the future peace-makers of their nation.
Bd. 4, 2016, 192 S., 29,90 €, br., ISBN 978-3-643-90823-0

Marianna Papastephanou; Torill Strand; Anne Pirrie (Eds.)
Philosophy as a Lived Experience
Navigating through dichotomies of thought and action
Imagine an international group of philosophers of education coming together on a Greek island three
years in a row to reflect and promote a conception of philosophy as a lived experience. This book is a
result of their discussions and makes an original contribution to the field.
The authors here present conceptual and critical works relevant to current theoretical developments
and debates within the fields of philosophy and education. The articles contribute both to philosophical clarifications and the advancement of research with solid arguments for theoretical and practical
redirections. To deploy their arguments, the contributors draw on classical thinkers such as Plato,
Kant and Dewey, and on contemporary prominent theorists, such as Derrida, Badiou and Deleuze,
with fresh and critical perspectives.
Bd. 3, 2014, 312 S., 34,90 €, br., ISBN 978-3-643-90290-0

Jesper Eckhardt Larsen (Ed.)
Knowledge, Politics and the History of Education
The humanities and social science disciplines have always been embedded in and responsive to their
contexts in cultural and political ways. The discipline of the history of education is no exception.
However, a change has occurred where these disciplines are increasingly expected to prove their relevance faced with the politics of knowledge in the knowledge economy. This tendency is investigated
in this book regarding the discipline of the history of education in America and Europe. As a reaction,
the contributions positively address the question of the raison d'être of the history of education. Is the
discipline to serve educationalists, the general public, social scientists, historians or all of them at the
same time?
Bd. 2, 2012, 264 S., 29,90 €, br., ISBN 978-3-8258-1561-5

Torill Strand; Merethe Roos (Eds.)
Education for Social Justice, Equity and Diversity
A Honorary Volume for Professor Anne-Lise Arnesen
Bd. 1, 2012, 304 S., 29,90 €, br., ISBN 978-3-643-90255-9

LIT Verlag Berlin – Münster – Wien – Zürich – London
Auslieferung Deutschland / Österreich / Schweiz: siehe Impressumsseite